CASS LIBRARY OF COUNTY HISTORIES

General Editors :
Dr. W. H. Chaloner, University of Manchester
Professor T. Barker, University of Kent

ESSAYS IN KENTISH HISTORY

ESSAYS IN KENTISH HISTORY

Edited and with an Introduction by

MARGARET ROAKE

M.A., University of Kent

AND

JOHN WHYMAN

Lecturer in Economic and Social History, University of Kent

With a Preface by

FELIX HULL

KENT COUNTY ARCHIVIST

FRANK CASS : LONDON

First published 1973 in Great Britain by
FRANK CASS AND COMPANY LIMITED
67 Great Russell Street, London WC1B 3BT, England

and in United States of America by
FRANK CASS AND COMPANY LIMITED
c/o International Scholarly Book Services, Inc.
P.O. Box 4347, Portland, Oregon 97208

These essays are reprinted from volumes of
Archæologia Cantiana
by kind permission of The Kent Archæological Society

ISBN 0 7146 2956 1

Library of Congress Catalog Card No. 72–90156

Printed in Great Britain by
UNWIN BROTHERS LIMITED, OLD WOKING, SURREY

ADDENDA ET CORRIGENDA for Late-Continued Demesne Farming at Otford, by F. R. H. Du Boulay, pp 51–59

Since this article was written two new sources of information about the fields of Otford have come to light. One is a list of the demesne fields as they were leased to Sir George Warham on 12 June 1524 (Dean and Chapter of Canterbury MSS. Register T, fo. 254b; cf. fos. 157, 313b. for similar leases of 1518 and of 1526). This list corresponds very nearly with that of 1515 printed on p. 53. The other is work in progress by Mr. G. P. Hewlett of Otford who is preparing a thesis in the Geography Department, University of Southampton, for which he is using the new technique of hedgerow species analysis. While agreeing more or less with the literary evidence presented in this paper, Mr. Hewlett hopes to be able to map more accurately the medieval landscape of the area: the acreages of cultivated lands, the deer park, and even the original areas of the individual tenant yokes.

p. 51 footnote 1. *For* problems *read* problem.

p. 52 line 30. *For* 'Alvetum' *read* 'Alnetum', i.e., 'alder-tree ground'.

p. 53 line 14. *For* 'Coridlebushe' *read* 'Cradlebush'.

line 34. *For* 'Blosse medes' *read* 'Closse medes'.

p. 55 *To the Table add year* 1397   160 acres arable (*Calendar of Inquisitions, Miscellaneous*, vol. vi, no. 328).

p. 58 footnote 6. *For* no. 258 (1464) *read* no. 259 (1454).

p. 59 last para. It is questionable whether the Multon water meadows took their name from the Multon family. The converse is more likely. The local name Milton, 'mill farm', south of the former Shoreham Place, can probably be traced back to 'Mylentun' and 'Meleton' of 822 and 1305 respectively. These suggestions were made by the late Dr. Gordon Ward.

CONTENTS

The italic Roman numerals and dates in parentheses after each title refer to the volumes of *Archaeologia Cantiana* from which the articles have been reprinted.

The page numbers refer to the numbers in bold print at the bottom foredge of each page throughout the text.

PREFACE

To be invited to write a preface to this volume is indeed both a pleasure and an honour. The editors are to be commended for bringing together in this form so varied and valuable a selection of papers regarding the social and economic history of Kent. One of the great advantages of modern re-print methods lies in the manner in which scattered material can be related and made accessible in an attractive form, as also in the much greater circle of readers who can be reached by this means compared with the membership of a learned society.

The Kent Archaeological Society has been far-sighted in agreeing to the re-issue of essays from *Archaeologia Cantiana*, for Kent is still a relatively unknown part of England. In many respects it has been neglected in the field of historical research and the establishment of a University at Canterbury is a vital link in the process of enlightenment. The vigour and enthusiasm of the Department of Economic History at that University is well illustrated by this venture by Miss Roake and Mr. Whyman and it is to be hoped that, as suggested in the Introduction, further volumes of essays will appear from time to time.

The papers chosen cover many aspects of local history and are of special value in so far as they indicate the nature and use of source material for such studies. Though perhaps none could be regarded as definitive, as a series they represent the development of scholarship in this field over the past half century and it is hoped their re-issue will stimulate fresh research and the opening up of new patterns of study from which still more adequate conclusions may be reached. I wish this venture every possible success.

Roundwell Cottage,   FELIX HULL.
Bearsted. 1971.

INTRODUCTION

Archaeologia Cantiana is the annual Journal of the Kent Archaeological Society, containing articles which contribute to the history and archaeology of Kent.

During the eighteenth century there was a notable growth of interest in archaeology and antiquarian studies which led to the nineteenth-century foundation of regional societies catering for these interests.[1] The Sussex Society was established in 1845, and others followed in Surrey, Middlesex and Essex within ten years.[2] The promoters were often the county gentry, and this was the case in Kent. Although there had been some unsuccessful attempts to form a Kentish Archaeological Society in the early 1850's, it was eventually launched on 19 September 1857 when a party of eleven noblemen and gentlemen of the county met for the inaugural meeting in the old state bedroom at Mereworth Castle at the invitation of the Viscount and Viscountess Falmouth.[3] Almost two years passed before the publication of the first volume of the journal *Archaeologia Cantiana* in July 1859.[4] Between then and 1970, eighty-five volumes have appeared.

These developments occurred at a time when a long tradition of writing general histories of the county had come to an end. The great but early writers, William Lambarde (1536-1601), William Camden (1551-1623), Richard Kilburne (1605-1678) and Thomas Philipot (d. 1682), belonged to a remote past. The eighteenth century was a fruitful age for Kentish historiography when a number of writers recorded the Kentish scene for the pleasure of the country gentry.[5] Without doubt the crowning achievement was that of Edward Hasted (1732-1812) whose work amounted to 7,000 pages.[6] His was a labour of love and, on the publication of the first volume of *The History and Topographical Survey of the County of Kent* in 1778, he observed:

> "The materials from which I have compiled the greatest part
> of the following work, are the result of twenty years constant
> labour and assiduity, and were collected for more than half
> that time without any further view, than that of affording me
> pleasure and employment."[7]

Modern historians refer frequently to these writers; a helpful evaluation of their work, and that of W. H. Ireland and John Furley, the latter writing in the Victorian age, is given by Dr. Hull in the first article reprinted here.

Current interest in local and regional history was expanded to the point of positive involvement by departments of history and economic history in many universities and schools of education, so that today a half of all post-graduate theses in English history in this country are devoted to some kind of localized study.[8] It is now widely recognized that the national economy has always been composed of a number of regional economies, and it follows that our knowledge of England as a whole is enhanced by an understanding of regional developments in the past.

In this respect the history of Kent is a valuable study to set against the emergence of industrial Britain which tends to loom large in the national picture. Kent is one of the largest and most populous of the southern counties and there are distinctive features in the development of the county which are worthy of attention. The influence of London has helped to mould its agriculture; proximity to the Continent and its long shoreline have encouraged trade. Compared with other counties there was remarkable development before 1700.

It has not been easy to select the 23 articles for this volume from the many valuable contributions over a long period to *Archaeologia Cantiana*. The editors in making their choice have sought to offer a reasonably balanced picture of the social and economic scene from the Middle Ages to the nineteenth century. Nine of the articles are specifically pre-1700 and thirteen concentrate on the later period. The fact that no article written before 1917 has been selected is explained by the changing nature of historical research and the current interests of economic and social historians. Since the essays which follow are reproduced in exactly their original form, readers will notice an inevitable variety in style and presentation.

The editors in making their selection were influenced also by the emphasis which some writers have given to the evaluation and use of sources. Many of the contributions deal with a particular source and thereby provide valuable models for students hoping to work on similar material. Miss Melling, for instance, demonstrates the value and use of account books and papers of insolvent debtors in relation to Kentish tradesmen in the early nineteenth century. Despite the difficulty of using and interpreting medieval documents, and the paucity of medieval statistics, good use is made of manorial accounts by Miss Smith and Professor Du Boulay and of early taxation records by Mr. Glasscock.

In the field of agrarian history Mr. Baker employs estate and ordnance maps in the study of medieval field patterns. Although his article now is somewhat dated, Mr. Tate shows how the historian can correlate the evidence of national authorities and contemporary writers, and he provides a useful list of Kent enclosure acts. The well-known Kentish phenomena of early enclosure and of gavelkind tenure are brought to the notice of readers by Messrs. Tate and Baker. The strength of Dr. Harvey's article on fruit farming lies in his appreciation of the many factors which influenced its spread and prosperity during the nineteenth century. The value of a purely visual source is illustrated in Mr. Bridge's account of Kent hop-tokens.

Miss Keen's work on the Best brewery at Chatham, Mr. Bridge's study of Maidstone Geneva, and Mr. Hiscock's article on the Dartford to Strood turnpike demonstrate the use of a variety of business papers. Mr. Minet's detailed analysis of the letter book of a Dover merchant is an early study in the commercial field. This article along with that of Miss Hardy, on the telegraphic link between London and the coast of Kent, are potent reminders of Kent's proximity to continental influences. The value and limitation of port books to the study of Kentish maritime trade before 1750 are discussed by Dr. Andrews. Messrs. Dulley and Chalklin employ wills and probate inventories to reconstruct aspects of urban history in the early modern period.

Three articles deal specifically with contemporary impressions gained from travelling through the county in 1735, 1759 and 1823. These examples reflect the value of historical information which may be gleaned from the many diaries which survive from the eighteenth and early nineteeth centuries.

The editors and publishers of these *Essays in Kentish History* have in mind for the future a companion volume which will introduce readers to further essays, based on research currently being undertaken in Kentish economic and social history. In the meantime, however, it is hoped that this selection of articles will be of value and interest both to students, and to those interested in a more general way in the history of this fascinating county.

University of Kent   MARGARET ROAKE
at Canterbury. 1971.   JOHN WHYMAN.

NOTES

1. See: Stuart Piggott, *William Stukeley: An Eighteenth-Century Antiquary* (Oxford, 1950), 7.
2. Frank W. Jessup, "The Origin and First Hundred Years of the Society", *Archaeologia Cantiana*, LXX (1956), 1.
3. *Ibid.*, 1.
4. *Ibid.*, 12-14.
5. Felix Hull, "Kentish Historiography", *Archaeologia Cantiana*, LXX (1956) reprinted below.
6. Alan Everitt, *New Avenues in English Local History* (Leicester, 1970), 4.
7. Edward Hasted, *The History and Topographical Survey of the County of Kent*, Volume 1, (Canterbury, 1778), Preface, i.
8. Everitt, *op.cit.*, 4; this finding comes from an analysis of the *Theses Supplement* for 1968 of *The Bulletin of the Institute of Historical Research*, the exact figure being 51%.

KENTISH HISTORIOGRAPHY

By FELIX HULL, B.A., Ph.D.

THE wider study of history embraces both the theory of historical research and the practice of historical writing. This latter topic, historiography, is equally significant whether in relation to the publication of works on local or national history and bears especially on the character and outlook as well as the scholarship of individual writers. In offering a paper on such a subject the author is not only aware of the limited research which he has been able to undertake, but also of entering what is for him a new field of study. Nevertheless, it seems that as the Kent Archæological Society and its journal reach a century of activity, some résumé of historical writing in Kent is not out of place.

The first volume of *Archœologia Cantiana* was produced at a time when general historiography in this county was at its lowest ebb for three centuries. The amazing industry of Hasted had been followed by the sterile work of Ireland, and although interest in archæology and things antiquarian was growing on an unprecedented scale, no new writer, as yet, had ventured into the wide and difficult field of county history. Today, one hundred years after, this is still largely the case. Of monographs and the results of detailed research we have unlimited evidence, the larger work of Furley and of the compilers of *Victoria County History* has opened up fresh paths, but no new volume has appeared which takes the place of those works, already old in 1858. As the days of Hasted and his predecessors become more and more remote, the works remain as monuments of scholarship but the authors become less vivid both as men and as historians. It is hoped, therefore, that a general paper on Kentish historiographers may stimulate others to follow the work of individual historians and topographers in greater detail and so to prepare the way for a definitive study of Kentish historiography.

In a single brief paper of this kind a measure of strict limitation is essential. Thus it is intended to refer only to some of the best-known historians who wrote of the whole or a major part of the county. Inevitably this means that so able a writer as William Boys of Sandwich is eliminated and with him many others whose names should be honoured among all who love Kent and its story. So, too, we must reject those antiquaries of Kent to whom we owe so much: Sir Edward Dering, John Philipot, Somerset Herald, or at a later date the Rev. Lambert Larking. Such men provided our historiographers with evidence.

1

They did not write history themselves, but their collections of MSS., and their transcripts and notes, were and remain in part, a store house for the searcher into the past of this corner of England.

Before discussing individuals and their works, certain general observations must be made. It is axiomatic that history is the story of the past written for the present. Seldom, if ever, does the historian consciously write for future generations. Nor would we expect that, for he, however shrewd his guess, has no special ability to judge future taste and fashion. We revere the names of Gibbon and Macaulay, but we do not expect modern scholars to adopt their style and conceits. While knowledge increases from age to age, literary taste and indeed society itself change and make their own demands on authorship. What was once the summit of research and stylistic writing becomes outdated and outmoded. An admirable example occurs in Vol. I of *Archæologia Cantiana*, p. 186, where that excellent antiquary Lambert Larking writes of Sir Roger Twysden as " . . . engrossed . . . in those learned researches to which we are largely indebted for the little we know of the early history of England". Who now looks to Twysden for knowledge of Anglo-Saxon society?

Again history is usually written with a definite purpose in mind. It may be the specialist monograph proving a point of detail, the broad sweep of a Trevelyan or the still wider view of a Toynbee or a Butterfield. Whether accuracy of factual account is related to prophetic message or not, written history cannot reside in a vacuum but for good or ill is purposive, since it involves a measure of interpretation.

Thirdly, the conception of history at any one time is largely determined by the political, religious and economic thought and practice of the day and of the place where it is written. Just as history written in communist Russia or catholic Spain varies from the English conception, so too the history of Livy, Camden or Gibbon varies from that of today.

These general factors influenced our authors just as they influence our approach to them and without due regard for them no comparative study is possible or reasonable.

The medieval period was not one of great historical scholarship. Various chronicles were compiled of a general and usually heroic character but local history as we know it did not exist. The stories of early mythical residents of this island coupled with the conquests of Brut of Trojan descent over the tyrannical giants of early days and later with the much expanded glories of King Arthur formed the basis for a " British history " which few dared to question. The sixteenth century saw the beginning of change with the pioneer topographical work of John Leland and the equally pioneer critical history of Polydore Virgil, an Italian living in this country. Such scholarship resulted in a growing interest in local and antiquarian study and it is from this date that the earliest of county historians appear, of whom William Lambarde represents Kent.

William Lambarde, 1536-1601, was born of parents connected with the business life of London, who were also fortunate enough to acquire " a house and land in Kent". Thus from his earliest years his connections with Westcombe Park, Greenwich, brought Lambarde into contact with this county, while family links brought him into touch with the life of the metropolis. At the age of twenty he was admitted to Lincoln's Inn, where under the tutorship of Lawrence Nowell he developed a lasting interest in the law and an appreciation of the legal outlook of the Anglo-Saxon period. Thus from the opening of his career his legal and antiquarian interests were welded together. By 1568 he had completed " Archionoma," a study of Saxon Law, and by 1570 his *Perambulation of Kent* was already prepared, though not published for another six years. Lambarde's subsequent career does not greatly concern us, for his later and greatest work was legal, but his close connection with Kentish justice kept alive his interest in the county and it is doubtful if anyone, as yet, has fully appreciated the value to Lambarde of his first marriage to Jane Multon. His wife died in 1575, but following his appointment to the Commission of the Peace four years later, he worked constantly by the side of his father-in-law for whom he seems to have had a deep affection and who may well have aided the younger man considerably in his career as a gentleman and justice in this county.

Lambarde's twin loves are fully apparent in the *Perambulation*. His pleasure in presenting the county of his choice is matched by his eagerness to display his knowledge of the pre-Conquest laws and the contemporary judicial picture. Thus we have his excellent " Estate of Kent " followed by topographical information of a modern Guide Book character. From thence, having dealt with the See of Canterbury, he covers such places of the county as he deems worthy of serious historical attention and completes the picture with the customs and laws of Kent. The whole presents an unusual form to modern eyes and something less than we now should regard as a county history. Nevertheless Lambarde produced a book of great interest and significance, not least in that it represented a pioneer activity.

This fact is linked with the author's day and generation. He is looking both backwards and forwards and this explains some of the peculiarities of the book. A follower of John Leland, he finds it necessary to uphold the badly shaken " British History " of Geoffrey of Monmouth although it has little to say of Kent. He accepts the wholly mythical Samotheans and the Brut legend and yet he does not lack critical ability. On the other hand, having made his apology, he admits that it is scarcely germane to his subject and, virtually omitting

3

the Roman occupation, dives into his own world of the Anglo-Saxon invaders.

Again he lived in a period of fierce religious passions and he takes delight in debunking monasticism and the medieval church, in this matter allowing his natural partisan feelings to overrule his critical faculties.

What, then, is the value of the *Perambulation* to us in the twentieth century? In the first place it is a pioneer work: no similar topographical account of a single county of like merit was attempted before this.[1] Secondly it presents clearly and concisely the Kent of the late Tudor period including judicial economic and social data of the greatest merit to the modern searcher. As a history of Kent it is good reading, contains much that is genuine and much that has been superseded. As a study of Kentish custom it is still valuable and not to be ignored, and it demonstrates the new and growing interest of that period in pre-Conquest affairs. But it is as a record of Elizabethan Kent, as a great lover of that county, who was also scholar and lawyer, saw it, that Lambarde's work stands the test.

It is reputed that Lambarde designed a much greater work than this, covering the whole country, but that he gave way to the younger Camden in this respect. This story, whatever its factual basis may be, serves to focus attention on Lambarde's near contemporary who far outstripped him in antiquarian and historical acumen. While William Camden hardly falls within the limits laid down for this paper, he did reside in Kent at Bexley, and he brought to the study of history and topography a fresh outlook and skill which make him justly revered. With Lambarde there is uncertainty and a distinctly medieval flavour, Camden is sure of his path and reaches out to the eighteenth-century writers and beyond.

More closely in harmony with the work of Lambarde, though lacking in its historical knowledge, is that of Richard Kilburne, 1605-78. Kilburne also was a lawyer and was five times Principal of Staple's Inn. His approach seems to have been a strictly utilitarian one. He presents the Kent of his own day with all its topographical divisions and, so far as he was able, he gives the reasons underlying these divisions. In this way he covers lathes, hundreds and parishes and also gives fresh information regarding the bailiwicks and liberties. In many respects his factual " Survey " is of more lasting value than the less sound historical narrative of the period. We do not turn to Kilburne for Kentish history, but for the pattern of seventeenth-century Kent, for he depicts the county as it was before the Civil War, despite the fact that his book was published in 1659.

---

[1] Carew's *Cornwall* appeared in 1602 and according to A. L. Rouse is a far more finished production than the *Perambulation*.

The second seventeenth-century author worthy of note is Thomas Philipot who died in 1682, son of the still better known John Philipot, Somerset Herald. With his *Villare Cantianum* we enter a new phase of Kentish historiography. The relationship with Lambarde and other earlier work is still apparent but the author is primarily an historian with all the advantages—scarcely acknowledged—of parental skill in the same field. Thus Philipot offers us a general if brief symposium of Kentish history supported by documents and evidence, as with the list of Sheriffs, from his father's work; and then follows with a much more detailed parochial study than any hitherto attempted. There is in this book a veneer of scholarly arrangement lacking in the rather haphazard plan of the *Perambulation* and we can see in this single volume the basis for Hasted's monumental work. There is, too, a changed approach. Lambarde's legal training repeatedly overcomes his antiquarian outlook, but Philipot has something of a truer historical sense. He emphasizes the significance of Kent from the naval and maritime aspect and is interested in the growth of local administration. In fact we are no longer presented with a " survey " but with an antiquary's " history." There are, of course, faults and difficulties: Philipot digresses with by no means happy results—as where he attempts to analyse the decadence of the monastics without any evidence in the modern sense; he has a most odd conception of alphabetical arrangement which seems to approach a phonetic list dependent on vowel sounds—thus Barfriston is followed by " Badhurst " and Blackmanstone is noted before Beakesbourne. In fact the whole arrangement suggests a dangerously haphazard approach and to the modern student is a warning that the contents may be equally haphazard and unreliable. In the third place there is an appendix setting out the supposed etymology of Kentish place names. That this list will not stand the tests of the English Place Names Society is not surprising, but it is more than a little significant that in the late seventeenth century an attempt of this kind should have been made on so full a scale.

The very character of this book makes it difficult to assess. Normally Philipot will be passed by for the fuller and better-developed Hasted, but that is unfair to one who took Lambarde's pioneer efforts and with his own and his father's researches produced a recognizable county history on the pattern which would be adopted and expanded for more than a century.

Our next author is the most difficult of all to assess. Scholar and mountebank Dr. John Harris, 1667-1719, has passed down to history as a charlatan who failed to bring his scheme to fruition, who uncritically copied his predecessors while claiming to be original and who equally uncritically added a good deal of rubbish to what passed for

5

county history. Yet is this wholly fair? Harris deserves more consideration than he has had if only because of his " grand design." To blame an historian for being a plagiarist is always dangerous, for nearly all depend on the work of others and may tend to accept generalizations and more detailed statements without due research. The seventeenth and eighteenth centuries were notorious for copyists who often slavishly followed another's work—even to the wording—and having added some small matter of personal knowledge or opinion claimed the whole as a new presentation. While Harris was uncritical and followed Philipot to a degree, his basic failure was his inability to complete the task he had set himself. Had his plan been accomplished the result might well have taken the place of Hasted's work, but the single volume appears bombastic and pretentious, to be regarded as a monumental failure and Harris's " folly."

The author of *Bibliotheca Cantiana* says that " though Harris was a man of unquestionable abilities and attainments, he was charged with culpable imprudence in his conduct; and, notwithstanding the preferments he enjoyed, was generally in distress". His ability as an historian tends to be damned in part on the grounds of his conduct as a clergyman, and it is more than difficult to judge these forerunners of Edward Hasted in a manner wholly fair to them or to their work. Harris's scheme was larger than Hasted's and indeed embraced almost as much as the more recent *Victoria County History*, excluding the economic sections. Hasted undoubtedly thought him valuable if not wholly reliable, and sought vainly the notes for his unwritten later volume. He took Philipot and expanded his work, even if he went no further in genealogical research and manorial ownership. He thought of civil and administrative history as a separate study—a most modern concept; and dealt with Roman roads and other archæological remains, matters untouched by earlier writers. Had he carried through his plan and finished off the ecclesiastical history of Kent, its natural history and the development of the Royal Navy, what a valuable whole might have resulted. As it is, Hasted supersedes Harris and we remember the earlier man's faults and failures rather than his breadth of purpose and modest achievement. It has been said that he would never have completed his task, for he was too unstable. Let that be as it may, he alone of the early historiographers attempted to describe in detail the Weald, Romney Marsh, the rivers and antiquities of Kent, or realized the full importance of maritime history to this county.

Edward Hasted, 1732-1812, presents so vast a canvas that several papers might be written on him and his work, rather than a single short paragraph. His alone of the early Kentish histories fully stands the test, and in his volumes no one who has been concerned with aspects of our history has sought wholly in vain.

A barrister, magistrate and deputy lieutenant, he spent forty years preparing his massive work, the footnotes to which alone testify to the quality of his researches. Naturally Hasted used the work of his predecessors: he owed much to all those mentioned already in these pages and he sought original or transcript evidence wherever it might be. With Hasted one is on surer ground than with the earlier men. Lambarde within his lights was clearly reliable and his whole account was limited in scope. Philipot and Harris spread themselves much further, but they seldom give chapter and verse for their statements and thus an element of doubt remains. Hasted was determined to prove everything to the best of his ability.

Even so, and surprisingly so, his scope and scheme is more limited than that of Harris. He packs general topography, civil history and the rest into a mere hundred pages, presenting for the main part a vast historical guide book parish by parish within the desperately confusing though topographically sound arrangement of lathes and hundreds. Because of this Hasted is not easy to use, and his overwhelming concern with the " descent of the manors " results in the omission of material which the modern historian would seek. Nevertheless his great value cannot be denied: not only is a vast amount of genealogical and topographical knowledge packed into these books, but for the student of the eighteenth century Hasted's evaluation of each parish in his own day is irreplaceable. That there are faults, omissions and evidence of lack of knowledge at times is no real criticism of a life work of outstanding merit and fundamental accuracy. The person who has worked in a county without a comparable eighteenth-century history knows from bitter experience the debt we owe to Hasted and his contemporary historians outside Kent.

The *New Topographical, Historical, and Commercial Survey* issued by Charles Seymour in 1776 raises yet again the problem of the copyist. Seymour claims to have had access to new material but his book is largely a re-hash of what previous writers had written, and his opening description of the county is almost word for word that used by the Rev. Thomas Cox in his *Britannia* (1720). Seymour, in fact, answers his own pretensions: in his introduction he speaks of the need for a concise but accurate account published at a price within the reach of most. This, despite his use of contemporary airs and graces, he gave to his public, and his book within its limits remains a useful guide book arranged alphabetically and therefore simple to use.

In contrast with Seymour, William Henry Ireland's *History of Kent* published between 1828 and 1830 has the sole merit of containing an attractive and useful set of prints for the early nineteenth century. Ireland, notorious for his Shakespearean forgeries, was a dilettante incapable of producing more than a pastiche of the work of his predecessors. What is of value comes from Hasted, but there is no attempt to enlarge or expand the earlier work and no real evidence either of knowledge of Kent or of original research.

With Ireland, however, we reach the end of an historiographical era, and were it not that the approach of these men whether giants or dwarfs varies so greatly from that of today it would be well to leave the story there. The changes of the last century and a half have been so great in historical thought and knowledge that it would seem wrong not to refer to them. All our historians from Lambarde to Ireland were topographers; they concentrated on actual administrative divisions (not their history) and on the history of the parish as seen through the descent of lordships and patronage of the living. All relied to a great extent on the material support of noble and gentle households, and their approach was governed by this mercenary factor. To make their work acceptable and profitable it must please, perhaps even flatter, those for whom it was intended: thus general history is glossed over except for the glories of Kentish Kings and the lists of nobles and gentry who served as sheriffs, justices, Knights of the Shire, and so forth. The economic growth and political democratization of the nineteenth century had their own reflection in historical writing, and it is with these facts in mind that we turn to *The History of the Weald of Kent*, by John Furley (1871).[1]

Nothing could be more distinct and different than the works of Furley and of Hasted. The Victorian owed much to his predecessor, but his whole approach is far removed. Here is local history written from the standpoint of national history. The earlier writers are concerned with Kent or even with the individual parishes of Kent; national affairs are incidental and neither make nor mar the story as it unfolds. Furley, in contrast, relies on national history as portrayed by his great contemporaries like Macaulay, as the basis for his work, fitting local incident into a larger pattern. Thus his chapters are arranged chronologically with the emphasis on the reigns of kings, and one is presented with a collection of facts woven into narrative for each epoch. The result is peculiar but typical of its period, and on the whole good compared with some other similar writers, for Furley never forgot Kent nor felt that a well-known incident must be retold irrespective of its Kentish connotation. Here is narrative history supported ably by original research as we understand it, and in Furley we can find much that is hidden or obscure in Hasted and the earlier books. Nevertheless it is unfair to compare two such dissimilar works, for they

---

[1] This is something of a misnomer. Furley, though emphasizing the Weald, deals with the history of the whole county and for that reason is included in this study.

require handling with due regard to their particular purposes. Hasted's is the great county history written for and of the gentry. From it we can see how estates rise and fall and can judge the collapse of monastic Kent from the statistics of the land market. Furley presents Kent's story for the newly educated masses who know vaguely of the major affairs of national history, but his own idiosyncrasies are apparent. Like many of his generation history to him became progressively less interesting and important as his own age was approached. Thus his chapter on the eighteenth century is a woeful affair, whereas the Civil War, Reformation and other periods of action are brilliantly presented. When all is said and done, however, Furley is telling a story which lasts until he nears the end of his third volume. Its faults are largely those of imperfect knowledge for which he can hardly be blamed, but in the last few chapters of the book we meet a new man. Here is Furley facing the problems and enigmas of Kent which still trouble us at times. In his handling of lathe, den, and other special features of Kentish topography and society he is giving us himself and the best years of research and thought. It matters not if his results do not always tally with our own, in his last chapters there is something new in Kentish historiography comparable only with Philipot's valiant efforts with place names.

Thus over a matter of three hundred years we can follow the writing of Kentish history from the brilliant but pioneer efforts of Lambarde to the amazing peaks of industry of Hasted and so to the very different and far from final work of John Furley. Approaches so different and scholarship so varied require a symposium such as it was hoped *Victoria County History* might present. The triumphs and failures of that scheme in Kent are not for this study, suffice to say that no previous writer other than the much maligned Dr. Harris conceived such a design for local history, and he could not carry it through. We still lack a definitive history of Kent, and *Victoria County History* as originally conceived would have wedded Hasted and his predecessors to the writers of Furley's approach. Yet it may be well that the great plan did not come to fruition, for recent research, archæological and documentary, has amplified and modified much of our historical thinking. This brings us to a final factor in the picture which is lacking throughout our historiography.

Lambarde dwelt on Saxon law and custom and this pattern was continued by his successors with due notice of the Kentish leaders and kings from Hengist to Baldred. So long as local history was centred in the landed families and their vicissitudes this sufficed, but it tended to reproduce those traditions of the conquering West Saxon house which survived the Norman conquest. So long, too, as Bede's story was the final word in early history Jutish and Saxon tradition were one.

In the 1930's a small volume was published on *The Jutes*[1] which with some justice was scathingly reviewed in this journal.[2] Nevertheless Jolliffe's main contention of a Jutish society, distinct from and overlain by that of the West Saxons remains, and until Kentish history is approached with the background however sketchy of three hundred years of independence, with a separate royal house, laws and economic system, the enigmas and curious survivals of this most fascinating county will not be solved. There remains for the future this great task of rewriting Kentish history from a new and more convincing standpoint.

To us, who study now, however, there are the books referred to above and many others, full of factual material for our purposes if we can but find it. These books, especially the best, are not easy to use: their approach is different, their wording peculiar, their material occasionally unreliable but they remain as a great monument to those who deeply loved Kent and regrettably, in some cases, as a warning to those whose designs overrun their skill or who regard the writing of history as a simple and casual affair. No one will re-write these books: some like Furley for all his good points will be superseded, some justly forgotten, but the two giants Lambarde and Hasted will remain to await some future unknown writer who may add yet another lasting pillar to the temple of Kentish historiography.

---

[1] *Pre-Feudal England: The Jutes*, by J. E. A. Jolliffe. O.U.P. (1933).
[2] *Archæologia Cantiana*, XLV (1933), pp. 290-4.

SOME FIELDS AND FARMS IN MEDIEVAL KENT

By ALAN R. H. BAKER

'Of all the features that go to make up the face of any
English country parish, the pattern of its fields strikes
me as the most puzzling. Why are fields the shapes
and sizes that they are? And is the present-day
pattern old, fairly old, or quite recent?'

A Correspondent, *The Times* (19th January, 1962), 12f.

THE fabric of the Kentish countryside shows some contrasting patterns.
The landscape of East Kent seems to have been woven on a broad loom:
its large fields and wire fences combine with a virtual absence of woodland to give it an open, extroverted appearance (Plate IA). The landscape of the Weald, on the other hand, seems to have been embroidered
in minute detail: its small fields and numerous, wide hedges combine
with abundant woods and coppices to give it an enclosed, introverted
appearance (Plate IB). From the crest of the North Downs escarpment these two views are one: in the foreground the expansive landscape
of the Vale of Holmesdale reflects in miniature that of East Kent and
beyond is the more confined landscape of the Ragstone Ridge and the
Weald (Plate IIA). These subjective mid-twentieth century impressions are confirmed in the objective late-eighteenth century drawings
of the surveyors engaged in producing the first edition Ordnance Survey
maps of Kent (Figs. 1-3).

Seventeenth century estate maps also reveal that fields to the north
of the chalk escarpment were generally twice as large as those in the
Weald. More specifically, fields in East Kent were more than three
times the size of those in the Low Weald (i.e. the Weald Clay Vale)
Fields in Holmesdale and the High Weald were larger than those in the
Low Weald although they were still only about half the size of those of
East Kent. There were regional variations, too, in the shapes and
boundaries of fields: the most striking contrast was between small,
irregularly shaped, hedged fields of the Weald and large, more rectangular, often unenclosed fields of East Kent. Estate maps also reveal
the existence of 'open fields,' i.e. fields subdivided into intermixed and
unenclosed parcels. But field and rural settlement patterns of Kent in
the seventeenth century differed little from those of the late-eighteenth

PLATE 1

A. A view in East Kent, of fields to the southwest of Eastry.

B. A view in the Weald, looking north across the valley of the
Kent Water near Tunbridge Wells.

PLATE II

A. A view across the Vale of Holmesdale, looking south from the North Downs escarpment near Wrotham towards the High Weald.

[*Photo by J. K. St. Joseph. Crown Copyright Reserved*

B. A view across Romney Marsh, looking northwest from New Romney. The marshland landscape, with its fenced and ditched fields and scarcity of hedges and trees, is the most open and exposed in Kent. Its fields and farms receive no consideration here because of their singular history of reclamation.

13

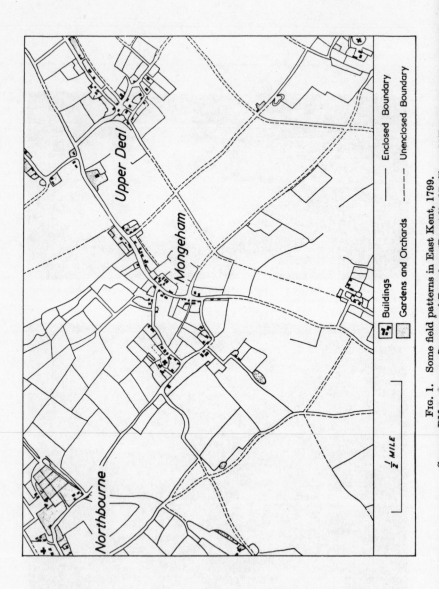

Fig. 1. Some field patterns in East Kent, 1799.

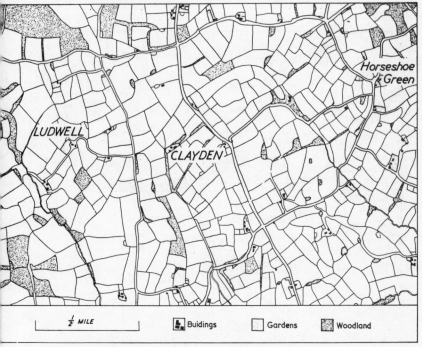

FIG. 2. Some field patterns in the Weald, 1799.
Source: BM Ordnance Surveyors' Drawings (Portfolio 5, Sheet 100).

or indeed of the mid-twentieth century. The origins of the present rural landscape are to be sought beyond 1600.[1]

THE PATTERN OF SETTLEMENTS

A precise picture of rural settlement and field patterns in the middle ages is, in the absence of estate maps, unobtainable but a partial picture can be derived from numerous and varied, but often fragmentary and intractable, verbal sources.[2] It will be the contention of this paper, based upon analysis of some of this material, that Kentish rural settlement and field patterns were already by the beginning of the fourteenth

[1] A. R. H. Baker, 'Some early Kentish estate maps and a note on their portrayal of field boundaries,' *Arch. Cant.*, 77 (1962), 177-184 and 'Field patterns in seventeenth-century Kent,' *Geography*, 59 (1965), 18-30.

[2] H. C. Darby, '*An Historical Geography of England*: twenty years after,' *Geographical Journal*, 126 (1960), 147-159.

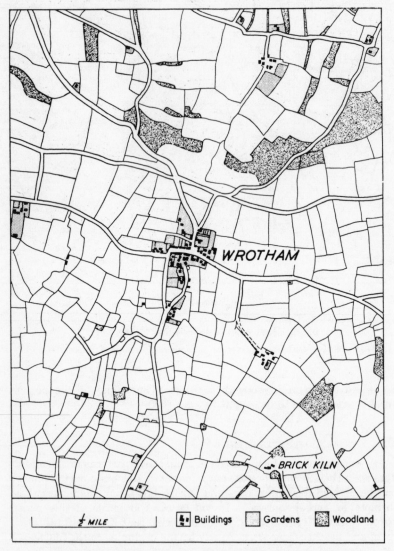

FIG. 3.   Some field patterns in the Vale of Holmesdale, 1799.
Source: BM Ordnance Surveyors' Drawings (Portfolio 16, Sheet 99).

century established in a form which has remained basically unchanged to the present day.[3]

The settlement pattern of the early fourteenth century in the Weald comprised mostly hamlets and isolated farmsteads, products of tardy colonization and a relatively low population density, and similar patterns probably existed on the heavily wooded Clay-with-flints capping the Downs and on the London Clay of the Blean.[4] Elsewhere —and most notably on the lower dip-slope of the Downs and in the Vale of Holmesdale—the earlier development of permanent settlement and greater density of population had produced a pattern of settlement which included villages as well as hamlets and isolated farmsteads.[5] From a rental of 1447, it has been possible to reconstruct the relative positions of most of the 50 or so yokes and other fiscal divisions on the manor of Gillingham and approximately to locate many of the tenants' messuages: there was in 1447 a nucleation of settlement around the church but in addition the landscape was dotted with houses and granges, grouped sometimes in twos and threes but also existing as isolated farmsteads. Comparison with a rental of 1285 suggests that settlement was similarly dispersed then.[6] A rental of 1494 of the manor of Wrotham reveals that few farmsteads had been erected in the heavily wooded Clay-with-flints country above the escarpment of the North Downs (some tenants who held land above the escarpment, *supra montem*, in fact had dwellings below it), most messuages were nucleated around the church at the foot of the escarpment, and there were hamlets and numerous isolated farmsteads dispersed throughout the township. Again, comparison with a rental of 1285 suggests a similar settlement pattern then.[7] At Ightham, immediately to the west of Wrotham, settlement at the end of the fifteenth century comprised a village, seven hamlets and numerous dispersed farms.[8] There had been a rapid growth of population in these and other Kentish townships during the twelfth and thirteenth centuries—some townships probably

[3] The marshland areas of Kent are excluded from this present study because of their singular history of reclamation.

[4] J. L. M. Gulley, 'The Wealden landscape in the early seventeenth century and its antecedents' (unpublished Ph.D. thesis, University of London, 1960), 356.

[5] S. W. Wooldridge and D. L. Linton, 'The loam-terrains of southeast England and their relation to its early history,' *Antiquity*, 7 (1933), 297-310 and 'Some aspects of the Saxon settlement in southeast England considered in relation to the geographical background,' *Geography*, 20 (1935), 161-175.

[6] Kent Archives Office (= KAO) U398 MIA and Canterbury Cathedral Library (= CCL) E24, ff. 29v-33v. See also A. R. H. Baker, 'Open fields and partible inheritance on a Kent manor,' *Econ. His. Rev.*, 2nd ser., 17 (1964-65), 1-23.

[7] KAO U55 M59 and CCL E24, ff. 76-84v. See also A. R. H. Baker, 'Field systems in the Vale of Holmesdale,' *Agricultural History Review* (forthcoming).

[8] E. Harrison, 'The court rolls and other records of the manor of Ightham as a contribution to local history,' *Arch. Cant.*, 48 (1936), 169-218 and 49 (1937), 1-95 and 'Some records of Ightham parish,' *Arch. Cant.*, 53 (1940), 17-23.

saw a four- or five-fold expansion of their tenant populations[9]—resulting not only in an increase in the sizes of villages and hamlets but also in a dispersal of settlement. Gavelkind tenure probably encouraged population growth, by providing for all male (or failing male, then female) heirs and it certainly encouraged settlement dispersal.[10] That the partitioning of patrimonial holdings sometimes produced isolated farmsteads is seen in a custumal of Wingham manor, 1285: 'if an inheritance . . . is divided into two or three portions when there are heirs, and each makes his messuage upon his portion,' then each will owe a separate hen-rent.[11]

THE PATTERN OF LAND HOLDINGS

Settlements were dispersed but individual holdings were more or less compact. The fields and parcels of an individual holding were not scattered throughout a township but tended to be concentrated within one section of it. At Gillingham in 1285, nearly three quarters (73·6 per cent.) of the tenants' holdings lay within a single, although not the same, fiscal division and most of the remaining quarter (23 per cent.) were within 2-5 divisions: the lands of an individual holding were not widely scattered. By 1447, the proportion of tenants with land in only one fiscal division had been reduced to a third (32·7 per cent.) and the proportion with land in 2-5 divisions increased to over two-fifths (43·7 per cent.): these changes indicate a wider distribution of the constituents of an individual holding in 1447 than in 1285 and reflect both the lower tenant population of the manor at the later date (there were about 300 tenants in 1285, about 110 in 1447) and the growing inequality of holding sizes during the later middle ages.[12] At Wrotham, 1285, where there were 6 boroughs or sub-districts, the inhabitants of which were grouped together for the maintenance of law and order, only about 20 of the 409 tenants, or about 5 per cent., held land in more than one borough; by 1494 the comparable figure was 25 per cent.[13] Individual holdings were more compact in the late thirteenth century than they were in the mid- and late-fifteenth century: they were also smaller.

It is impossible to discover the exact sizes of many individual holdings from the 1285 rentals: the Wrotham rental, for example,

[9] F. R. H. Du Boulay, 'Partible inheritance in medieval Kent' (unpublished paper). I am most grateful to Prof. Du Boulay for kindly allowing me to see a typescript of this paper.
[10] C. I. Elton, *The Tenures of Kent* (London, 1867), 39-44 and N. Neilson, 'Custom and the common law in Kent,' *Harvard Law Review*, 38 (1924-25), 482-498.
[11] CCL E24, f. 15.
[12] Baker, *loc. cit.* (1964-65), 7, 14-15 and 17.
[13] KAO U55 M59 and CCL E24, ff. 76-84v.

frequently lists five or more tenants as paying the rent on a single piece of land, but the general picture is one of small holdings such as William Blacson's 1 acre and John son of Dunstan's 7 acres. Inequality of holding size was increasing (already by 1285 one large holding had come to be termed a 'manor') but even in 1494 most holdings were small: one-fifth of the 131 holdings then owed rents of 1s. or less, nearly two-fifths owed rents of 2s. or less and just over one-half owed rents of 3s. or less. The lowest rent owed by a single holding was 2d., and the highest was £4 6s. 3d.: a rental of the same manor in 1538 shows that since 1494 the inequality of holding size had increased considerably. A typical holding at Wrotham at the end of the fifteenth century comprised a messuage, an adjacent garden, and a number of small crofts and larger fields, lying often as a compact unit and never widely scattered.[14] At Gillingham, 1285, probably one half of the holdings were of two acres or less: by 1447 the comparable proportion was one quarter. At this later date, however, 66 per cent. of the holdings were still of 10 acres or less; 19 per cent. were of 10·1-50 acres; 9 per cent. were of 50·1-100 acres and 6 per cent. were of more than 100 acres.[15] It was suggested earlier that population growth combined with gavelkind tenure to accentuate the dispersal of settlement in Kent during the thirteenth century. This same combination produced also a multiplicity of small holdings.[16] In some places partitioning of inheritances resulted in holdings too small to be economically viable: in 1276 the lands of John of Cobham were disgavelled on the grounds that excessive partitioning had reduced holdings below subsistence size.[17]

The Effects of Partitioning

P. Vinogradoff noted the impact of gavelkind tenure upon the Kentish landscape and suggested that settlement expansion might take three forms:

(1) Secondary colonization, i.e. the migration of one set of tenants to some outlying part of the estate or to an altogether new place of abode. This would have created a dispersed settlement pattern of compact farms

---

[14] *Ibid.*, and KAO U55 M60/2. A typical holding at Wrotham in 1494 was that of Richard Cooke, who held in the borough of Hale for a rent of 2s. 10d. 'one piece of land called Bakisland, one parcel of land and meadow called Stokemede and one piece of land called Taylers': KAO U55 M59, ff. 4-4v.

[15] Baker, *loc. cit.* (1964-65), 7 and 15.

[16] Elton, *op. cit.*, 41, 290-291, 369 and 384; H. L. Gray, *English Field Systems* (Cambridge, Mass., 1915), 272-304; G. C. Homans, 'Partible inheritance of villagers' holdings,' *Econ. His. Rev.*, 8 (1937-38), 48-56 and 'The rural sociology of medieval England,' *Past and Present*, 4 (1953), 32-43; F. R. H. Du Boulay, *Medieval Bexley* (Bexley, 1961), 20-24.

[17] *Cal. Ch. Rolls.*, 1257-1300, no. 198.

and would have only been possible in an area of relatively low population density where there remained sufficient waste to allow expansion of the cultivated area (Fig. 4b).

(2) Fragmentation of holdings into minor yet compact parts. This would have created a dispersed settlement pattern only if a new farmstead were also erected, but it would certainly have led to lowering of the average size of the farms (Fig. 4c).

(3) Subdivision of the fields of a holding into intermixed parcels, tending to equalize advantages and disadvantages in the distribution of land on soils of differing qualities. This again would have created a dispersed settlement pattern only if a new farmstead were also erected but it would certainly have led to a pattern of subdivided fields (Fig. 4d).[18]

Examination of Kentish Feet of Fines throws some light on the effects of gavelkind tenure upon the size of holdings and the pattern of fields.[19]   A Fine was an instrument for transferring property and it represented, during the thirteenth century at least, an agreement made in the settlement of an action at law.   For the period 1182-1272 there are nearly 1,500 Fines relating to land in Kent and of the 420 parishes into which the modern county is divided 370 are represented.[20]   Gavelkind tenure is mentioned explicitly in only 5 of these Fines,[21] but two characteristics of the tenure—a widow's claim to half of her husband's property and the equal claims to the other half by the other heirs—are discernible in many others.   The Fines show beyond doubt that holdings were partitioned.   A Fine relating to lands in East Peckham, 1248, demonstrates how the property of Blakemany de Stockingebir, amounting probably to about 30 acres, in the course of 4 generations became split up in a complex series of interests among 12 of his descendants.[22]   Only occasionally is precise indication given of the form partitioning was to take but there is no doubt that both the subdividing of fields and the fragmenting of holdings took place.

At Wye in 1227 individual fields were halved and halves of fields were halved again to effect subdivision.   The holding of Richard le Brun comprised fields and halves of fields and after his death his four sons acknowledged one half of the holding to a third party and retained the other half themselves, so that the resulting parcels comprised halves

[18] P. Vinogradoff, *English Society in the Eleventh Century* (Oxford, 1908), 274.

[19] Transcriptions of Kentish Fines are conveniently contained in I. J. Churchill, R. Griffin and F. W. Hardman (eds.), 'Calendar of Kent Feet of Fines to the end of Henry III's reign,' *Kent Records*, 15 (1956).   This volume contains a comprehensive introduction by F. W. Jessup.

[20] *Ibid.*, xiii, xxxvii and cviii.

[21] *Ibid.*, lxv.

[22] *Ibid.*, 200.

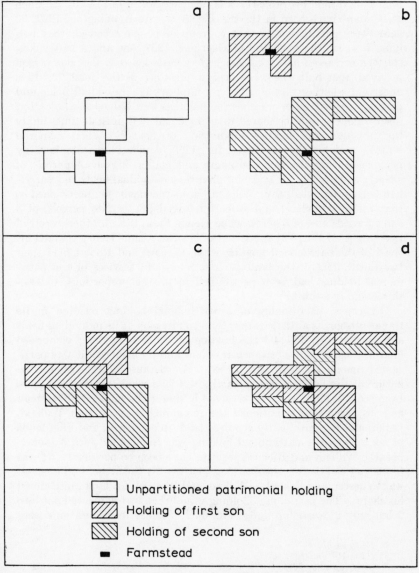

Fig. 4. Some hypothetical field and settlement patterns associated with a growing population and partible inheritance.

and quarters of fields. As Richard's four sons seem to have been joint-cultivators, his property was not partitioned in practice as much as it might have been in theory (Fig. 5).[23] At Kennington, 1227, 30 acres were partitioned so that a group of people received 'that half lying towards the east' and at Ospringe, 1227, one and a half yokes, thirteen acres and half a messuage were partitioned so that one person received 'that half which lies everywhere towards the north.'[24] It is uncertain whether this phraseology implies that individual fields and parcels were halved or whether the holdings were halved as wholes, but if soil values were to be shared with any equality it must at times imply the bisection and further subdivision of fields.[25] When manorial rentals, such as that of Wrotham, 1285, depict tenements held by persons bearing the same surname and comprising small parcels of exactly equal sizes it may be inferred that individual fields and parcels had been subdivided: thus William Fara's tenement was partitioned so that his sons Richard and Robert received jointly two parcels, of 3 acres 3 roods and of 6 acres, while Henry Fara, their brother, received two parcels of 1 acre 3½ roods and of 3 acres. Thus Henry claimed his third of the patrimonial holding while Richard and Robert held their two-thirds jointly: the land parcels, rents and services of the patrimonial holding had been partitioned in precise proportions, of two-thirds and one-third.[26]

At times, partitioning of a patrimonial holding resulted in its fragmentation as a whole rather than subdivision of its individual fields and parcels. In 1262-63 the holding of William Peyforer comprised land in 8 parishes in north-central Kent and on his death it was partitioned among his wife and three sons. Because of the fragmented nature of the holding, it was partitioned as a whole rather than piece by piece. William's widow received in dower the manor of Sharstead and his three sons partitioned the remaining lands so that William, junior, and Richard jointly acquired lands in one parish and Fulk lands in six. Thus the patrimonial holding was fragmented into 3 (not 4, because William and Richard seem to have been co-partners). It was further agreed that on the death of their mother the manor of Sharstead was to descend undivided to William and Richard, for Fulk quitclaimed his share. The patrimonial holding would then be fragmented not into 3 but only 2 ownership units (Fig. 6).[27] Similar fragmentations were

[23] *Ibid.*, 94-95.
[24] *Ibid.*, 101 and 105.
[25] Gray, *op. cit.*, 296: 'Division among co-heirs probably involved giving to each his share of the several qualities of land within the *iugum* . . . Since allotments of different quality must frequently have been non-contiguous, the tenants of a subdivided *iugum* would find their holdings consisting of scattered parcels.'
[26] CCL E24, ff. 81v-82.
[27] Churchill *et. al.*, *op. cit.*, 339-340.

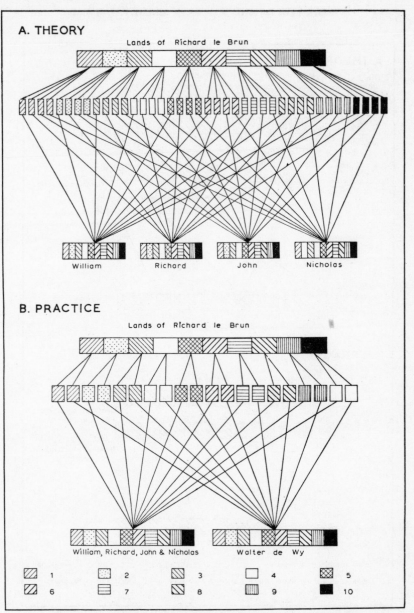

FIG. 5.   Inheritance of the holding of Richard le Brun in 1227.
Source: Churchill *et. al., op. cit.,* 94-95.

Key to the unpartitioned holding:
    1. Half of Redebrock; 2. Half of Wiredesham; 3. A croft; 4. Half of Kingesfield; 5. Half of Santesdane; 6. Half of the land of Fannes; 7. The Vale of Biltesberh; 8. Half of la Falaise; 9. Half of Meleland; 10. Land which lies under the garden.

23

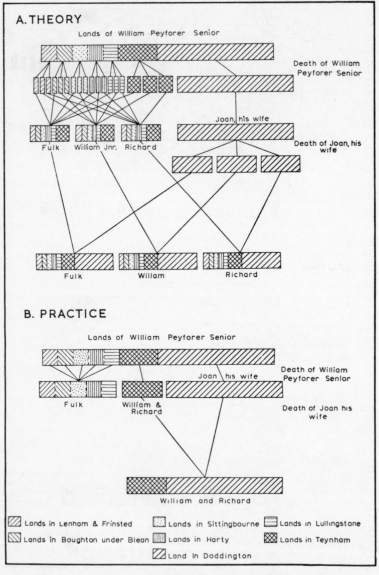

FIG. 6.   Inheritance of the holding of William Peyforer in 1262-63.
Source: Churchill *et al.*, *op. cit.*, 339-340.

effected on the holding of John de Esthall in the Orpington area in 1241 and on the scattered holding of William de Faulkham in 1249-50.[28]

Partitioning of holdings, together with the subdivision of rents and services attached to them, led to the disintegration of yokes (*iuga*). Yokes in Kent were fiscal divisions, for the assessment of rents and services. Although the sizes of yokes at Gillingham, for example, varied considerably, the labour services and customs due from them had been largely uniform. While services and customs were exacted, it was principally in the money rents they owed that yokes at Gillingham differed from each other. The rent due from each yoke was related not to the area of each unit but to the quality of its soils: jugation at Gillingham was an assessment of land potential.[29] The *iugum* was devised at the end of the third century by the Romans as a means of assessing rapidly the contribution of taxes from parts of a large land area[30] and by the early middle ages it had become a system, an adaptable system, of assessing rents and services due from land holdings. The woodland area which belonged to the manor of Aldington and which was divided into denns had, by 1285, been arranged into half and quarter yokes, burdened with carrying services and suit of court.[31] Of Haythurst and Finchurst, two Wealden denns of the manor of Gillingham, it was said that 'the tenants of these denns associate together as two yokes (*pro duobus juga*) when a collection happens to be made for Rochester Bridge or for a taxation of yokes.'[32] Many rentals and surveys show that thirteenth century yokes—and *logi*, virgates and *tenementa*, the other principal fiscal units of assessment— had personal names, which suggests that they had often formerly been in the hands of a single tenant, or at least of a small group of tenants, probably collaterals. Some were held in this way at the beginning of the thirteenth century and as late as 1285 John Brutyn was the sole tenant of *Jugum Brutyn* in Gillingham.[33] But many yokes had been partitioned by that time. In *c.* 1214 the 17 yokes of gavelkind land at Bexley were held by 47 persons. Of these 17, three were held by only one tenant, five more were probably held in a previous generation by only one tenant and two more were probably held by single tenants two generations back. Even in the early thirteenth century few of these yokes were held by more than two or three partners, who were often brothers. By 1284, however, these same yokes were divided among at

---

[28] *Ibid.*, 158-159 and 230.

[29] A. R. H. Baker, 'The Kentish *iugum*: its relationship to soils at Gillingham,' *English Historical Review*, 81 (1966)—forthcoming.

[30] F. Lot, 'Le jugum le manse et les exploitations agricole de la France moderne', in *Mélanges d'Histoire offerts à Henri Pirenne*, vol. 1 (1926), 307-326.

[31] F. R. H. Du Boulay, 'Denns, droving and danger,' *Arch. Cant.*, 76 (1961), 75-87.

[32] *Ibid.*, 82.

[33] CCL E24, f. 30v.

least 150 persons.[34]   At Gillingham, *Pieresyok* had 8 tenants in 1285 but it is described as 'the yoke formerly of Peter'; *Soperesyok* had 5 tenants but in the previous generation it probably had only 3; and 10 tenants held 'the yoke of Reginald at Upeton.'[35]   *Tenementum Osberti*, in West Wickham, had 5 tenants in 1310 and *Tenementum Elfryk atte Derefold*, in Lenham, had 13 in 1302.[36]   The fact that a fiscal unit had at one time been in the hands of a single tenant or small group of tenants, together with the fact that at the end of the thirteenth century the lands of an individual holding were still concentrated in one part of a township, shows that the original fiscal assessment was concerned with more or less compact family holdings.   A yoke was not necessarily a single family farm, however; rather single family farms were assessed as single yokes or as multiples or fractions of a yoke, according not simply to the size of the farm but to the qualities of its soils.   By the end of the thirteenth century—with the growth of population, the partitioning of holdings and the impact of an active market in land—a single yoke had often lost its character as an agrarian unit, for by then it was occupied by many tenants.   Nevertheless, it retained its importance as a fiscal unit, the services and rents of which were minutely subdivided among these tenants.   With the commutation of services, a yoke lost even its fiscal validity and gradually it disappeared from the records.   Thus a rental of Wrotham in 1285, by which time most services on the manor had probably been commuted (they certainly had by 1309), contains references to only 7 full or half yokes and a rental of 1494 makes no reference to yokes at all.[37]   By contrast, a rental of Gillingham in 1285, when most services were still exacted, contains references to 31 full, double or half yokes and a rental of 1447, when services had only recently been commuted (commutation having taken place between 1442 and 1447) contains references to 29 full or double yokes.[38]

The effects of partitioning were not as far-reaching as they might have been, for they were counterbalanced by a number of processes. Holdings were not partitioned either as often or as minutely in practice as they might have been in theory.   Some were probably farmed jointly by co-heirs.   Nearly 40 Fines for the period 1182-1272 record brothers purchasing or renting land and they may have been agricultural as well as financial partners.   In 1255, the holding of William de Mares in northwest Kent was partitioned among his widow and four sons: the apportionment of lands is described in detail and it appears that William and Richard each held his lands on his own while John and

[34] Du Boulay, *op. cit.*, 21-22.
[35] CCL E24, f. 29v.
[36] KAO U312 M21 and U55 M210.
[37] CCL E24, ff. 76-78; Lambeth Palace Library (= LPL) CR119; KAO U55 M59.
[38] CCL E24, ff. 29v-33v; KAO U398 MIA; LPL CR461.

Henry held theirs jointly.[39] Where brothers appear as joint-holders of land, it seems reasonable to assume that they may have been joint cultivators as well. Rentals frequently refer to *heredes, socii, parcenarii* and *pares*, which may be interpreted either as implying the joint-holding of a tenement or as representing no more than a clerically convenient way of recording the responsibility for rents and services from a partitioned holding. There is no way of solving this problem, and it can only be said that some of these phrases probably indicate joint-holding. It is certain, however, that the partitioning effects of gavelkind tenure were counteracted and to some extent reversed by another characteristic of that tenure, namely free alienation *inter vivos*. Any one of a number of co-heirs could alienate all or part of his share of an inheritance, either to one or more of the other co-heirs (in which case the effects of partitioning would be mitigated, possibly nullified) or to an outsider (in which case the patrimonial holding would still have been broken up).[40] Freedom to alienate holdings certainly stimulated the market in land, enabled the more enterprising and more prosperous tenants to augment their holdings by purchase or lease and resulted in a growing inequality in the size of land holdings.[41]

SUBDIVIDED DEMESNE FIELDS

Not all of the fields which appear on early estate maps as being subdivided into unenclosed parcels of land were a consequence of the operation of gavelkind tenure. Some originated from the leasing of former demesne fields not in their entirety but in parcels to different tenants. While demesne fields in Kent were being directly cultivated by manorial lords and their officials, they were frequently sown in sections with more than one kind of crop in a field in any given year.[42] And as the fields had often been sown in sections with different crops, so they came to be leased out in parcels to different tenants. At Otford small portions of demesne fields were being leased to tenants by the

[39] Churchill *et al.*, *op. cit.*, 411-412.

[40] The Feet of Fines contain many examples of such modifications to inheritances: Churchill *et al.*, *op. cit.*, *passim*. For more detailed discussion of this topic, see A. R. H. Baker, 'The field systems of Kent' (unpublished Ph.D. thesis, University of London, 1963), 272-288.

[41] F. R. H. Du Boulay, 'Gavelkind and knight's fee in medieval Kent,' *English Historical Review*, 77 (1962), 504-511 and *op. cit.*, 22-25; Baker, *op. cit.* (1964-65), 7 and 18-21; Gulley, *op. cit.*, 354-356.

[42] This practice has been observed on a number of manors. For example, at Wrotham; Baker, *loc. cit.* (forthcoming): at Westerham; T. A. M. Bishop, 'The rotation of crops at Westerham, 1297-1350,' *Econ. His. Rev.*, 9 (1938), 38-44: at Otford; F. R. H. Du Boulay, 'Late-continued demesne farming at Oftord,' *Arch. Cant.*, 73 (1959), 116-124: at Bexley; Du Boulay, *op. cit.*, 7: at Westwell; A. Smith, 'A geographical study of agriculture on the Kentish manors of Canterbury Cathedral Priory, 1272-1379' (unpublished M.A. thesis, University of Liverpool, 1961), 47: and at Thurnham; KAO U512 T2.

early fifteenth century.[43] The leasing of small parcels of demesnes acquired increasing importance during the fourteenth century on some of the manors of Canterbury Cathedral Priory, such as Monkton and Ickham in East Kent.[44] At Wrotham, 1399-1400, the lord was cultivating most of his 250 or so acres of arable but about 12 acres were leased to his tenants in various of the manor's fields (*in diversis campis huius manerii*), for a total rent of 11s. 2d. By 1406-7 this practice had been extended, for although most of the demesne was being cultivated by the lord, leased portions produced a rent of £2 16s. 0d.[45] Comparison of names of demesne fields in a custumal of 1285 and later account rolls with names of subdivided fields on a map of part of Wrotham manor in 1620 shows that some subdivided fields in Kent developed from the cropping and then the leasing of demesne fields in sections.[46]

CO-ARATION AND FIELD PATTERNS

It has often been suggested that strip fields in the midlands were closely associated with co-aration, that each contributor to a joint plough team was allotted a strip or strips of each day's ploughing.[47] The extent to which subdivided arable fields in Kent were similarly produced is difficult to determine. An examination of the relationship between ploughing techniques and field shapes in Kent concluded that with the turn-wrest plough most commonly used in the county it was just as possible to plough squarish plots as rectangular strips and assumed that intermixed strips in the county resulted from co-aration.[48] The practice of co-aration in medieval Kent can be substantiated. A custumal of the manor of Wingham, 1285, states: 'every tenant who resides in the hundred and who has a fully-yoked plough shall, by reason of his tenements within the precinct of the manor, plough one acre of *gerserth* and he who has less shall plough proportionately, in such a way that if any tenant shall join with a non-tenant or with anyone who does not owe ploughing service, he shall come to plough with as many beasts as he has at the plough and the bedel shall make up one plough from the horses of those who do not have a full plough.'[49] In the portion of the custumal dealing with Grain, it is stated: 'every joint-plough within the precinct of the manor shall plough half an acre (of the demesne).'[50] Similar references to co-aration come from Lyminge, Northfleet and

---

[43] Du Boulay, *loc. cit.* (1959), 121.
[44] R. A. L. Smith, *Canterbury Cathedral Priory. A Study in Monastic Administration* (London, 1943), 192.
[45] LPL CR 1142 and 1145.
[46] CCL E24, f. 76; KAO U55 M64-67 and U681 P31.
[47] C. S. and C. S. Orwin, *The Open Fields* (2nd edn., Oxford, 1954), 1-68.
[48] M. D. Nightingale, 'Ploughing and field shape,' *Antiquity*, 27 (1953), 20-26
[49] CCL E24, f. 11v.
[50] *Ibid.*, f. 33.

Teynham.[51]   At Sundridge, c. 1258, ploughing services were assessed
in proportion to a tenant's ownership of a whole or part of a plough
team: presumably those who owned only a part joined with others to
make a full team.[52]   Co-aration might have given rise to a pattern of
unenclosed parcels in some parts of Kent, although there is no evidence
that it actually did so.   The fact that settlements were dispersed and
that individual holdings were more or less compact suggests, as does
the wording of the Wingham custumal, that co-aration in Kent was a
venture in agricultural co-operation by friends and neighbours.   Some
of the many subdivided fields shared by only a few tenants might have
been products of such private agreements.

COMMON ARABLE FIELDS?

It now becomes necessary to ask whether agricultural co-operation
in medieval Kent included not only co-aration but also cultivation and
grazing of arable fields in common: were subdivided arable fields in fact
common arable fields?   Most land in Kent was held in severalty.[53]   In the
Weald in the early fourteenth century enclosed pastures held in severalty
covered substantial acreages and Feet of Fines suggest that land was
held in severalty throughout the county.[54]   It was in fact pleaded in
1322 that no man in Kent could pasture his livestock in common on
gavelkind lands and it seems that most cultivated land was held in
severalty.[55]   Nevertheless, it would have been difficult to graze unenclosed parcels of land and this difficulty was overcome in two ways;
first, individuals sometimes put up temporary folds around their own
unenclosed parcels; secondly, groups of owners with unenclosed parcels
in the same field sometimes came to private agreements about pasturing
the field in common.

Farming practices on tenant holdings in the middle ages are difficult
to discern, partly because they were not controlled by a manorial court.
In an exchange of lands at Kennington, 1268-9, one man was granted
in the woods of another 'reasonable estovers for housebote and haybote
for burning and fencing and for repairing his folds.'[56]   Many tenants of
archiepiscopal manors had to provide hurdles for the lord's folds and it
may be assumed that some tenants followed the demesne practice of
folding livestock.[57]   Folding was practised on the demesne at Deal in

---

[51] *Ibid.*, ff. 40, 64 and 87v.
[52] H. W. Knocker, 'The evolution of the Holmesdale. No. 3. The manor of
Sundridge,' *Arch. Cant.*, 44 (1932), 189-210.
[53] J. E. A. Jolliffe, *Pre-Feudal England: The Jutes* (London, 1933), 7 and 14.
[54] Gulley, *op. cit.*, 322; Churchill *et al.*, *op. cit.*, *passim*.
[55] A. Fitzherbert, *Grand Abridgement of the Common Law*, II (1516), xiv-xv,
cited in Gulley, *op. cit.*, 320.
[56] Churchill, *op. cit.*, 355.
[57] Folding was practised on the demesnes at Wrotham (CCL E24, f. 84) and
Gillingham (CCL E24, ff. 29v and 33, and BM Add. Ms. 29, 794, m.3).

the fourteenth century and on the unenclosed arable lands of the tenantry in the seventeenth century, and sheep folding was required by covenant in some leases on land in the Folkestone area in the eighteenth century.[58] It seems that individuals folded their own stock on their own lands, there being no evidence of fold-courses such as were used in East Anglia.[59] An alternative to folding was the common pasturing of subdivided fields by private agreement. Some tenants were compelled to graze their livestock collectively on the arable demesne and again it may be assumed that tenants sharing subdivided fields sometimes followed this practice by mutual agreement.[60] Such agreements would have represented no more than common sense arrangements which were rarely written down. One such agreement, made in 1246, relates to lands in Bekesbourne. William de Beck qui claimed to his brother, Richard, a moiety of 48 acres of land in Bekesbourne which he claimed as 'his reasonable part of the inheritance of William de Beck their father whose heirs they are.' Richard granted to William in exchange a rent of 20s. yearly from a tenement in Bekesbourne which Henry de Bourne had held from their father. In addition, Richard agreed that William and his heirs might have 'pasture for 4 cows yearly in the pasture of Richard in the said vill from Easter to Michaelmas except the pasture of the garden of Richard and his heirs . . . and if Richard and his heirs do not wish to put their cows in the pasture nevertheless it shall be lawful for William and his heirs to turn their cows in whenever they will without hindrance of Richard and his heirs.'[61] Most subdivided fields in Kent were shared by small numbers of tenants: agricultural co-operation, where practised, involved only few tenants and not the entire community of a township. For the end of the eighteenth century we have the testimony of John Boys, 'an able and successful farmer [at Betteshanger, in East Kent], and a famous breeder of South Down sheep,' who wrote in his report to the Board of Agriculture: 'there is no portion of Kent that is occupied by a community of persons, as in many other counties.'[62]

[58] A. R. H. Baker, 'The field system of an East Kent parish (Deal),' *Arch. Cant.*, 78 (1963), 96-117; G. E. Mingay, 'Estate management in eighteenth-century Kent,' *Agricultural History Review*, 4 (1956), 108-113.

[59] Gray, *op. cit.*, 305-354; K. J. Allison, 'The sheep-corn husbandry of Norfolk in the sixteenth and seventeenth centuries,' *Agricultural History Review*, 5 (1957), 12-31. Individuals certainly folded their own stock on their own unenclosed parcels in fields on the Sussex Downs; A. M. M. Melville, 'The pastoral custom and local wool trade of medieval Sussex, 1085-1485' (unpublished M.A. thesis, University of London, 1931), 75 and 128; J. C. Cornwall, 'The agrarian history of Sussex, 1560-1640' (unpublished M.A. thesis, University of London, 1953), 98-100.

[60] CCL E24, f. 84.

[61] Churchill, *op. cit.*, 192.

[62] C. Matson, 'Men of Kent, 1. Boys of Bonnington,' *Arch. Cant.*, 79 (1964), 70-76; J. Boys, *General View of the Agriculture of the County of Kent* (2nd ed., 1813; first published 1796), 61.

Conclusions

Although some subdivided fields in Kent originated from the leasing of demesne fields in parcels and some may have been produced by co-aration, it seems that most resulted from the partitioning of formerly more or less compact family holdings among co-heirs and from the early development of the land market: both partibility and free alienation were features of gavelkind tenure. Partitioning produced numerous small holdings and the form that it took varied regionally. In predominantly arable regions it produced subdivided fields as the more fertile soils were often claimed equally by co-heirs, whereas in predominantly pastoral regions, where soils were less conducive to arable cultivation, fragmentation of holdings caused less disruption of animal husbandry than subdivision of fields and parcels.[63] Most subdivided arable fields in Kent were located on fertile soils in Holmesdale, in the valleys of the Darent, Medway and Stour, and on the lower dip-slopes of the Downs. In contrast, few were located in the Weald, in the Clay-with-flints country at the crest of the Downs and in the Blean on London Clay.[64] Another reason for the relative absence of subdivided fields in these last-mentioned areas was that, being heavily wooded and having generally poor soils, they were brought into cultivation by secondary colonization and had lower densities of population than other parts of the county in the early fourteenth century. In these areas, with only slight pressure of population upon land resources in the early middle ages, much land was enclosed direct from the waste and was rarely subdivided into unenclosed parcels.[65] The highest densities of population were in north and east Kent and it was here that most subdivision of fields took place.[66] Pressure of population upon land increased during the thirteenth century, resulting in much partitioning of holdings. By the fifteenth century, with pressure upon land much reduced and with the growing practice of disposing of land by will, the partitioning of holdings was probably more the exception than the rule; it was certainly so by the sixteenth century. By the mid-six-

[63] By c. 1300 agricultural regions in Kent were well established, the most striking contrast being between the wheat-barley-sheep husbandry of north and east Kent and the oats-cattle-pigs economy of the Weald. R. A. Pelham, 'The relation of soils to grain-growing in Kent in the thirteenth century,' *Empire Journal of Experimental Agriculture*, 1 (1933), 82-84; Gulley, *op. cit.*, 319-348; A. Smith, 'Regional differences in crop production in medieval Kent,' *Arch. Cant.*, 78 (1963), 147-160.

[64] Baker, *loc. cit.* (1965), Fig. 2, p. 22: 'Distribution of subdivided fields indicated in pre-1700 estate maps'; D. Roden and A. R. H. Baker, 'Field systems of the Chiltern Hills and parts of Kent from the late thirteenth to the early seventeenth century,' *Transactions of the Institute of British Geographers*, 38 (forthcoming), Fig. 6: 'Distribution of subdivided fields indicated in the Feet of Fines, 1182-1272'.

[65] Gulley, *op. cit.*, 354-355 and 364-365.

[66] H. A. Hanley and C. W. Chalklin, 'The Kent lay subsidy of 1334/5,' *Kent Records*, 18 (1964), 58-172, especially pp. 63-67.

teenth century density of population in the Weald had become greater than in some other parts of the county (Fig. 7) but by then the growth of alternative employment (in the cloth and iron industries especially) had combined with the physical restraints on arable farming to limit subdivision of fields.[67]

Gavelkind tenure not only encouraged the creation of numerous small holdings and subdivision of fields, it also facilitated the growth of large holdings and early enclosure of land parcels. Free alienation of land encouraged early leasing, exchanging and selling of land, and thus the consolidating and augmenting of individual holdings. As the parcels and fields of an individual holding were usually located within one part of a township rather than distributed throughout it, consolidation was a less exacting process in Kent than it was in the midlands. Moreover, those fields which were subdivided into unenclosed parcels were usually small, with few tenants, and they were not grazed in common by the livestock of an entire farming community. Piecemeal consolidation of holdings resulted in their early enclosure. By the seventeenth century, the Kentish landscape was largely enclosed. Other factors— such as proximity to London and the precocious spread of commercial influences,[68] or the use of the turn-wrest rather than the mould-board plough[69]—may have contributed to early enclosure of open fields in Kent but more significant were the free market in land, the pattern of compact land holdings and the private nature of agricultural practices.

Not all Kentish fields were enclosed early, some remained unenclosed (although not necessarily still containing land parcels in intermixed ownership and/or occupation) until the nineteenth century and even until the present day.[70] Their survival can be explained in three ways: first, unenclosed fields survived longest where their subdivision into intermixed open parcels had been most acute and the process of consolidation most complex; secondly, many survived in the prosperous arable areas, on the most fertile soils, where hedges would have reduced

[67] Christopher Baker, an Admiralty official, reported in 1578 that the number of iron furnaces and mills in the Weald 'is greatlie to the decaie spoile & overthrowe of woodes & principall tymber with a greate decaie also of tillage for that they are Contynewallie imploied in Carrying of Furniture for the said works': State Papers Domestic, Elizabeth, Book 117, no. 39, cited in D. and G. Mathew, 'Iron furnaces in south-eastern England and English ports and landing places, 1578,' *English Historical Review*, 48 (1933), 91-99.

[68] R. H. Tawney, *The Agrarian Problem of the Sixteenth Century* (London, 1912), 405; C. S. and C. S. Orwin, *The Open Fields* (Oxford, 2nd edn., 1954), 68.

[69] Nightingale, *loc. cit.*, 25: Nightingale suggests that the turn-wrest plough could be used to produce square plots just as easily as the strips usually produced by the fixed mould-board plough and concludes that 'the great number of plots that were ploughed in parts of Kent probably accounts for early inclosure there.'

[70] For example, in the Isle of Thanet and parts of East Kent. For a specific example, Deal, see Baker, *loc. cit.* (1963), 96-103.

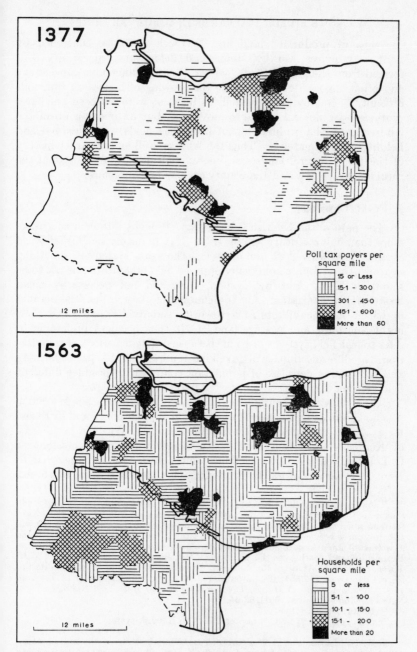

FIG. 7. Some population densities in the diocese of Canterbury, 1377 and 1563
Source: 1377 Poll Tax—PRO E 179/123/32, 33, 35, 38-42 and E 179/129/760
and 762.

1563 Ecclesiastical Enumeration—BM Harl. Ms. 594(8), ff. 63-84.
Areas for which no information is available have been left blank.

33

the area of productive land and livestock could be controlled by temporary fences; thirdly, unenclosed fields survived on dry soils formed from the Upper Chalk, where ditch draining was unnecessary and often exposed locations made the growing of hedges on thin soils difficult.[71] But by 1600 most fields in Kent were enclosed and later centuries saw not an enclosure movement but an opening up of the landscape by the grubbing-up of hedges as fields were enlarged and holdings amalgamated.[72] Thus the later as well as the earlier history of the Kentish rural landscape differed considerably from that of the rural landscape of a midland county such as Leicestershire.

A FINAL COMMENT

The phrase 'the Kentish field system,' brought into common usage more than half a century ago by H. L. Gray in his classic *English Field Systems*, has outlived its usefulness.[73] The word 'system' is something of a misnomer, for a communally imposed field organization is not to be found in Kent. But by 'system' Gray did not necessarily mean 'systematic organization,' for he defined 'field system' as 'the manner in which the inhabitants of a township subdivided and tilled their arable, meadow and pasture land.'[74] It thus becomes preferable to refer to 'the field systems of Kent' because different periods of colonization, the differing impact of gavelkind tenure, varied types of farming and contrasting densities of population combined to produce different field systems in physically contrasted parts of the county.

The evolution of contrasting field systems within a single county was not peculiar to Kent—field systems in Warwickshire and in Essex, for example, show marked regional differences.[75] Was the peculiarity of 'Kentish' field systems their close association with gavelkind tenure? C. I. Elton believed that gavelkind tenure *sensu stricto* was peculiar to Kent but that one of its characteristics, partible inheritance, was found

---

[71] A. D. Hall and E. J. Russell, *A Report on the Agriculture and Soils of Kent, Surrey and Sussex* (London, 1911), 101-102: the greatest difficulty of East Kent farming upon the Chalk is to retain enough moisture in the soil and 'hedges will not grow in a very satisfactory manner.' Similar reasons for the long-continued existence of unenclosed fields on Chalk formations have been noted in Wiltshire, Hampshire and Yorkshire: E. Kerridge, 'Agriculture c. 1500-c. 1793,' *V.C.H. Wilts.*, 4 (1959), 43-64, on p. 46; M. Naish, 'The agricultural landscape of the Hampshire Chalklands, 1700-1840' (unpublished M.A. thesis, University of London, 1961), 82 and 185-186; A Harris, *The Rural Landscape of the East Riding of Yorkshire* 1700-1850 (London, 1961), 62-64.

[72] Baker, *loc. cit.* (1965), 25.

[73] Gray, *op. cit.*, 272-304: Chapter VII 'The Kentish system.'

[74] *Ibid.*, 3.

[75] R. H. Hilton, 'Social structure of rural Warwickshire in the middle ages,' *Dugdale Society Occasional Papers*, 9 (1950); F. Hull, 'Agriculture and rural society in Essex, 1560-1640' (unpublished Ph.D. thesis, University of London, 1950), 11-82.

in many parts of Britain.[76]   Partible inheritance has been observed as producing small holdings in many parts of England: in the fenland of Lincolnshire, for example, partible inheritance produced numerous small holdings during the thirteenth century and was still conducive to their preservation in the sixteenth century.[77]   In other places, partible inheritance produced a pattern of fields subdivided into unenclosed parcels: in the Ouse Basin in Yorkshire, for example, assarts originally cleared and cultivated by individuals were, during the thirteenth century as a consequence of the growth of population, divided up by being shared among the heirs of the original assarters.[78]   Where partible inheritance was not the law it may have been the custom to make provision for the livelihoods of younger sons.   The influence of partible inheritance—or at least of some form of partible succession to land—on the evolution of English field systems needs more careful investigation.[79] Even in Leicestershire, in the heart of the area characterized by the 'midland field system,' some holdings in the middle ages were subdivided by inheritance and newly made assarts and crofts were partitioned into unfenced parcels, and in the sixteenth century the parcel pattern was still being modified by partitioning among co-heirs.[80]   If the so-called 'Kentish system' has been shown to have had little 'system,' it would also seem to have not necessarily been peculiarly 'Kentish.'

ACKNOWLEDGEMENTS

I wish to thank Professor H. C. Darby, Mr. H. C. Prince, Dr. Joan Thirsk and Professor F. R. H. Du Boulay for many helpful comments and criticisms of the work on which this paper was based.   I also owe thanks to the University of London for a grant from the Central Research Fund towards research expenses.

[76] Elton, op. cit., 45-56.
[77] H. E. Hallam, 'Some thirteenth-century censuses,' Econ. His. Rev., 2nd ser. 10 (1957-58), 340-361; J. Thirsk, English Peasant Farming. The Agrarian History of Lincolnshire from Tudor to Recent Times (London, 1957), 44.
[78] T. A. M. Bishop, 'Assarting and the growth of the open fields,' Econ. His. Rev., 6 (1935-36), 13-29.
[79] J. Thirsk, 'The common fields,' Past and Present, 29 (1964), 3-25.
[80] R. H. Hilton, 'Medieval agrarian history,' V.C.H. Leics., 2 (1954), 145-198, on pp. 138, 166 and 170; W. G. Hoskins, Essays in Leicestershire History (Liverpool, 1950), 136.

REGIONAL DIFFERENCES IN CROP PRODUCTION IN MEDIAEVAL KENT

By Ann Smith

THE archives of the Chapter Library of Canterbury Cathedral include a collection of Beadles' rolls (serjeant's compotus rolls, bailiffs' account rolls or manorial accounts) which relate to 31 of the 33 manors[1] held by Canterbury Cathedral Priory in Kent during the mediaeval period.

The following description of crop patterns on the Priory estate in the period 1271-1379 is based on a geographical analysis of four of the many sets of figures relating to agricultural production and management which are contained in the rolls.[2] The rolls have already been studied in detail by R. A. L. Smith[3] in his work on the organization of the Priory estate. R. A. L. Smith's central theme was financial administration and in considering the costs of the agrarian economy he was led to describe methods of agriculture. However, he did not make a detailed statistical analysis of agricultural production to which the rolls are particularly well suited. T. M. Bishop[4] and F. R. H. du Boulay[5] have written accounts of mediaeval agriculture on single manors in Kent using beadles' rolls; and R. A. Pelham[6] has shown the value of a mediaeval estate document, less detailed than the beadles' rolls, for a geographical study of agriculture in Sussex.

However an exhaustive analysis of the information contained in the large number of beadles' rolls which exist has still to be done.[7]

THE DOCUMENTARY EVIDENCE

The beadles' rolls are the annual accounts made by the stewards of the Priory manors which were sent to Canterbury for audit each

---

[1] No rolls are available for the Barton or for the joint manor of Seasalter with Whitstable. A list of the other manors appears on Fig. 1.

[2] This article derives from part of the author's thesis, ' A geographical study of agriculture on the Kentish manors of Canterbury Cathedral Priory, 1272-1379 ' (University of Liverpool, M.A. thesis, 1961).

[3] R. A. L. Smith '*Canterbury Cathedral Priory*' (Cambridge University Press, 1943).

[4] T. M. Bishop ' The rotation of crops at Westerham 1297-1350 ' (*Economic History Review*, IX, 1938).

[5] F. R. H. du Boulay ' Late continued demesne farming at Otford ' (*Arch. Cant.*, LXXII, 1959).

[6] R. A. Pelham ' The agricultural geography of the Chichester Estates in 1388 ' (*Sussex Arch. Colls.*, LXXVIII, 1937).

[7] A detailed analysis is to be found in J. A. Raftis ' The Estates of Ramsey Abbey ' (*Pontifical* Inst. of Medieval Studies and Texts No. 3. 1957, Toronto).

Michaelmas (September 29th). Numerous detailed rolls are available for the reigns of the first three Edwards (1272-1379), and the few less detailed rolls which exist for earlier and later dates have been omitted from the study.

On the inside of each roll is recorded the receipts and expenses of the manor and on the outside is the grange exit in which is recorded the agricultural production of the demesne.[8] Crops and stocks in kind and animal products are enumerated and it is part of the former information which will be analysed here. As the extract below shows there are two sections for each crop, the first describing the total quantity of the crop held on the manor, and secondly a statement of what was done with the crop.

Extract from the beadles' roll for Monkton, 1315-1316

Frumentum:	Idem respondit de CVii semis de exitu frumenti apud Moneketon. Et de XXVii semis Vi buss de exitu frumenti apud Brokeshende. Et de i sema iii buss de excremento seminis. Et de ii semis ii buss de emptis.
	Summa CXXXViii semis ii bus
Wheat:	The same answers for 107 seams of wheat of the issue of Monkton. And for 27 seams, 6 bushels of wheat of the issue of Brokesend. And for I seam 3 bushels left over from sowing. And for 2 seams, 2 bushels bought.
	Total: 138 seams 2 bushels.
Inde:	In semine apud Moneketon super LXX acras XXXVii semis super acram di sema et ii semis ultra in toto. Item in semine apud Broke super xv acras, viii semis, super acram di sema et di sema ultra in toto.
Thence:	In seed at Monkton over 70 acres 37 seams over the acre half a seam and two seams beyond this amount. Item in seed at Broke over 15 acres 8 seams over the acre half a seam and half a seam beyond this amount.

From the above information for every manor the following items were extracted for the year 1291 which was chosen to represent the beginning of the period.

(i) The acreage sown for each crop.

(ii) The number of bushels sown per acre.

(iii) The number of bushels sown of each crop.

(iv) The number of bushels harvested in the following year 1292.

Where the beadles' roll is not extant for 1291 the year nearest in date was chosen. To ensure that the year chosen was representative of

---

[8] The demesne was that part of the manor retained by the Priory and farmed by its servants; the rest of the manor being leased to tenants.

normal conditions on the manors the statistics were checked against the results of a standard deviation analysis of rolls for the period 1285-1296. Where relevant agricultural production in 1291 was compared with that of 1371, a date chosen to represent the end of the period; and the figures for this latter date received a similar statistical treatment.

COMPOSITION OF THE SOWN DEMESNE ACREAGE

In order to compare the crop patterns of the manors, the acreages under individual crops on each manor were expressed as percentages of the total sown demesne acreage and plotted as proportional pie graphs (Fig. 1, and Appendix A). As the manors were distributed throughout Kent, they serve as samples of regional conditions on different geological outcrops, and hence on different soil types. The location of the manors in relation to the geological formations is given in simplified form below Fig. 1. The numbers given in brackets after each manor in the text, refer to their numbering on the maps. In fact many manors were situated at the junction of two geological formations or held land in more than one place; and therefore a description of their location and of their different soil qualities would be long and detailed and has been omitted. The significance of the location of individual manors will become apparent within the text.

In 1291 four distinct groups of manors with the same crop economies were apparent and showed a close correlation with geology. One manor Cliffe (7) had an acreage pattern which could be related to one of these groups, although it lay some distance from the group, and four manors Blean (17), Lydden (32), Meopham (8) and Orpington (9) had unique acreage patterns.

Barley was the dominant crop on a group of manors situated in the northern half of East Kent (Group I) and lying on Chalk or Thanet Beds. Wheat was of secondary importance except at Monkton (1), and Copton (13) where legumes exceeded wheat in acreage. On all the manors oats were relatively unimportant. Cliffe (7) situated on the isolated Chalk outcrop in the Hoo Peninsula, also had the same pattern as this group.

Lydden (32), and Blean (17) were anomalies within the above group. The small acreage of wheat, in contrast to the moderately large acreages of oats and rye, reflects Lydden's situation within the ill drained Sandwich marshes, for both crops were favoured in the medieval period on economic margins of cultivation.[9] At Blean, which lay wholly on the very stiff London clay, oats was by far the most important crop, and rye was again prominent, but the wheat acreage was greater than at Lydden.

[9] R. A. L. Smith, *op. cit.*, 137-138.

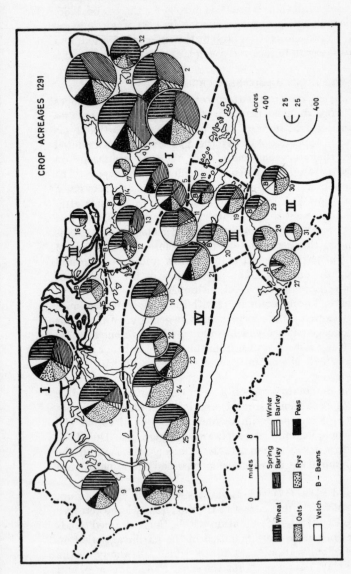

CROP ACREAGES 1291

Chalkland Manors. 1. Monkton ; 2. Eastry ; 3. Ickham ; 4. Adisham ; 5. Godmersham ; 6. Chartham ; 7. Cliffe ; 8. Meopham ; 9. Orpington ; 10. Hollingbourne ; 11. Welles.
Manors on Thanet Beds and Brickearth. 12. Elverton ; 13. Copton ; 14. Ham.
Clayland Manors. 15. Barksore ; 16. Leysdown ; 17. Blean ; 18. Brook.
Lower Greensand Manors. 19. Mersham ; 20. Great Chart ; 21. Little Chart ; 22. Loose ; 23. East Farleigh ; 24. West Farleigh ; 25. Peckham
Marshland Manors. 27. Ebony ; 28. Appledore ; 29. Ruckinge ; 30. Agney cum Orgarswick ; 31. Fairfield ; 32. Lydden.
Manor 26. Westerham, has been omitted from this particular study as it did not belong to Canterbury Cathedral Priory.

Figure 1

40

On the manors of Romney Marsh (Group 2) oats were dominant particularly at Appledore (28) and Ruckinge (29). The acreages of wheat and barley were approximately equal and within the marsh were surprisingly high considering the ill drained nature of the reclaimed marshland. R. A. L. Smith found that from the late thirteenth century onwards the Priory made efforts to increase the acreage and yield of the more profitable cereals on its marshland manors, by marling the land heavily and buying in seed corn.[10] Minor but significant features of the arable economy of this group were the presence of rye and beans and the absence of peas; also the prominence of barley as a winter crop whereas elsewhere it was chiefly spring sown.

Group 3, comprises manors in two separate areas. Intermediate in position between the two groups already described, were the clayland manor of Brook (18), and the western Lower Greensand manors of Mersham (19), Great Chart (20), and Little Chart (21), all of which had fairly heavy soils. Fringing the North Kent marshes and situated on the London Clay were the manors of Barksore (15), and Leysdown (16). On all these manors wheat ranked first in acreage with oats as the secondary grain crop but exceeded in acreage by legumes. Beans were again of minor importance.

A mid-Kent group of manors (Group 4) comprised the eastern Lower Greensand manors of Peckham (25), East and West Farleigh (23 and 24), and Loose (22) whose soils were relatively light; together with Welles (11) and Hollingbourne (10), which lay on Chalk marls. Wheat was the major crop but was nearly equalled by oats. The barley acreage was very small, although noticeably larger on the two chalkland manors than elsewhere, and was exceeded by the legume acreage.

Finally two chalkland manors, Meopham (8) and Orpington (9) had unique acreage patterns, a reflection of their differing physical situations. Orpington was situated on thin soils which included valley gravels, whilst Meopham lay on Clay-with-Flints.

Wheat ranked first in acreage on both manors, and their barley acreages which were approximately equal were greater than on the manors of the previous group. However, the oats acreage on the heavy soils at Meopham was second only to that of wheat, whereas Orpington grew very few oats and had quite a large acreage under legumes which were grown to maintain the fertility of the light soils.

In 1371 (Appendix B) several crop patterns had altered, chiefly the result of changes in the acreages of barley and oats. These changes again show a regional distribution. An increase in legumes also occurred on some manors reflecting their increasing use in crop rotations.

[10] R. A. L. Smith, *op. cit.*, 178.

A similar legumes increase was observed during the same period at Westerham by T. A. M. Bishop.[11]

In 1371 barley was far less dominant and was only the first-ranking crop on those chalkland manors, which had soils derived from deposits of Brickearth and Thanet beds and on the clayland manor of Brook. On the other chalkland manors (Godmersham (5), Chartham (6), and Cliffe (7)), wheat had replaced barley as the dominant crop. However, the barley acreage showed an increase on the Lower Greensand manors, particularly on those western manors lying on light soils.

Oats had declined in acreage by 1371. On manors on the Lower Greensand and Chalk marls oats had ranked second to wheat in acreage in 1291, but by 1371 it had fallen below barley and legumes. On the clayland manors oats had also declined and on Romney Marsh it was only dominant at Ruckinge (29) and Ebony (27). At Agney cum Orgarswick (30) they were exceeded in acreage by barley and wheat, and at Appledore (28) by wheat. This increase in the acreages of the more profitable cereals on the marsh was possible in 1371 because as the reclaimed land gradually dried out it was no longer necessary to grow so much oats, 'the usual crop on new land'.[12]

The range of crop economies described above chiefly reflects the soils preferences of individual crops but also their commercial and utilitarian value.

The bulk of the grain was sold and therefore obviously grain crops would occupy the major part of the sown acreage. Wheat fetched the highest prices with barley next in value.[13] A small amount of grain was also used for human consumption whilst oats was used as fodder for horses and cows. Barley was particularly important since it was used for brewing ('in braseum'), and was issued to the farm servants as payment for their services ('lib. famulus'). Although the leguminous plants were used for human consumption ('in potage') they were primarily used for stock fodder. The animals were sometimes fed on the fields ('in campo') particularly on the chalklands,[14] or the crops were threshed and used as winter fodder ('in potage').

As today wheat was easily the most important grain crop, and had a very regular distribution being a major crop on all the manors. Its importance reflects both its commercial value and its adaptability to a variety of soils.[15] It was the dominant crop on manors on the heavier

[11] T. M. Bishop, *op. cit.*

[12] R. A. L. Smith, *op. cit*, 178.

[13] Thus at Ickham in 1371 wheat sold for 6s. a quarter, and barley for 4s.

[14] For example in the account roll for Adisham (Edward III, 45-46) it is stated that no vetches were harvested from 25 acres because they were fed to sheep in the field—'de xxv acras nil quia forage—multones in campo'.

[15] A. D. Hall and E. J. Russell, *The agriculture and soils of Kent, Surrey and Sussex* (H.M.S.O., 1911), 140.

soils of the clays and chalk marls, as well as on manors on the lighter soils of the Lower Greensand. It was also important on the manors of Romney Marsh and on the manors of the chalklands and Thanet Beds, although on these latter manors it usually ranked second to barley.

In contrast to wheat, barley was an important crop only on the chalkland manors of East Kent, and particularly on those manors which had fertile soils derived from Brickearth and Thanet Beds. This grain is essentially a light land crop.[16] This explains why acreages were small on the clayland and marshland manors. The Report of the Land Utilization Survey of Kent[17] contains the following summary of the distribution of barley-growing in the county in the early 1930s—'in contrast to wheat the growing of barley is very markedly localized on the chalky and sandy loams of East Kent including Thanet. There is some on most parts of the chalk belt but very little in the Weald proper, south of the chalk scarp, where soils are too heavy and too poor.' This might equally well be a description of barley-growing on the manors of Canterbury Cathedral Priory in the medieval period. The presence of soils suitable for barley-growing in close proximity to Canterbury was fortunate, since the Priory used large quantities of the grain for brewing and for payment to its servants. The Bartoner's accounts, described by R. A. L. Smith,[18] record the quantities of grain sent to the Priory. They reveal that the bulk of the grain came from the East Kent manors.[19] This probably explains why barley-growing was not more important on the light soils of the Lower Greensand manors since they lay at a considerable distance from Canterbury.

Oats showed a much more even distribution than barley since it was a useful crop being suited particularly to heavy, ill-drained soils. Thus it was dominant on the marshland manors and of secondary importance on the Chalk marls and clays. On the lighter soils of the Lower Greensand and Chalk, acreages were small since the more profitable grains, wheat and barley, were suited to these soils.

Rye was of minor importance and was only grown on poor lands. For example acreages occur on the marsh soils of the manors of Romney Marsh, and on the lighter soils at some Lower Greensand manors such as Peckham (25).

Legumes were particularly important on the claylands and marshes since beans was a heavy land crop.[20] The emphasis on bean-growing on the Romney Marsh manors is interesting since this area today is

---

[16] A. D. Hall and E. J. Russell, *op. cit.*, 143.

[17] L. D. Stamp (edit.), *The Report of the Land Utilization Survey of Britain*, part 85—Kent 1943, 578.

[18] R. A. L. Smith, ' The Barton and Bartoner of Christ Church, Canterbury '. (*Arch. Cant.*, LV, 1942.)

[19] R. A. L. Smith, *op. cit.* The Bartoners Account for 1311-12 is printed.

[20] L.U.S. Report, *op. cit.*, 578.

noted for the growing of beans for stockfood.[21]   Elsewhere beans was chiefly a garden crop and consequently was not included in the percentage calculations.[22]   Peas were absent or insignificant on many bean-growing manors as for example those of Romney Marsh since their place in the rotation was taken by beans.

The influence of the edaphic factor can be considered further by studying the number of bushels sown per acre (Fig. 2), and particularly by analysing crop yields (Fig. 3).

FIG. 2.   The number of Bushels sown per acre in 1291.

Manor	Spring Barley	Winter Barley	Oats
Chalkland Manors			
1. Monkton	7	6	3½
2. Eastry	6	5	3
3. Ickham	6	5	3
4. Adisham	6	–	3
5. Godmersham	6	–	3
6. Chartham	6	–	3
7. Cliffe	6	5	3
8. Meopham	4	3	4
9. Orpington	4	3	4
10. Hollingbourne	5	5	3½
11. Welles	5	5	3½
Manors of Thanet Beds and Brickearth			
12. Elverton	6	5	3
13. Copton	6	–	3
14. Ham	–	6	3
Clayland Manors			
15. Barksore	5	5	3
16. Leysdown	–	5	3
17. Blean	–	–	3
18. Brook	5	–	3½
Lower Greensand Manors			
19. Mersham	5	–	3½
20. Gt. Chart	5	–	4
21. L. Chart	5	–	3½
22. Loose	5	–	3
23. E. Farleigh	5	–	3½
24. W. Farleigh	5	–	3½
25. Peckham	5	–	3½
Marshland Manors			
27. Ebony	–	4	4
28. Appledore	–	4	4
29. Ruckinge	–	4	4
30. Agney cum Orgarswick	5	4	4
31. Fairfield	5	–	–
32. Lydden	6	5	5

[21] G. H. Garrad, ' A survey of the Agriculture of Kent '—(*County Agricultural surveys*, no. 1, Royal Agricultural Society, 1954, 82.)

[22] For example at East Farleigh in 1308 (Edward II, 1-2) three bushels of beans were planted ' in gardina '.

FIG. 3. Yields per bushel sown, 1291.

A—Actual yield per bushel sown.

B—The actual yield per bushel sown of each crop expressed as a percentage of the total yield of all four crops.

Manor	Wheat		Spring Barley		Oats		Peas and Vetch		
	A	B	A	B	A	B	A	B	Total
Chalkland Manors									
1. Monkton	4·2	44	2·0	21	2·7	30	0·7	7	9·6
2. Eastry	3·7	39	2·0	21	2·8	30	1·0	10	9·5
3. Ickham	4·9	48	2·4	24	2·2	21	0·7	7	10·2
4. Adisham	2·6	37	1·9	26	1·5	22	1·0	15	7·0
5. Godmersham	2·8	28	3·6	36	2·2	22	1·5	14	10·1
6. Chartham	2·1	31	1·9	28	1·8	27	1·0	14	6·8
7. Cliffe	2·0	30	2·4	36	1·3	20	1·0	14	6·7
8. Meopham	3·8	36	2·6	24	2·1	19	2·4	21	10·9
9. Orpington	3·3	31	3·2	29	2·7	23	1·9	17	11·1
10. Hollingbourne	1·9	28	2·0	29	2·2	32	0·8	13	6·9
11. Welles	2·0	28	2·1	30	1·3	18	1·9	26	7·3
Manors of Thanet Beds and Brickearth									
12. Elverton	2·9	36	2·6	32	1·5	18	1·1	14	8·1
13. Copton	5·5	38	4·0	27	4·5	31	0·7	4	14·7
14. Ham	1·6	19	3·2	37	2·0	24	1·7	20	8·5
Clayland Manors									
15. Barksore	2·0	22	2·6	29	2·3	26	2·2	23	9·1
16. Leysdown	3·7	42	—	—	2·6	29	2·5	29	8·8
17. Blean	—	—	—	—	—	—	—	—	—
18. Brook	4·8	39	2·5	20	3·8	30	1·4	11	12·5
Lower Greensand Manors									
19. Mersham	3·1	30	3·3	33	2·6	26	1·2	11	10·2
20. Gt. Chart	3·1	30	2·8	27	2·7	27	1·7	16	10·3
21. L. Chart	1·3	23	2·0	36	1·7	31	0·6	10	5·6
22. Loose	2·3	26	2·8	32	1·6	18	2·2	24	8·9
23. E. Farleigh	3·3	47	1·6	23	1·6	23	0·5	7	7·0
24. W. Farleigh	1·5	23	1·7	26	1·8	27	1·6	24	6·6
25. Peckham	2·7	39	1·5	22	1·4	20	1·3	19	6·9
Marshland Manors									
27. Ebony	2·8	41	—	—	4·1	59	—	—	6·9
28. Appledore	2·5	29	2·6	31	2·7	32	0·7	8	8·5
29. Ruckinge	3·5	29	4·0	33	3·3	27	1·4	11	12·2
30. Agney cum Orgarswick	2·3	23	3·4	34	2·8	28	1·5	15	10·0
31. Fairfield	3·8	46	—	—	3·4	41	1·1	13	8·3
32. Lydden	2·7	35	2·4	32	2·0	27	0·4	6	7·5

THE NUMBER OF BUSHELS SOWN PER ACRE

The sowing rates of barley and oats varied on individual manors and can be correlated with their relative importance in the demesne arable economy. This suggests an awareness of soil potentialities and adaptation of agricultural practices with this in view.

The manors which sowed the largest number of bushels per acre of barley were those in East Kent on which barley was the dominant crop. These manors sowed 6 or 7 bushels of spring barley per acre and 5 or 6 bushels of winter barley. Chalkland and Lower Greensand manors where barley was moderately important sowed 5 bushels of both spring and winter barley per acre. On Romney Marsh, where barley was not important in 1291 since the soils were newly reclaimed, four bushels of winter barley and five of spring barley were sown. However, in 1371 when much more barley was sown on the marsh the sowing rate of winter barley increased from four to five bushels per acre.

The differences in the sowing rates of oats although small show a gradation the reverse of that for barley. Thus on the manors of Romney Marsh where oats was the dominant crop, four bushels were sown per acre; whilst on the chalkland manors where oats were unimportant only three bushels were sown per acre.

A standard sowing rate of four bushels per acre of wheat is puzzling since it was the major crop in the economy, but it is probably a reflection of its adaptability to varied soils. The minor crops, rye, peas, beans and vetch show no significant regional variations in sowing rates.

CROP YIELDS

Since the sowing rates for individual crops varied regionally the yield per bushel sown was analysed (Fig. 3) rather than the yield per acre sown. Ideally the average yield per bushel sown for a consecutive number of years should have been studied thereby eliminating the distortions caused by the occurrence of good and bad years. However, as account rolls for a sufficient number of consecutive years occurred so rarely this was not possible, and therefore the analysis was restricted to the year 1291.

To make possible comparison between the manors the yields per bushel sown of wheat, spring barley, oats and peas/vetch were expressed as a percentage of the sum of the yields of all four crops on each manor. Rye, winter barley and beans were not grown in sufficient quantities on enough manors to make yield calculations worthwhile. The actual yield has also been tabulated because the percentage analysis presents the yields of a particular crop relative to the yields of the other crops on the manor, and therefore masks the presence of high or low total yields on a manor. Therefore despite the fact that the actual crop yields

46

of 1291 may have been influenced by abnormal weather conditions they have been calculated and are referred to where relevant.

The percentage yields of wheat showed the largest range varying from 23-47 per cent. since large acreages of wheat were widely grown it must sometimes have been cultivated on soils which were not particularly suited to it and consequently yields would be low. It would seem also that the sowing rate of four bushels per acre which was almost universal on the manors, did not always give satisfactory results.

Wheat yields in general decreased westward and southwestward from N.E. Kent. On the manors lying on the drift-mantled lower slopes of the Chalk together with two of the Lower Greensand manors, and Brook and Meopham, wheat comprised over 35 per cent. of the total yield. The latter manor (8) lay on Clay-with-Flints which 'with careful farming and manure will yield excellent crops of corn and especially of wheat'.[23] Brook (18) lay on the Gault Clay which is rather less intractable than the London Clay on which wheat yields were lower. On all these manors wheat was first-ranking in yield and many actual yields were high. Thus wheat was particularly suited to the soils derived from Brickearths and Thanet Beds and yet the manors on these soils concentrated on barley-growing. The remaining manors with wheat percentage yields of 35 per cent. and below were situated on the thinner chalk soils, on the Lower Greensand and on Romney Marsh. Significantly yields were slightly higher at Mersham (19) and Great Chart (20) which lay on the heavier Lower Greensand soils east of the Medway. Wheat was first-ranking in yield only on three manors and actual yields were also quite small; and yet, because of the commercial value of the crop, wheat occupied a larger acreage than any other crop except on the manors of Romney Marsh.

The spring barley percentage yields ranged from 20 to 36 per cent. Thus the highest percentage yield for barley was eleven per cent. less than that of wheat, a reflection of the former crops' smaller degree of adaptability. The highest values (27 per cent. and over) occurred on Romney Marsh manors, and on some manors on the Lower Greensand Chalk, Thanet Beds and Brickearth. Barley was the first-ranking yield on these manors and many of the actual yields were high. These facts correspond with Hall and Russell's findings that 'the most favourable barley soils lie on the Lower Greensand' and that 'the light loams derived from the lower drift-mantled Chalk are next in favour'.[24] However it has already been explained that owing to the organization of the estate economy barley acreages were small on the Lower Greensand. The increase in barley acreages on Romney Marsh manors in 1371 suggests that the high yields obtainable from these soils had been

[23] A. D. Hall and E. J. Russell, *op. cit.*, 140.
[24] A. D. Hall and E. J. Russell, *op. cit.*, 148.

recognized. The importance of barley on the chalklands has already been noted.

The lowest percentage values for barley (under 27 per cent.) occurred on manors on the clays, and on the chalklands of N.E. Kent despite the high sowing rate on the latter manors and their importance for barley-growing. A possible explanation is that they were sowing more seed than was necessary and that the larger acreages would tend to lead to lower yields. This apparent anomaly also results partly from the statistical method adopted because wheat is a higher-yielding crop than barley, particularly on these soils, and in consequence the percentage yields on these manors were mostly higher than elsewhere which confirms that barley was grown not only because of the proximity of the manors to Canterbury but also because of the suitability of the soils.

The percentage yields of oats ranged only from 18-32 per cent. and the distribution pattern was relatively simple. Values were lower than for barley and only at Hollingbourne (10) were oats first-ranking in yield. Manors with percentage yields over 25 per cent. were situated on the heavier soils of the clays, Alluvium, Chalk Marls, and western section of the Lower Greensand, or worked reclaimed marsh soils as part of the demense. On practically all these manors the actual yields were fairly high and oats was the second-ranking yield. Thus the highest percentage yields for oats were on the manors where oats was important. Manors with percentage yields for oats of under 25 per cent. were situated on light soils derived from Chalk, Thanet Beds or Lower Greensand. Despite the low yield, oats was an important crop on the Lower Greensand in 1291 but it is significant that its acreage had declined very considerably by 1371 and ranked only fourth in size.

The percentage yields of peas and vetches were extremely low and variable ranging from 4-27 per cent., and it is difficult to assess which soils were most suited to legumes, although yields were generally higher on the light soils.

CONCLUSION

In the above study an explanation was sought for the distribution patterns of crop acreages on the manors in 1291 and 1371, and it was inferred that they could be correlated with the geological sequence. Crop sowing rates and yields provided further support for this conclusion. Moreover, the picture that emerged was not merely a simple correlation with the major geological formations, for a close relationship between cropping patterns and strata within the major formations, and with drift deposits, was revealed. Thus there were differences in cropping patterns on the Gault and London clays, both major formations;

whilst the changes from Chalk to Chalk Marl, a strata within the major formation, and from Chalk to Clay-with Flint, a drift deposit, were similarly marked. Thus the Priory estate with utilitarian and commercial value in view, utilized the physical environment to their best advantage organizing arable farming on a rational basis.

APPENDIX A. CROP ACREAGES 1291

Manor	*Wheat*	*Barley*	*Oats*	*Rye*	*Peas*	*Vetch*	*Beans*
Chalkland Manors							
1. Monkton	72	166	51	—	60	58	—
2. Eastry	89	159	43	18	52	42	9½
3. Ickham	161	177	21	—	46½	92	—
4. Adisham	121	147	68	—	48	56	—
5. Godmersham	56	40	15	—	23½	18	—
6. Chartham	68	54	10	—	18	37	—
7. Cliffe	82	92	24	33	27	25	—
8. Meopham	120	52	86	—	11	22	—
9. Orpington	103	44	39	—	19	29	—
10. Hollingbourne	81	33	78	—	53	and vetch	—
11. Welles	70	52	91	—	58	and vetch	—
Manors of Thanet Beds and Brickearth							
12. Elverton	33	36	3¾	9	36	and vetch	3½
13. Copton	52	47	6½	—	34	and vetch	—
14. Ham	7	—	12	—	—	3¼	4½
Clayland Manors							
15. Barksore	22	10½	24½	—	25	and vetch	2
16. Leysdown	16½	½	7	—	10	—	—
17. Blean	6	—	15	3	—	11	—
18. Brook	29	9	18½	—	3½	4½	11½
Lower Greensand Manors							
19. Mersham	40¾	18	33¾	—	10	19	—
20. Gt. Chart	54	13	68¼	—	73	and vetch	18
21. L. Chart	49	4½	52¼	3	12½	25¼	—
22. Loose	46	7½	31	4½	37	and vetch	—
23. E. Farleigh	56¾	11	64	10	14	24¼	—
24. W. Farleigh	102	8	94	5	51	and vetch	—
25. Peckham	44	3½	38	3½	18¼	and vetch	—
Marshland Manors							
27. Ebony	12¼	—	117	6	—	—	8¼
28. Appledore	15¾	—	65¾	3¾	—	—	—
29. Ruckinge	27¼	8½	42¼	—	—	—	13¾
30. Agney cum Orgarswick	37¾	20¼	39	3	1	14	15
31. Fairfield	11½	—	18½	—	—	13	—
32. Lydden	98	10	16	8	13	—	—

APPENDIX B   CROP ACREAGES 1371

Manor	Wheat	Barley	Oats	Rye	Peas	Vetch	Beans
Chalkland Manors							
1. Monkton	12½	15	3	—	5	4	—
2. Eastry	80	98	10	—	14	32	—
3. Ickham	156	156	12	—	40	44	10
4. Adisham	82	91	16	—	19	31	—
5. Godmersham	48	36	11	—	10	14	—
6. Chartham	62	48	13	—	13	20	—
7. Cliffe	80	72	8	—	18	43H	—
8. Meopham	80	36	36	—	17	16	3
9. Orpington	72	40	26	—	12	14	—
10. Hollingbourne	54	26	13	—	12	18	—
11. Welles	51	35	24	—	25	22	—
Manors of Thanet Beds and Brickearth							
12. Elverton	31	32	3	—	16	12	2
13. Copton	41	42	11½	—	9	24	—
14. Ham	—	—	9	—	—	—	—
Clayland Manors							
15. Barksore	22	—	13	—	10	—	8
16. Leysdown	15	—	7	—	5	1	—
17. Blean	16	3	8	—	5	—	—
18. Brook	12	13	11	—	2	8	2
Lower Greensand Manors							
19. Mersham	47	33	6½	—	11	21	5
20. Gt. Chart	41	17	11	—	13	15	9
21. L. Chart	35	10½	32	—	14	18	2
22. Loose	32	12	12	—	8	12	—
23. E. Farleigh	50	20	18	—	16	24	—
24. W. Farleigh	53	26	22	—	8	19	3
25. Peckham	28	35	24	—	3	17	—
Marshland Manors							
27. Ebony	—	—	87	—	—	4	18
28. Appledore	106	41	91	—	6	10	44
29. Ruckinge	9	9½	19	1½	1	1	11
30. Agney cum Orgarswick	14	31	10	—	5	9	4
31. Fairfield	—	—	—	—	—	—	—
32. Lydden	—	—	3	4	—	2	4

H—Haras

LATE-CONTINUED DEMESNE FARMING AT OTFORD

By F. R. H. Du Boulay, M.A., F.R.Hist.S.

As it is not very usual to find a demesne continuously exploited by its lord as late as the mid-fifteenth century, with detailed accounts of the process, the manor of Otford is worth a short paper to show how an attenuated cultivation by the archbishop was carried on until 1444.

The numerous demesnes of the archbishopric, mostly lying in Kent, Sussex and Surrey, had with few exceptions been leased out by 1422 when a surviving *valor* gives a fairly comprehensive view of the estates.[1] The Cathedral Priory had gone over to rents as a matter of policy in the 1390's, and it is not unlikely that the archbishop's council had the same policy in train. The fact that a few widely-spaced manors like Tarring, Stoneham and possibly Wadhurst in Sussex, Otford, Wingham Barton, and possibly Teynham in Kent were still directly exploited, in whole or in part, as late as 1422 strengthens the impression that the supply of the archbishop's itinerant household was one reason for continued demesne-farming on selected manors.

It should be noted at the outset, however, that the demesne lands on the archbishop's manors were often rather small in comparison with the lands of the tenants. To put it another way, the major part of the archbishop's income from land, throughout the medieval period, was from rents. So the interest of his demesne exploitation derives less from watching a "high-farming" policy like that of certain monasteries than from the information its records give us about farming methods and, indeed, the local communities.

In the thirteenth century the issues of Otford demesne and the rents of tenants were jointly answered for by a bailiff and a reeve in one great undifferentiated account.[2] Accounts of the same sort survive from 1315-16 and 1322-3, where the accounting officer is called a serjeant (*serviens*), and from 1355-6 where he is called reeve (*prepositus*)[3] But from 1382-3, when something like a consecutive series begins again, the demesne is always left to the serjeant;[4] the collection of the tenants' rents to the reeve.[5] This process of differentiating accounts is con-

---

[1] Lambeth Palace Library, Cartæ Miscellanæ, vol. xi, no. 89. It is hoped to discuss the whole problems of farming the demesnes in a forthcoming book on the archbishop's estates in the middle ages.

[2] *Brit. Mus. Add MS* 29,794 (account of 1273-4) ; Lambeth Court Roll collection (abbreviated *L.R.*) no. 831 (account of 1296-7).

[3] *L.R.* 832-4.

[4] *L.R.*, 835-6, 838, 841, 846, 846a, 849, 850, 853, 857-8, 860, 863, 865, 868, 871.

[5] *L.R.*, 839, 842, 844-845a, 847, 854, 854a, 859, 861, 864, 866, 869-70, 872, 874.

tinued and emphasized in the fifteenth century. We have a series of parker's accounts from 1400.[1] After the demesne is wholly leased out in 1444 we have not only the farmer's account, but a continued serjeant's account, answering for the profits of the leased demesne and for the residence at Otford which the archbishop retained and used. And then, from about 1450, the large manor of Otford was broken up into a number of separately-accounting collectorates : the *borgha* of Otford under its reeve, the *borgha* of Shoreham, and the once-dependent settlements at Chevening, Sevenoaks and Weald, each under its collector (usually styled reeve), and Whitley (*Whytclyff*) woods under a forester. All these accounts continue with few important breaks till Cranmer's time.[2]

The present concern is with the extent of the demesne and with what the serjeants' accounts tell of its cultivation. The Domesday survey simply says that the manor of Otford was assessed at eight fulungs, that there was tenant-land for forty-two ploughs and demesne for six. The bare statement of Domesday is borne out and vastly amplified by two detailed medieval descriptions of the demesne. A custumal of *c.* 1284 shows some 665 acres of arable scattered in four-teen parcels, ranging in size from 1 to 153 acres, about 55 acres of meadow in twelve parcels, and an indeterminate amount of wood, park and pasture land. The demesne description in this custumal is set out here in translation :[3]

In ' La Combe ' 68 acres ; by the sheepfold 1 acre 1 virgate ; *sub orto Pycard* 23a. ; in ' Wycham ' 26a. 3v. ; in ' Northfield ' 153a. 3v. ; in ' Estfeld ' 83a. 3v. ; in the croft of ' Wenlagh ' 1a. 3v. ; in ' Tylefeld ' 12a. 3v. ; in the field by Preston 58a. 2v. ; in the field on the north and east side of Shoreham church 55a. $\frac{1}{2}$v. ; in the field by the sheepfold and vill of Shoreham 26a. $\frac{1}{2}$v. ; at ' Wodelond ' 34a. ; at ' Halstede ' 80a. ; in ' Morelegh ' 40a. *preter Alvetum*.

Pasture in 'Robeloteslond' 25a. besides *Alvetum*; a park and some other woods there ; in ' Gevelmed ' 6a. ; in ' Littelmed ' 1a. 2v. ; by the house of John Planez 3a. ; in ' Meleton ' 11a. ; in the same meadow 4a. 2v. ; in ' Rodbrok ' 9a. 2v. ; in ' La More ' 6a. 2v. ; at ' Southmell ' 1a. 3v. ; between the course of two streams (*aquarum*) 3a ; in ' Redon ' and water 2a. 2v. ; in ' Stywmed ' 6a. ; in ' La Wore ' 1a.

A description of the demesnes as they were in 1515-16 has also

---

[1] *L.R.*, 847, etc.

[2] The numerous later accounts, mostly in Lambeth Palace and the Public Record Office, need not be referred to here.

[3] Dean and Chapter of Canterbury MSS., E24, fo. 69v. This is a copy, probably of the late fifteenth century, of a custumal and rental remade under Archbishop Pecham from a roll of Elias of Dereham, archbishop's steward *c.* 1207-14, covering almost all the archbishop's estates.

chanced to survive on the parchment cover of an Otford court-roll belonging to Elizabeth's reign.[1] It is a hasty scrawl, but provides a comparison interesting enough to reproduce here :

A mesurement of the demeanes of Otteforde anno vij° H.viij.
In Estfeld lyeng frome the lompytt and the path way leding frome Otteforde to Seale uppon the hill ward, 62 acres 8 dayworks 3 perches.

In Northfeld in one pece called the Eighteen acre there is [sic] 18 acres 18½ dayw.

In a nother feld called the 14 acres there is 14 a. and no mow.

In Whythill there is . . . ½ a. 3 dayw. 3 p.

In the Faston there is 43a. 7 dayw. 1 p.

In a feld called the Combe and that half (?) to the hill there is in one pece lieng in le[n]ght toward Shorham 66½ a. 6½ dayw.

In a nother pece lyeng in the bottom under Coridlebushe (?) there is 10 a. 15½ dayw.

Item in the fosse Undergrenhill called the Drowwaye [Droveway] for the farmershope there is 2 a. 3 dayw.

Item in a nother pece that is the hanger and side of the Mydlehill and so compasse [sic] the side of Stomblebussh and the Shotte above Cradlebushe there is 25 a. 12 dayw.

Item in 2 peces mowe that lyeth at the Foxe . . . and Blackbushe, and boundith to the Highways leding from Ottford toward Woodland there is 15 a., and 1 a. lyeng between the parsons 3 a. and Mr. Palmer.

The sum of acres with the Combe 120½ a. 7 dayw., beside 31 a. that I cannott calle to mynd.

Item there is in Oxenlease 10½ a.

Item there is in Little Newe Park as to met him [measure it?] square 26 a. 18 dayw.

Item there is in Gret New Park as we met him in 2 parts without the diche of the mede called Multon 60½ a. 14½ dayw.

Item there is taken into the mede that was Gret Nupark 3 a. and 5 the . . . of the 2 nuparks and Oxenlease is 100 a. 3 r[ods] 2 dayw.

Item there is in Wickham 24 a. 3 r. 5 dayw. 7 p.

Item there is in the medes called the Blosse medes 7½ a. 8 dayw. and thereof in 2 parks . . . must have one . . . and then hath the lond in Redbrok 3 r. 6 dayw.

Item there is in Mylton mede as far . . . now within the diche 16½ a., and thereof the tenants hath one acre.

Item there is in the . . . mede 8 a., and the tenants have 1 a. 15 dayw.

Although this description is in places obscure or defective, a general comparison with the description of the thirteenth century is possible.

---

[1] De L'Isle and Dudley MSS, Roll 478.   I am indebted to Viscount De L'Isle, V.C., for his kind permission to make use of his family papers.

Of the thirteenth-century demesne fields, only four can be readily identified in 1515. Of these, the Combe and Wickham remain much the same, but North field and East field have been to a greater or lesser extent split up. The entirely changed nomenclature of the other fields cannot disguise the fact that some further splitting up has taken place. Names of demesne fields sown with various crops in the fourteenth and fifteenth centuries are given in the serjeants' accounts, and some of these do not appear in either of the lists printed here. From an inspection of all these sources, one must conclude that North field, East field, the Combe and Wickham had a continued identity from Edward I's day to that of Henry VIII, and that the field of 50-60 acres at Shoreham lasted through the fourteenth century, though all of these were liable to a certain morcellation while retaining their names. But the other parcels changed their names, and probably their boundaries, much more freely. In addition, meadow land and park land could in the later middle ages be cropped, while portions of supposedly arable land seem to pass out of cultivation altogether.

It is hard to calculate the nominal size of the demesne in 1515, but it seems a little smaller than it had been in 1284. A very different question is how much of the demesnes were actually laid under crop during the period of the archbishop's demesne exploitation. The situation is set out concisely in the Table. This shows that even in the thirteenth and early fourteenth century a much smaller proportion of the demesne was cultivated than can be accounted for by fallow, and that even this amount contracts strikingly in the second quarter of the fourteenth century. From the middle of the fourteenth century to the middle of the fifteenth the contraction of the cropped area goes on, with ups and downs in particular years. From 1419 onwards the serjeant even seems to become self-conscious about the total area cropped, for he develops the habit of comparing the current acreage with that of the previous year.

Parallel with the contraction of the cropped acreage went the reduction in the number of full-time ploughmen employed by the lord. Domesday said there were six ploughs on the demesne, and six *famuli caruce* we find in the accounts until about 1393. Thereafter the number is four.

The Table also shows the relative importance of the different crops. Wheat production was predominant, and of this a high proportion was sold on the local market or delivered to the archbishop's household. Production of oats declined steadily from 1418, but the stability of spring barley cultivation is remarkable. The sowing of legumes was of minor importance, and by 1432 had almost ceased. The whole picture is one of an attenuated but viable economy lasting out the near-century 1355 to 1444, and kept going more to supply the household in London or north-west Kent than for any other ostensible reason.

TABLE

ACREAGES OF DEMESNE SOWN

Year	Wheat	Barley[1]	Oats	Peas	Vetches	Beans	Total
1273-4[2]	94½	42¼	118	7	15¼	—	277
1315-16	135	24+28	113	9	6½	—	315½
1322-3	108	17+23	125	2	7	—	282
1355-6	66	15¾+30	58	7	15½	6¼	198½
1382-3	88	8 +32	60½	12	12	—	212½
1391-2	69½	5 +28	44	11	11	—	168½
1399-1400	70½	8¼+25½	47½	6	10½	—	168¼
1405-6	70½	8¼+28½	40	4	8	—	159¼
1410-11	69	8¼+36½	55½	6	7½	2	184¾
1413-14	69½	6 +25	53½	4½	12	—	170½
1417-18[3]							187
1418-19	87	5 +20	59½	4	6½	—	182
1422-3	73½	4 +19	34	8	8	—	156½
1426-7							163
1427-8	71½	35	33	8	8	—	155½
1428-9	64¼	30	48	—	8[4]	—	142½
1430-1							151¾
1431-2	65½	43½	43½	—	—	—	152½
1436-7							136
1437-8	54¼	44	33	12	—	—	143¼
1438-9							143¼
1439-40	64	48	28	12	—	—	152
1440-1	71	44½	30	8	—	—	153½
1443-4	63	57	27	5	—	—	149½

Fifteen accounts over the period specify what crops were sown on particular fields. This is not enough to demonstrate a particular rotation technique, though clearly some sort of alternation was practised in the larger fields, while some of the marginal pieces seem only to have been laid under oats. Looking at a cropping table over the available years, the most striking fact is the way in which the larger fields were themselves divided among different crops in any one year, and also were liable to have only a small proportion of their area cropped in any particular year. East Field was the most continuously and fully cropped one. In 1284 we are told it contained about 84 acres. From 1315 to 1440 it can be seen at intervals, now wholly under wheat, or wheat and winter barley, now under spring barley,

[1]. Where two figures are given under barley, the first signifies winter, the second spring, barley. Note decline of winter barley cultivation.
[2] Calculated this year from amounts of seed sown (Add MS 29,794).
[3] Total acreage of years where crops are not specified is known through the account for the subsequent year.
[4] All destroyed by flood.

55

oats and legumes in some unpredictable combination, occasionally under barley alone. Although there are one or two years when the field was wholly blank, it was, in recorded years, rarely cropped over less than 60 to 80 acres. But East Field was the exception. North Field was in operation over the whole period, yet after 1322 never more than about 40 of its supposed 154 acres were sown ; during the later middle ages some 20 to 40 acres of its surface were generally sown with blocks of wheat, spring barley and, occasionally, oats. In 1432 it was specified that 26a in the south of the field were under wheat, 18a in the northern part under barley.[1] Roughly the same things could be said of the Combe, though this was cropped a little more fully. The big field in Shoreham was quite fully cropped till 1391, after which no record of cropping exists at all. Other fields seem only occasionally and marginally cropped, though a demesne field at Milton was considerably used in the fifteenth century.

If, as is apparent, the demesne arable was increasingly under-exploited from the mid-fourteenth century onwards, what was happening to it ? The evidence is fragmentary, but there may be two or three complementary explanations. Small portions of the demesne fields were being let off to tenants by court-roll, for rent.[2] Also, some demesne land, like some tenant-land, was going out of cultivation for lack of people willing or able to cultivate it.[3] Finally, it is possible that some of the demesne went out of cultivation because the soil was not good and was easily abandoned during a period of economic recession.[4] The leasing process is visible in a small way at least by the early years of the fifteenth century. Decayed rents and land left in the lord's hand are more apparent in the second quarter of the fifteenth century. But they are also concurrent processes.

This tale of diminishing tillage is only one aspect of the archbishop's demesne economy at Otford. It is necessary to look briefly at the proceeds and expenses of demesne farming.

---

[1] *L.R.*, 860.

[2] E.g., in 1404-5 the assized rents are swollen by a number of "new" rents (not necessarily new that year), including 1s. 4½d. from William and John, sons of Adam Sweyneslond, for 2a. 3r. lying in North Field and the Combe, let to them by court roll, and 4 dayworks by the sheepfold let to Adam Sweyneslond and his heirs forever for 4d. and the service of supplying lime to Otford manor whenever necessary (*L.R.*, 839).

[3] E.g., in 1437-8 some 23a. of demesne land in Shoreham was let to various persons at 8d. an acre. But all other demesne lands and pastures there brought in nothing for lack of a *conductor*, and were occupied by the lord's sheep (*L.R.*, 863).

[4] There seems to be an analogy in an *Inquisition post mortem* (vol. xi, no. 363), where an estate in Ickham is described in 1362 as consisting of " a capital messuage and 120 acres of arable, dry and sandy, of which 80 acres may be sown every year, but this year only 31 acres are sown, and of these 8 acres are sown with beans, peas and vetches."

Demesne income is clearly set out in the serjeant's acco
consisted first and foremost of the proceeds from selling
differently to the archbishop's household or on the local
livestock and the wool and woolfells of the lord's flock of 2.. ..
sheep. After these things in order of value came the miscellaneous
group which the account-rolls call " Issues of the manor ", and which
include rents from hiring out the archbishop's pastures and his carts,
and selling pannage, brushwood from his copses, pigeons from his
dovecote, and so on. Up to *c.* 1428 the sale of corn and stock accounts
for about two-thirds of demesne proceeds, but thereafter only for a
half or less, because in 1428 the annual fee-farm of Sundridge, worth
£22 12s. and for long leased to the Isley family, was brought on to the
serjeant's account. The general truth about demesne proceeds is
that they fluctuated considerably from year to year, according to the
abundance and price of corn, but that no clear trend upward or down-
ward is discernible.

Demesne costs in the fifteenth century likewise fluctuated. For
instance, nearly £14 were spent in 1382-3 in repairing the manorial
buildings used for the archbishop's registrar, clerks and esquires. In
1402 a further £20 were spent on building repairs, and about £20 on
buying sheep. On this side of the account, however, a marked trend
can be observed in the rising cost of labour. Up to *c.* 1428 the annual
labour bill was rarely near £10. From then until 1444 it was always
well over £10, and in the last year of demesne farming amounted to
nearly £23. That year the lord's surveyor had to make new agreements
with the *famuli* for their wages.

When the buildings were repaired, the workers paid, and the fields
tilled, the lord should have something to show for it, and this something consisted in the money and provisions supplied to the household,
at Lambeth or elsewhere. While reeve and serjeant each to some extent
paid over both cash and kind, the vast bulk of the reeves' liveries
were in money, the serjeants' in wheat, oats, meat, ale, hay and wood.
Such deliveries, whether *victualia* or *pecunia numerata*, are always
entered on the " discharge " side of the account, but must, of course,
be distinguished from expenses. When the archbishop's household
took supplies, it normally purchased at, or allowed the serjeant,
current market prices. In some ways the year-by-year delivery to the
lord is a good index of the estate's profitability, especially if the arrears
are inconsiderable and the capital investment reckoned in, for such
payments represent a physical flow of wealth more certain and cal-
culable than the " charge " side of accounts, which were simply
statements of what was in theory owing. The Otford serjeants
certainly supplied their lord steadily right up to the end of demesne
farming.

The difficulty of striking a modern balance with a medieval account, or even appreciating a medieval account with medieval eyes, has often enough been remarked.   It is not possible to point to a clear accounting reason why the lord leased off his whole demesne in 1444.   Several developments may have played a part in the decision.   Archbishop Stafford succeeded Chichele in 1443, and the arrival of a new lord was sometimes the occasion for a new start by the financial organization. Secondly, the cost of working the demesne was undoubtedly becoming high.   Thirdly, there were men ready to take on the demesne-lands, work themselves, pay a regular rent to the lord, and go on supplying his household with provisions against cash when required.   The questions of labour and of the new farmers may, in conclusion, be briefly discussed.

The rising cost of labour has already been alluded to.   In 1443-4 the surveyor, William Stevens, had not only to convert the corn liveries of the *famuli* to money at a rate favourable to them, but had to arrange for the serjeant to be subsidized by payments from outside *super husbondriam faciendam*.[1]   Even though the standing labour force had been reduced since the earlier fourteenth century, and now stood at four ploughmen, a carter and a shepherd,[2] they came expensive when their wages and liveries were added up.   Nor was the difficulty one of commanding customary services, as it was in other parts of England, since the customary services of tenants on these west Kentish manors of the archbishop did not count for very much.   On the analogy of Wrotham and Bexley, it was more difficult in the later middle ages to keep the Kentish *famulus* sweet.[3]

Labour-services at Otford, such as they were, came to an end with the final leasing of the demesne.   Portions of the demesne were being let out before the complete leasing of 1444.   The first farmer who comes to notice was the then serjeant, Thomas Brounswayn, who in 1402-3 took the demesne lands and pastures with 9 acres of meadow in Shoreham for seven years at £3 6s. 8d. *per annum*.[4]   In 1414 he was holding them for term of life,[5] but by 1418 they had passed to a member of the well-to-do Otford family of Dorkynghole,[6] and by 1427 to Robert Tymberden,[7] whose family were also local tenants of

---

[1] *L.R.*, 871, 872.

[2] *L.R.*, 853.

[3] E.g., at Bexley in 1350 the bailiff reported that the value of liveries claimed by the *famuli* must be allowed, *et famuli aliter non potuerunt haberi* (*L.R.*, 240) ; at Wrotham in 1401 extra pay was allowed *in rewardo facto omnibus famulis manerii ut melius se haberent in servicio domini* (*L.R.*, 1142).

[4] *L.R.*, 838.

[5] *L.R.*, 850.

[6] *L.R.*, 853.   That this family was of some financial standing is indicated in *Early Chancery Proceedings* (Public Record Office, Class C1), File 24, no. 258 (1464).   I owe this reference to my former pupil, Miss Margaret Avery.

[7] *L.R.*, 857.

long standing. In 1437-8, a bad year, only 23 acres of the Shorham demesnes could be leased, and those were taken up by various persons for a short term at 8d. the acre.[1] But in 1439 the Shoreham demesnes were all let again, by court roll, at £3 *per annum*, to four men who continued to hold them severally for some time : John Sepham, John Reeve, butcher, Thomas Blakenham and Thomas Lane.[2] At the same time John Multon took up an acre of the Otford demesne which lay next to property of his own for 1s. p.a. In 1440 an acre of North Field was rented at 6d. a year to Thomas Court, whose own lands lay adjacent.[3] Finally, in 1444, the whole demesne of Otford (less Shoreham, which by now was considered separate) was let to one Richard Clerk, clerk, for eight years at £15 6s. 8d. p.a., on condition that the archbishop should maintain the buildings belonging to the husbandry unless the farmer himself, his servants or animals were responsible for the damage.[4] Major leases like this were made not by court roll but by private indenture between the parties. Henceforward, the Otford demesnes, less the small pieces previously leased off, were held by a single farmer, who took over the whole stock, including the demense sheep, which was priced at £20. The farmer held the outer court of the manor, with buildings including the " Baileychamber ". The palace remained to the archbishop, to be used and coveted by the Tudors.[5]

The hidden strength of the early farmers, whose story does not concern us here, is suggested as well by place-names as in any other way. There is a Multon meadow in the demesne survey of 1515. Multons were again farming the demesne in 1536, and George Multon,[6] the father-in-law of Lambarde, was by then styled " gentleman ". As for the other first farmers, the one-inch O.S. map perpetuates two of their names in Timberden Bottom and Sepham Farm. The latter is a patronymic traceable back to the thirteenth century.

---

[1] *L.R.*, 863.
[2] *L.R.*, 865.
[3] *L.R.*, 868.
[4] P.R.O. Ministers' Accounts (S.C.6), 1129/1.
[5] See a paper by the present writer in *English Historical Review*, lxvii, 20.
[6] *Westminster Abbey Muniments*, no. 14303 ; cf. Prerog. Court of Canterbury, Will Register " Thower " quire 20 (will of Robert Multon of Otford, 1532).

FOUR KENT TOWNS AT THE END
OF THE MIDDLE AGES

By A. J. F. DULLEY

BETWEEN 1915 and 1938 the late Arthur Hussey published in these
pages and elsewhere abstracts of the surviving wills for eight Kent
parishes down to 1558.[1] Four of them were towns, and for these the
evidence of the wills is especially valuable, since the smaller, non-
corporate market town is usually ill-documented so far as its early
history is concerned. Of the four, only Hythe was corporate, and
none was very large: Hythe had about 700-800 inhabitants *c.* 1570,
Milton about a hundred less; Ashford was about the same size as
Milton, and Sittingbourne rather smaller.[2] Except for Hythe, where
the haven on which it depended was rapidly silting, all had probably
grown in the previous century, the period in which most of the wills
were made. The four rural parishes—Ash and Eastry, south-west
of Sandwich, and Herne and Reculver with its chapelry of Hoath, on
the coast north-east of Canterbury—because of their geographical
grouping are not fully representative of the Kentish countryside.
Their value for the present enquiry is principally as a foil to the towns,
though Herne and Reculver have an independent importance when
it comes to a consideration of the fishing industry, which is better
attested than most in these documents and merits more detailed study
than it has commonly received.

An enquiry of this sort, if it is not to be a collection of subjective
impressions, must be based on statistical methods. Wills, full as they
are of miscellaneous information, are not ideally suited to this purpose.
They have two principal drawbacks. Firstly, only the richer inhabitants
owned enough goods or property to justify their making a will at all.
How far down the social scale the habit extended may be disputed:
doubtless it varied from individual to individual. But it has been
estimated with a good show of reason that between a third and a half

---

[1] Ash: *Arch. Cant.*, xxxiv (1920), 47-62; xxxv (1921), 17-35; xxxvi (1923),
49-64; xxxvii (1925), 35-47. Ashford: *Ashford Wills*, publ. Ashford U.D.C., 1938.
Eastry: *Arch. Cant.*, xxxviii (1926), 173-82; xxxix (1927), 77-90; xl (1928), 35-47.
Herne: *ibid.*, xxviii (1909); 83-114; xxx (1914), 93-126. Hythe: *ibid.*, xlix (1937),
127-56; l (1938), 87-121; li (1939), 27-65. Milton: *ibid.*, xliv (1932), 79-102; xlv
(1933), 13-30; xlvi (1934), 36-51; xlvii (1935), 177-88. Reculver and Hoath:-*ibid.*,
xxxii (1917), 77-141. Sittingbourne: *ibid.*, xli (1929), 37-56; xlii (1930), 37-56;
xliii (1931), 49-71.
[2] C. W. Chalklin, *Seventeenth Century Kent* (1965), 30.

61

of townsmen lived at or near the level of bare subsistence, and few of these can have made wills.[3] Confirmation of this can be derived from the wills themselves. Of the 57 testators other than farmers and priests who specify their occupations only one was a labourer. Yet out of 380 comparable entries among the lists of persons in Kent pardoned for participation in Jack Cade's rebellion in 1450 no less than 18 per cent. were labourers.[4]

The second difficulty is that wills never give exhaustive information. The fact that the deceased did not bequeath land, for example, does not imply that he did not possess any. But if one takes groups as a basis for study, it is possible to distinguish significant variations from what might be expected from a purely random mention of these things. The larger the group, the smaller the variation that will count as statistically significant and therefore the finer the comparisons that can be made. Thus, while it is impossible to infer from the wills alone what proportion of testators were landowners, it is possible to show that in one parish or period the proportion was higher than in another.

TABLE 1

	Urban parishes				Rural parishes			
	Up to 1500	1501-1530	1531-1558	Total	Up to 1500	1501-1530	1531-1558	Total
Males	248	276	219	743	181	148	73	402
Females	39	53	29	121	24	16	12	52
Total	287	329	248	864	205	164	85	454
Children per male	1·67	1·39	1·77	1·60	2·08	1·90	2·62	2·10
Real estate (%)								
Land (± house)	43·1	32·2	28·6	34·9	77·6	69·5	58·8	71·1
House only	34·9	25·6	30·2	30·0	8·3	4·9	4·7	6·4
None	22·0	42·2	41·2	35·1	14·1	25·6	36·5	22·5
Cash Legacies (%)								
All cash legacies	84·0	75·9	68·9	76·5	82·4	82·4	77·7	81·5
Legacies over £1	61·6	52·6	58·1	57·2	52·7	59·1	67·1	57·6
,, ,, £3	48·4	33·1	42·0	40·7	34·6	42·1	50·6	40·3
,, ,, £10	25·4	14·7	28·3	22·3	16·1	20·7	37·7	21·8
,, ,, £30	8·7	5·5	16·5	9·7	3·9	4·3	24·7	7·9
,, ,, £100	1·7	0·6	4·4	2·1	1·0	0·6	8·2	2·2

So far as town and country as a whole are concerned, it is in land ownership that the most obvious contrast lies. Real estate is the most likely of all forms of property to receive a mention in a will. In the rural parishes 71 per cent. bequeath farmland and a further 6 per cent.

[3] Julian Cornwall, 'English Country Towns in the 1520's', *Econ. Hist. Review*, 2nd Series, xv (1962), 52-69.
[4] W. D. Cooper, 'Jack Cade's Followers in Kent', *Arch. Cant.*, vii (1868), 233-71.

houses only. For the towns the corresponding figures are 35 per cent. and 30 per cent. Even in Ashford, where the farming element is most evident, the number of persons leaving land is only 49 per cent. of the total. A large proportion of the townsmen who owned land must have been rentiers only. Less than one man in five can be proved to have been a farmer, sometimes in addition to following a trade, whereas in the country nearly one half left corn, cattle, tools or other evidence of farming. A good deal of the land owned by townsmen was marsh grazing, in Romney Marsh if they lived in Ashford or Hythe, in Sheppey or nearer home if they came from Milton or Sittingbourne. This could be stocked with sheep or store cattle or let to upland farmers while the owner gave his attention to some other means of livelihood. Of those who were definitely farmers many undoubtedly lived outside the towns. Hythe was the only parish to have an insignificant amount of agricultural land within its boundaries, and it had correspondingly the smallest proportion of farmers—22 out of 260 males. Altogether agriculture accounted for about a third of those townsmen whose occupation can be ascertained (44 per cent. of the total), and only 2 per cent. of that number combined it with another occupation. In the country only 36 men, apart from clergy, had occupations other than farming, and of these at least 16 farmed in addition to following their trade. The craftsman-smallholder was a feature of the countryside but not of the towns, at least so far as these eight parishes are concerned.

Comparatively little can be gleaned about farming practice. Sheep were everywhere important and outweigh the other livestock bequeathed in point of numbers in most parishes. At Ashford they were less prominent, but there were several legacies of horses, which, to judge from the number of mares and colts among them, were being bred for sale rather than used about the farm. The earliest Customs Port Books (1565+) show a thriving export trade in horses to France from Hythe and other ports along this stretch of coast. Wheat and barley are the only crops commonly mentioned, though there are occasional bequests of saffron gardens, which, like the sheep, doubtless owed their existence to the cloth industry. At Milton much of the land still lay in open fields of the Kentish type. Small plots, some of half an acre or less, are described as lying in Sayersfield, Buggesfield, Leyfield, Akirmansfield or Schamellisfield, of which the first two at least derived their names from local farming families.

The pattern of land ownership was not static. Both in town and country there was a pronounced and steady decline in the number of testators leaving land and also, though less pronounced and steady, in ownership of other forms of real estate. Only in a very few cases are details given of the area or value of the land concerned, but it would seem that land in East Kent was being concentrated in fewer

63

and fewer hands, with a rising proportion of landless men being left to seek employment as labourers or drift to the towns.

The extent of that drift cannot be traced directly, but its existence is clearly implied by the number of children who receive legacies or are otherwise mentioned in wills. In the four country parishes they averaged 2·1 per male (childless included) as against 1·6 in the towns. These figures probably underestimate the numbers of children surviving their fathers, particularly in the poorer families, where it was impossible to provide for each separately, but the relative difference is noteworthy: families were undoubtedly smaller in the towns, whether through lower fertility or higher mortality rates. The crowding together of people even in small towns created problems of sanitation that did not exist in the countryside. Nor were they altogether unnoticed by the townsfolk themselves. John Edwey of Hythe left 3s. 4d. in 1473 'to making of one common latrine in the town'.

Family size shows variations not only between town and country but also from period to period, being lowest between 1501 and 1530 and rising later. This trend corresponds with similar fluctuations in the value of legacies expressed in cash terms. These provide a very rough and ready index to the wealth of groups. In tabulating them I have taken the maximum value possible where the terms of the bequest are conditional or ambiguous, and annual payments have been assumed to have been paid for an arbitrary seven years: possible errors in these cases tend to cancel each other out when only the relative wealth of groups is considered. The same fluctuation between generations is apparent, though there is no overall distinction between town and country. The towns, however, seem to have been wealthier than the countryside up to 1500, while in the recovery after 1530 the country outpaced the town. Throughout, those who left large sums of money tended to name more children than those who left little or none, and it is unlikely that this correlation is purely a product of the random variation in the amount of detail that different testators give about their family affairs, for there is evidence from other sources that in pre-industrial England the well-to-do succeeded in rearing more children than the poor.[5] The chronological variations, particularly the general increase in the value of legacies after 1530, may in part be due to the declining value of money. But at any rate so far as the towns are concerned, taking the statistics for family size and wealth together, it would seem that in all of them there was a period of stagnation, if not decline, in the early decades of the sixteenth century.

The reasons for this fluctuation are not apparent. There was considerable variety in the economic basis of the individual towns. Trade was an important source of prosperity to each, but none was dependent

[5] Peter Laslett, *The World We Have Lost* (1965), 69.

TABLE 2

Occupation stated in will	Ashford	Hythe	Milton	Sitting-bourne	Total
Priest	2	2	3	3	10
Draper (incl. d. or weaver)	2			2	4
Smith (blacksmith)		3		1	4
Weaver	1		3		4
Butcher	1	1	1		3
Clothier (clothman, -maker)	2		1		3
Fisherman		3			3
Shoemaker		1		2	3
Tailor	2			1	3
Brewer	1		1		2
Fletcher (bow and arrow maker)	1			1	2
Glover				2	2
Miller			2		2
Servant	2				2
Waxchandler (candlemaker)	1			1	2
Bricklayer			1		1
Cooper			1		1
Cutler	1				1
Dyer		1			1
Fuller	1				1
Hermit			1		1
Innholder				1	1
Labourer				1	1
Parish Clerk		1			1
Surgeon	1				1
Tanner	1				1
Waterman			1		1
Total	19	12	15	15	61

TABLE 3

Occupation Group	Ashford	Hythe	Milton	Sitting-bourne	Total
Whole-time farmers	46	17	33	23	119
Seamen and fishermen	—	74	13	2	89
Textile workers	9	6	14	3	32
Clergy, etc.	2	3	4	3	12
Miscellaneous	21	21	18	14	74
Total	78	121	82	45	326
Occupation unknown	107	139	88	83	417
Total males	185	260	170	128	743

on trade alone. Indeed, to judge from the occupations stated in the
wills, few townsmen were retailers pure and simple. Most were craftsmen or processers supplying the everyday needs not only of their
fellow-townsmen but also of the inhabitants of the surrounding
countryside. Nearly all the commoner crafts are named at least once.

Carpenters are unaccountably absent. More significant perhaps is the absence of purveyors of luxuries and practitioners of the more highly specialized crafts and services, such as spicers, grocers and mercers, goldsmiths, scriveners or notaries. As the list of Cade's followers shows, at the beginning of the period at least these were mainly concentrated in the larger towns, notably Canterbury, Sandwich, Maidstone and Rochester.

In each of the four towns trade centred round the weekly market. At Hythe this gave its name to one of the four wards, and here were located all the shops whose situation is specified. Neither here nor elsewhere are they mentioned often in wills. Only 5 per cent. of the men bequeathed shops or stalls, but as most shops were no doubt simply the front room of the house, many must have gone unmentioned. Milton had semi-permanent stalls or shambles in its market place, apparently arranged in accordance with the commodity for sale, for William Maas in 1465 left two fish shambles and two tanner shambles. The area served by these markets was not normally large. Kent was well supplied with market towns: Symonson's map, published in 1596, shows 27 cities and towns, and few parts of the county were more than five miles from one of them. Milton and Sittingbourne were in fact only about a mile apart, although as Sittingbourne's market was on a Wednesday and Milton's much larger one on a Saturday, they were probably complementary rather than competing. No tradesman has left any means of identifying the extent of his custom, but Thomas Norden of Sittingbourne, who acted as a moneylender, was creditor to three men in Borden, two each at Milton and Sittingbourne itself, and one at Rodmersham, Stockbury, Tonge and Tunstall, all of which lie within a four-mile radius. A study of all connections outside the testator's home parish—property, legatees, witnesses, etc.—shows that with the exception of Ashford there was no great difference in this respect between town and country. Two-thirds of the wills reveal none at all, and only a few had any beyond ten miles from home: 5 per cent. in the country and 10 in towns. For Ashford the corresponding percentages are 58 and 17; lying as it did at the junction between the predominantly pastoral and industrial Weald and the arable districts to the north, it probably served a wider area than the average market town.

This local market absorbed the products of most of the urban craftsmen, but there is one large group who formed part of an industry of national rather than local importance, namely the cloth trade. Though they were peripheral to the main centre in the Cranbrook district, all four towns had weavers and other textile workers among their inhabitants. It is not always easy from the wills alone to distinguish manufacturers from retailers, and even contemporaries sometimes found the distinction obscure. Thus John Shavelok of Sitting-bourne in 1486 described himself as 'draper or weaver'. For statistical purposes, therefore, drapers and all who left legacies of cloth have been classed as belonging to the industry, which, as so defined, accounted for 14 men at Milton (17 per cent. of known occupations), 9 at Ashford (12 per cent.), 6 at Hythe (5 per cent.) and 3 at Sitting-bourne (7 per cent.). By comparison, in 1450 in the industrial villages of Smarden and Pluckley, where virtually the whole able-bodied male population seems to have joined Cade's revolt, the textile workers numbered 16 out of 98 in the former and 8 out of 50 in the latter. The towns seem to have concentrated on the finishing processes, and Milton in particular was surrounded by 'tenter grounds', in which the cloth was stretched and dried after fulling in the local mills.

The cloth trade and the weekly market were not the only sources of employment. Except for Ashford, all the towns under discussion were to some degree sea-ports. Milton and Sittingbourne shared the same creek, which, opening on to the Swale, provided a sheltered route for small vessels to London and one that was much used, particularly for the supply of grain from the fertile soils of North Kent to the metropolitan market. The earliest indications of the extent of this trade come from the last quarter of the sixteenth century. From Michaelmas 1573 to Michaelmas 1574, the Port Book for the Creek of Milton (which included Sheppey and the coast as far west as Rainham) recorded 111 shipments, 74 outwards (49 to London, 12 to other English ports and 13 overseas) and 37 inwards (18 from London, 9 from other English ports and 10 from overseas).[6] The nature of all the cargoes is not stated, but from Easter to Michaelmas 1574 the 27 outward consignments included 15 of grain, mostly wheat, and 4 of fish to London, and 8, half of them malt, to other ports. About half were conveyed in local boats, 13 Milton vessels and 3 from Sitting-bourne. All were small: the largest was of only 20 tons burden, and the average was 14 tons. According to a list of shipping compiled in 1566, there were then 26 vessels at Milton and 3 at Sittingbourne.[7] The largest was of 24 tons, but 20 were of 10 tons or less. Four quays are named at Milton and two at Sittingbourne. Probably most or all were in private ownership, for they are mentioned several times in wills. Thus Hamond Key got its name from Ralph Hayman, who purchased it c. 1464 on the death of Joan Hert, the widow of its previous owner, and left it in turn to his son Ralph, who died in 1534, having acquired an additional wharf and a boat in the meantime. He was the only one of the four quay-owners to bequeath a vessel. The majority of ship-owners were mariners or fishermen rather than merchants, though

[6] P.R.O., E.190/639/7, 10.
[7] Brit. Mus., Cott. MS. Julius B iv, fol. 95.

some might attain to moderate wealth. Robert Ruffyne, senior, who described himself as 'yeoman', in 1549 left six boats, one of them a 'dredging skeye', as well as three houses and £13 in cash. It was in fact normal to own more than one boat and to own them outright rather than in partnership. At least one was often a fishing-boat, and oyster-dredging probably alternated seasonally with transport of merchandise. Altogether mariners and fishermen made up a large section of the population at Milton. Among 29 followers of Jack Cade 13 were described as 'shipman', and the same number of fishermen and mariners occur among the 82 testators whose occupation is known. At Sittingbourne the proportion was much smaller: two wills out of 45. Situated as it was on the main road from London to Canterbury, traffic by road probably provided more employment here. The only innholder named among the wills was a Sittingbourne man, and a rippier (carrier of fish by pack-horse from the coastal ports to London) received a legacy.

The distribution of rippiers among Cade's followers shows that Watling Street was not the only route by which fish reached the capital. The roads from Folkestone and Hythe via Ashford and from Rye via Tonbridge also had their share of the traffic, a traffic which does something to discountenance the criticisms sometimes voiced about the state of early Wealden roads. For the trade was essentially one in fresh fish, and speed of delivery was important. By contrast the fish sent by sea from Milton to London was ling and cod, not locally caught and presumably either salted or dried.

The sources from which the rippiers drew their supplies were varied, and the variations are well represented among the published wills. The oyster fishery at Milton and Sittingbourne has already been discussed.[8] It was only part of an industry that was widespread along the Swale and the Medway estuary from Rochester to Whitstable, and also in the Wantsum Channel behind Sandwich, where in 1467 the corporation, anxious to preserve the haven, forbade oyster-dredgers to throw back the stones dredged up.[9] At the same time they legislated against 'werys, groynes and kiddles' erected by various owners of the foreshore between Sandwich Haven and North Mouth. The Sandwich authorities were not the only body to legislate, usually without effect, against these obstructions to navigation. In the thirteenth and fourteenth centuries the Corporation of London made several attempts to put down kiddles in the Thames Estuary. In 1237 they fined 28 men, including 7 from Strood, 4 from Rochester and 3 from Cliffe, the large sum of £10 each for erecting kiddles at the seaward end of Yantlet

---

[8] See also R. H. Goodsall, 'Oyster Fisheries on the North Kent Coast', *Arch. Cant.*, lxxx (1965), 118-51.

[9] W. Boys, *Collections for a History of Sandwich* (1792), 675.

Creek, while in 1406 another confiscation of nets resulted in a riot led by men of Barking, Erith, Woolwich and elsewhere to the number of 2,000.[10] Nor was the Thames shore the only place where they were to be found. They were also put up in the creeks behind New Romney, where a lawsuit was fought over them in 1358 and a part of the town was called 'Kydelmannehope'.[11]

The nature and working of these structures is illuminated by the wills for Herne and Reculver, where they existed in some number. Altogether 31 men out of 197 in the two parishes bequeathed them, usually describing them as 'weirs'. They consisted of a stout wooden framework, the 'steddle', V-shaped in plan, to which were attached nets which guided the fish into a trap at the apex of the V. Fish were forced into the net by the set of the tide, and consequently we find both flood- and ebb-weirs, arranged to take advantage of the currents in either direction. They were set up several deep along the coast and a boat was needed to reach the furthest. The right to build them seems to have belonged to the owner of the adjacent cliff, and was regulated, at Reculver at least, by the manor courts, which exacted a nominal rent and forbade the extension of old or the building of new weirs. Working the weirs was only a part-time occupation, for the trap only needed emptying once per tide and the only other work required was routine maintenance of the frame and nets, and all the owners of weirs were farmers or at least smallholders. As a group, however, they seem to have been rather poorer than the majority of their fellow villagers.

The fishermen described so far were all inshore fishermen and formed a minority of the working population of their respective communities. At Hythe the situation was rather different. There 61 per cent. of the testators whose occupation is traceable left boats or nets. Not all were themselves necessarily engaged in fishing, for one man from Ashford left a share in a boat and fishing gear at Folkestone, and several Hythe men left gear to their wives or daughters, to be used on their behalf. But there are other reasons for thinking that a high proportion of the population were fishermen. The 1566 census of shipping reports that there were 122 houses in the town and 160 of their occupants were engaged in fishing. The same was true of fishing towns generally on this coast. At Hastings a similar list compiled the previous year estimated that 146 out of 280 householders were fishermen, and at Rye 225 out of 530.[12] This was a much higher percentage than could

---

[10] *Munimenta Gihallae: I, Liber Albus* (Rolls Ser., ed. H. T. Riley (1859)), 500-1, 514.

[11] *Register of Daniel Rough* (Kent Records, xvi, ed. K. M. E. Murray (1945)), 142-4, 187.

[12] P.R.O., S.P.D., Eliz., xxxviii, No. 28.

have been found following any single occupation or group of occupations in either Ashford, Milton or Sittingbourne, or, probably, in other inland towns, even the larger manufacturing towns of the Midlands. Nor is it easy to find parallels in succeeding centuries. Seventeenth-century Tonbridge seems to have had an occupational structure very much like Ashford,[13] and even at Chatham, almost exclusively dependent on the Royal Dockyard, its employees only accounted for one-third of those whose probate inventories have survived.[14]

Hythe had had a long history as a fishing port, for it had been a founder member of the Cinque Ports confederacy, which had been called into being in part to regulate the Yarmouth herring fishery. It also handled a certain amount of commercial traffic, but with the decay of the haven and the growth in the size of ships, it was steadily declining and had become insignificant by the end of the sixteenth century. At the beginning of the period covered by the wills it may have been of some importance. There are records of Hythe ships being engaged in passenger traffic with the continent and in victualling the garrison at Calais in the reign of Henry VIII. Two of the three masters so engaged in 1533 were also fishermen, and it is likely that most of the larger vessels were used for both purposes.[15]

Fishing continued to flourish, even though commerce declined. The number and proportion of men bequeathing fishing gear remained fairly constant throughout the period covered by the published wills— despite the fact that one source, probably tendentious, reported a decline in the number of ships and fishing boats in the port from 80 in 1533 (the most in any of the Cinque Ports) to only 8 in 1563.[16] The bequests made by fishermen often go into considerable detail and, taken in conjunction with other evidence, they make it possible to reconstruct the workings of the industry in outline.

The most valuable single item of equipment bequeathed was normally a boat. More than half owned at least part of one. Out of 39, 11 owned only a part share, 8 had a single boat, 3 had shares in two, and the rest had two or more. In contrast to Milton, it seems to have been usual for two or more to share the cost of a new boat, partly because the boats were generally larger, and also because, being involved in deep-sea work, they were exposed to greater risks. Shared ownership, which was normal at Rye and Hastings also, was a form of insurance. Many must have been built locally (one will mentions 'the house where the shipwright dwells'), but not all: John Clerke in 1487 left part of a boat bought in Normandy.

[13] *Arch. Cant.*, lxxvi (1961), 159.
[14] *Ibid.*, lxxvii (1962), 162.
[15] *Cal. S.P., Hen. 8*, iv, No. 6022; vi, No. 1530.
[16] P.R.O., S.P.D., Eliz., xxviii, No. 3.

Several types of vessels are enumerated, both in the wills and in the list of 1566. In 1566 the largest were crayers, 4 of 40 tons and 3 of 30 tons. There were 7 shotters of 15 tons and 18 tramellers of 5 tons. The distinction between them, apart from size, was primarily one of function. The crayers were used for trade and deep-sea fishing, the other vessels for various methods of fishing. To what extent they differed in appearance as well is uncertain. The best evidence for the rig of six-teenth-century vessels on this coast is the chart of Rye harbour made by John Prowze in 1572, which illustrates at least four distinct types, from fully rigged ships to rowing boats.[17] It has been suggested that the vessels of intermediate size shown off Winchelsea, apparently clinker-built with a raised deck or cabin at the stern, a sprit mainsail and in one case a small mizzen, should be identified with the crayers of written records, and the smaller, undecked boats, square-rigged on a single mast, with the shotters, tramellers and hookers of the documents. This may well have been generally true, but at least some crayers were fitted out as fully rigged ships, for in 1536 a crayer of Sandwich was attacked by pirates off Hythe and 'broke both his topmasts'.[18]

The smaller boats at Hythe were sometimes referred to by the generic name of 'stade boats', the Stade being the open beach where they were hauled up by means of 'vernes' or capstans worked by horses. These capstans, as well as lodges on the Stade, are a common item in wills. William Rust's seven 'sea horses' presumably earned their keep by turning them.

Much more widely distributed than boats, vernes or lodges were nets and lines. Six different types of net and two types of line were in use. Flews and shot-nets were bequeathed by a majority of fishermen; sprat and tramel nets were also in common use; and deepings and seine-nets receive an occasional mention, as do harbour hooks and small hooks.

The uses of these pieces of equipment and the routine of the fishing year can be gathered to some extent from comparison with the practice of the Brighton fishermen, which was described in detail in 1580.[19] There the fishing year was divided into seasons called 'fares', some for local in-shore fishing and some in deeper waters. They may be repre-sented in tabular fashion as follows:

[17] H. Lovegrove, ' Shipping in a Sixteenth-Century Plan of Winchelsea and Rye', *Mariners' Mirror*, xxxiii (1947), 187-98. See also: *Rye Port Books* (Sussex Record Society., lxiv (1966), ed. R. F. Dell), xxxvii-xxxix.

[18] *Cal.S.P., Hen. 8.*, xii, Part 1, No. 718 (iii).

[19] C. Webb and A. E. Wilson (eds.), *Elizabethan Brighton: the Ancient Customs* (1952).

Date	Fare	Place	Catch	Tonnage of Boat
Feb.-Apr.	Tucknett	Upon coast	Plaice	c. 3
Apr.-June	Shotnett	To sea	Mackerel	6-26
May-June	Drawnett	By the shore	Mackerel	c. 3
Summer	Harbour	—	Conger	c. 8
June-Sept.	Skarborow	Scarborough	Cod	18-40
Sept.-Nov.	Yarmothe	Yarmouth	Herring	15-40
Oct.-mid-Dec.	Cok	—	Herring	2-6
Nov.-end Dec.	Flew	—	Herring	8-20

Of these eight, at least four were followed at Hythe, viz. shotnet, harbour, Scarborough and Yarmouth fares, but plaice were caught with tramels and there was an additional season for sprats. Both these latter had been features of the Rye fishery since the thirteenth century but never spread further west. The sprat season was not particularly valuable, but trammelling was more important. The interests of the local trammellers were vigorously defended by the local authorities against various threats from foreign fishermen and English trawlers during the late sixteenth and early seventeenth centuries, and from their regulations and representations various details emerge. The season for tramels and draw-nets ran from 16th March to 31st October.[20] The boats used were small, of only five tons, as we have seen, and carried a crew of seven.[21] The net consisted of a triple wall of mesh, resting on the bottom and of up to 18 furlongs in length, in which plaice, soles and other bottom-feeding fish entangled themselves.[22] It was essentially a complicated, vulnerable and expensive adaptation of the drift-nets used for catching herring and mackerel, and it is a mark of conservatism that it persisted so long after the introduction of the more economical and effective trawl.

While the smaller boats were catching plaice in the bay, the larger boats drifted for mackerel until early summer, when some at least sailed north for the Scarborough voyage. Originally this seems to have been devoted to catching herrings. There are references to the herring fishery there in the fourteenth century, and in 1412 the earliest Hythe municipal records show that John Leghe paid local custom for five lasts of herring of 'Schardeburgh fare'.[23] In 1528 Hythe, Folkestone and Romney between them sent 20 crayers on this 'North Seas' voyage, and it is an additional sign of the traditionalism of Cinque Ports fishermen that though they contributed in all about half of the North Seas

[20] J. M. Baines, *Historic Hastings* (1955), 227
[21] *Ibid.*
[22] P.R.O., S.P.D., Jas. 1, xci, No. 12.
[23] H.M.C., *Fourth Report* (1874), Appendix, 435.

fleet on this occasion, they sent not a single vessel on the newer and more distant Scottish and Iceland voyages.[24] The emphasis at Scarborough later changed from herring to cod and ling. In 1565 a memorandum about the proposed rebuilding of Scarborough pier stated that 'the moste store of this Coste, Lynge and Haberdyne, is there made and dried by reason the fyshers straungers and others that fishe in thes northe Seas do theare unlade theire ffishe new takyn and fishith agayne of newe once or twise and unladith theare before they departe awaye ladyn'.[25] In 1580 the Brighton boats took herring nets but probably used them mainly to catch bait for the lines with which they fished for cod—the lines of 'small hooks' that the wills refer to in contrast to 'harbour hooks' used at the same season for conger fishing in home waters.

After the Scarborough voyage followed the other expedition to distant waters, Yarmouth fare, which traditionally occupied the bulk of the Cinque Ports fishermen for the six-week season and was probably still the most profitable of the year's ventures. When the Herring Fair was over, the boats returned to Hythe and continued to fish for herring in the Channel until the end of the year imposed a brief lull in activity until the spring.

The profits of each voyage were distributed by a system of shares, so many to the boat, so many to the gear and so many to the crew. The system varied in detail from port to port and voyage to voyage, but some version of it seems to have been normal in all Channel ports and dates back at least to the twelfth century. The understanding seems to have been originally that each member of the crew contributed a proportion of the nets, a 'fare' or 'mansfare', which at Brighton was either three or four and at Hythe probably four for herring and mackerel nets (it apparently did not apply to tramels). Testators clearly regarded this as the minimum to set up a servant or apprentice as an independent fisherman, but many possessed a great deal more. Some were capable of fitting out a complete voyage with comparatively little aid. Thomas Staple in 1520 left a crayer, a new 'hoker', a boat, tramel and sprat nets, 30 mackerel nets, and 30 herring nets. A Brighton boat normally carried about 80 shot-nets for mackerel fishing and about 70 flews and norward nets on Yarmouth fare. Consequently a place had to be found for hands who contributed nothing but their labour. A medium-sized shotter required a crew of ten in addition to her master, and a Yarmouth boat about twelve. At Brighton it was forbidden to make up the complement by employing wage-labour, and crew and nets were counted separately in calculating shares, one man

[24] *Cal. S.P.*, *Hen. 8*, iv, Part 2, No. 5101.
[25] P.R.O., S.P.D., Eliz., xxxviii, No. 47. Haberdine, according to the *New English Dictionary*, is a variety of large cod, salted or dried.

73

receiving the same as three or four nets. In the Cinque Ports it seems
to have been common for fishermen to hire 'servants' on a more or less
permanent basis. At Hastings there were 57 'servants' among 239
seafarers in 1565, and at Rye 450 out of 785 (this is probably a scribal
error: other estimates of the seafaring population in the Elizabethan
period are around 300). For Hythe itself there is no list which divides
seamen into categories, but 12 out of the 75 mariners and fishermen
who left wills gave fishing gear to servants or, in two cases, to an
apprentice, a significantly higher proportion than obtained among the
rest of the population.

But even among the townsfolk at large, servants and wage-earners
formed a large group. Very few made a will, and though some received
legacies (usually among the gentry or where the testator was childless),
they are too few to draw conclusions. Many in this category were no
doubt domestics, some apprentices, journeymen or farm labourers.
In general, as returns to the 1524 Lay Subsidy show, they made up a
large section of the town population: at Chichester 42 per cent. of the
men were assessed on wages, usually £2 per annum or less, and this
seems to have been a fairly constant proportion over the years, for in
1380 30 per cent. of the men assessed to the poll tax had been servants.[26]

Beneath them still, at the base of the social pyramid, were the casual
workers and paupers, too impoverished to attract the tax collector or
to aspire to make a will. In the wills of their richer neighbours there are
hints that they were not few. The making of a will served as an opportunity to make up for deeds of piety left undone in the testator's life-
time, and while these usually take the form of payments for masses
for the deceased's soul or contributions to the upkeep of the church,
the poor are not forgotten, and it seems a general assumption that the
executors can always find six stalwart paupers to bear the coffin for a
penny or forty deserving recipients for a dole of bread and ale.

[26] Julian Cornwall, *op. cit.* The poll tax assessment is printed in *Sussex Arch.
Coll.*, xxiv (1872), 67-69.

THE DISTRIBUTION OF LAY WEALTH IN KENT, SURREY, AND SUSSEX, IN THE EARLY FOURTEENTH CENTURY

By R. E. GLASSCOCK

IN his part of the valuable introduction to the recent publication of the 1334 Lay Subsidy for Kent, C. W. Chalklin uses the subsidy as an indicator of the distribution of wealth within the county and discusses the average tax payments by individuals in different areas.[1] This short paper aims to take this line of study a stage further by producing a map of the 1334 assessment for Kent, commenting on the regional variations, and comparing the lay wealth of Kent with that of its neighbours Surrey and Sussex.

1334 is a particularly valuable date at which to survey the distribution of wealth within the county for it enables us to see the situation as it was just before the Black Death and before the great social and economic changes of the years after 1350. Moreover 1334 is the only year when the situation in Kent may be compared with that in the rest of England as the 1334 Lay Subsidy is the only one of the early fourteenth century taxes upon movables whose coverage enables us to reconstruct a picture of the country as a whole.[2] This is possible because the quotas of taxation agreed upon in 1334 were standardized in 1336 and did not finally disappear until 1623. This means that for almost every county in England where the 1334 rolls do not survive, the information may be obtained from later tax rolls. Kent is the one county where this might be impossible as the system of individual taxation continued in the county and instead of the 'freezing' of the 1334 tax quotas, the assessments changed at subsequent grants. Luckily the problem is averted as the detailed 1334 roll for Kent survives in the Public Record Office, London.[3]

A number of maps and commentaries have already appeared dealing with regional prosperity and the distribution of wealth for

---

[1] C. W. Chalklin, in H. A. Hanley and C. W. Chalklin eds., 'The Kent Lay Subsidy of 1334/5,' *Kent Records*, 18 (1964), 58-172.

[2] The standard work on the early fourteenth century lay subsidies is J. F. Willard, *Parliamentary Taxes on Personal Property, 1290-1334*, Cambridge, Mass., (1934).

[3] E 179/123/12.

various counties in 1334.[4] The map for Kent, Surrey and Sussex included here adds a further piece to the jigsaw.[5] The ever-widening picture must, however, be treated with caution. We must be under no illusions about the two great drawbacks in the source material. Firstly, the 1334 assessments were not on total wealth. Many people were exempt below the taxable minimum and no doubt there was widespread evasion and under valuation.[6] Secondly, as Willard has shown, most of the movable wealth of the Church was excluded from the lay subsidies.[7] Ideally therefore we want a map of the clerical wealth in Kent in the early fourteenth century to complement that for lay wealth before we can be sure of the real distribution of wealth within the county. Until this is done a picture of total wealth is impossible: the best that we can hope for is that the 1334 assessments are a useful guide to relative wealth from place to place.

Apart from these exemptions there are in Kent the special exemptions of the moneyers of Canterbury and the men of the Cinque Ports, and in addition, the nature of the Kent returns prevents any comparison of either the size or prosperity of the urban centres.[8] With these limitations in mind there follows some general remarks on the distribution of lay wealth in rural Kent in 1334.

THE DISTRIBUTION OF LAY WEALTH IN KENT

Kent is considered in terms of the county as it was in the mid nineteenth century before certain parishes were detached to form part of the administrative county of London. Unfortunately, as the Kent roll is unique among 1334 rolls in not giving place-names we can get no

---

[4] E. J. Buckatzsch, 'The geographical distribution of wealth in England 1086-1843,' *Economic History Review*, 2nd series, 3 (1950), 180-202; F. W. Morgan, 'The Domesday geography of Devon,' *Transactions of the Devonshire Association*, 72 (1940), 321; B. Reynolds, 'Late medieval Dorset: three essays in historical geography' (unpublished M.A. thesis, University of London, 1958); C. T. Smith, in *Victoria County History, Leicestershire*, 3 (1955), 134; H. C. Darby, *The Medieval Fenland* (1940), 134-5; W. G. Hoskins and E. M. Jope, in A. F. Martin and R. W. Steel, eds., *The Oxford Region* (1954), 109; R. E. Glasscock, 'The distribution of lay wealth in south-east England in the early fourteenth century (unpublished Ph.D. thesis, University of London, 1963); R. E. Glasscock, 'The distribution of wealth in East Anglia in the early fourteenth century,' *Institute of British Geographers, Transactions and Papers*, 32 (1963), 113-123; R. E. Glasscock, 'The Lay Subsidy of 1334 for Lincolnshire,' *The Lincolnshire Architectural and Archæological Society, Reports and Papers*, 10, part 2 (1964), 115-133.

[5] The author has prepared a map for the whole of England. This is expected to appear in H. C. Darby, ed., *An Historical Geography of England before 1900* (forthcoming).

[6] See Willard, *op. cit.*, 139-41, and Chalklin, *op. cit.*, 63-4. For an interesting local example of the sort of bribery that took place when goods were assessed, see P. D. A. Harvey, *A medieval Oxfordshire village: Cuxham, 1240 to 1400*, (1965), 105-7.

[7] Willard, *op. cit.*, 102-9.

[8] Chalklin, *op. cit.*, 67.

idea of the relative prosperity of towns and villages, and it is only possible to map the assessments as they appear on the roll, by hundreds. Yet while we know the position of the hundreds in the early fourteenth century[9] their exact outlines and areas are not known. In calculating average assessments per square mile I have used the late nineteenth century acreages of the parishes in each hundred, as listed by Wallenberg.[10] The slight inaccuracies of such an approach are obvious but unavoidable, and they certainly do not alter the general picture. The quotas of Canterbury and Rochester are excluded from the calculations.

From his study of local rolls before 1334 Willard has suggested that the goods taxed as movables represent the surplus over and above the basic essentials that a family needed to live and work.[11] This idea is supported by the detailed work of Gaydon for Bedfordshire,[12] and Salzman for Sussex.[13] Certainly it would help to explain, in addition to the non-assessment of poorer people, why so few people are listed on the tax rolls, as few people in any village would have produced a surplus. In the Weald for example, where farms were small and scattered, agriculture was not geared to the production of surplus by contrast to north-east Kent where it was.

Accepting Willard's thesis a map showing the average 1334 assessments from place to place (Fig. 1) in fact shows the distribution of surplus or saleable produce from which income could be gained. On the assumption that the tax assessment reflects the ability of an area to pay we can get an approximate idea of the distribution of lay wealth in the county.

The most striking feature of the map is the comparative poverty of the Weald and Romney Marsh relative to the north-east. The map supports Chalklin's view that 'the wealth of the inhabitants depended fairly closely on the fertility of the soil.'[14] As the main geographical regions of Kent emerge fairly clearly from the map it will be convenient to discuss the map under the headings of the two principal divisions, the Weald and Romney Marsh, and North Kent.

THE WEALD AND ROMNEY MARSH

Whereas the Weald Clay and the High Weald were areas of low assessments, for the most part under 15s. per square mile, by comparison

---

[9] *Ibid.*, map following page 172.

[10] J. K. Wallenberg, *The Place-names of Kent*, Uppsala (1934).

[11] Willard, *op. cit.*, 84-5.

[12] A. T. Gaydon, 'The Taxation of 1297,' *Bedfordshire Historical Record Society*, 39 (1959).

[13] L. F. Salzman, 'Early Taxation in Sussex,' *Sussex Archæological Collections*, 98 (1960), 29-43, and 99 (1961), 1-19.

[14] Chalklin, *op. cit.*, 68.

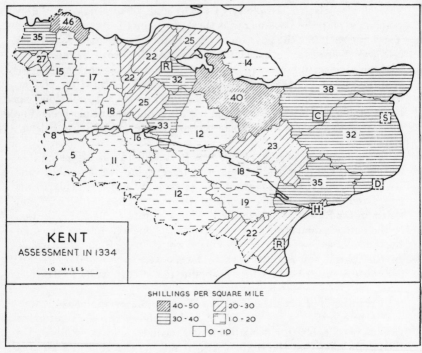

FIG. 1.

Canterbury and Rochester, and the Cinque Ports of Dover, Hythe, New
Romney and Sandwich are denoted by initials.
The northern boundary of the Weald Clay is shown.

with north-east Kent, the Weald was by no means poverty stricken.
The traditional view of the Weald as an unsettled area, hostile to settlement and agriculture, and used only for swine pannage was a thing of
the past by 1300.   J. L. M. Gulley, in his account of the geography of
the Weald in the early fourteenth century,[15] has shown that while much
woodland remained, the Weald was an area of mixed farming with an
emphasis on animal husbandry.   Cattle and swine were reared and
grazed on both enclosed and common pastures.   While oats was the
commonest grain crop wheat was grown on the heavier soils, especially
on the Weald Clay.   By 1334 the landscape had already begun to
assume many of the characteristics known today, with woodland,
hamlets and farms in small clearings, agriculture on the more favourable

[15] J. L. M. Gulley, 'The Wealden landscape in the early seventeenth century
and its antecedents' (unpublished Ph.D. thesis, University of London, 1960),
294-387.

soils, orchards and even parkland. Much heathland must have remained in the western Wealden districts of Kent. Clearly the Weald was an area of subsistence rather than commercial agriculture and as such we are unlikely to find many people producing much surplus to be taxed as movable wealth. Nevertheless for what the Weald lacked in movables it was amply compensated in its timber resources which by 1334 were already becoming the basis for the iron and glass industries of the later middle ages. Also, just at this time, the cloth industry was beginning to grow in and around Cranbrook in the central Weald.[16]

As an area of intense agricultural activity it is no surprise that the assessments of around 20s. per square mile of Romney Marsh and its surrounding area were higher than those in the Weald proper and in much of north-west Kent. The lists of personal names in the subsidy suggest that the population density of Romney Marsh and its surrounds was comparable to that of north-west Kent and very much higher than that of the Weald.[17] We know from the work of R. A. L. Smith,[18] and Miss Ann Smith,[19] on the Canterbury Cathedral Priory estates that while Romney Marsh was a great centre of pasture farming and especially of cheese-making, it was also important for crops, as oats were particularly suited to the heavy lands, as were beans. The enormous efforts of the monastic houses to reclaim, drain and work the marshland in the late thirteenth and early fourteenth centuries testify to the value of the land and to the wealth which it must have carried.[20]

NORTH KENT

Apart from the great difference between the movable wealth on the chalk downs and that on the rich loams of the north-east lowlands the assessments in the north do not reflect the various east-west regions of this part of the county. The highest assessments, between 32 and 40 s. per square mile, were in the north-east lowland, Thanet, and along the northern edge of the Downs. The figures are slightly higher than those around Rochester and the Medway. Generally speaking the western part of north Kent carried only about half the movable wealth of the north-east, although it seems to have been an area of extremes. For example, whereas the Thames-side hundreds of Blackheath and

[16] Gulley, *op. cit.*, 377.
[17] Chalklin, *op. cit.*, 65.
[18] R. A. L. Smith, *Canterbury Cathedral Priory* (1943).
[19] Ann Smith, 'A geographical study of agriculture on the Kentish manors of Canterbury Cathedral Priory, 1272-1379' (unpublished M.A. thesis, University of Liverpool), undated.
[20] R. A. L. Smith, *op. cit.*, 146-189, and also N. Neilson, *The Cartulary and Terrier of the Priory of Bilsington, Kent* (1928).

Little were surprisingly rich, the inland hundreds of Ruxley, Axton, Codsheath and Wrotham, which must have contained much heathland and scrub, were rather poor, with average assessments only slightly higher than those of the Weald.

The lay wealth of north-east Kent was the highest in England south-east of a line Great Yarmouth to Southampton. Only parts of the Sussex coastal plain and the Thames valley carried comparable wealth. As Chalklin has shown, the 1334 subsidy suggests that north-central and north-east Kent were the most populous parts of the county. Pelham has shown that in 1297 north-east Kent was barley and wheat country,[21] the more valuable commercial grains by comparison with oats, the chief crop of the Weald and Romney Marsh. Miss Smith has shown that wheat was the most important crop overall on the manors of Canterbury Cathedral Priory in the north-east, on account of its adaptability to a wide variety of soils and its high market value. Barley was the most important crop of the light soils, for example on the easily worked Brickearths of Thanet.[22]

While the prosperity of north-east Kent may be partly explained by soil fertility part of the answer must also lie in agricultural practice and organization. It was in north-east Kent that some of the most highly specialized and efficient grain farming of medieval England had been developed in the late thirteenth and early fourteenth centuries. On their large estates midway between the markets of London and the continent the Benedictines of Canterbury improved the yields of both seed and land in their drive to take advantage of rising grain prices in the years after 1300.[23] The extent of their achievement may be seen in Prior Eastry's remarkable survey of 1322 which shows the great area under wheat in east Kent, under oats on the marshland manors, and the importance of peas and beans in the various rotations.[24] While the efficiency of the Benedictines alone cannot account for the great prosperity of this corner of the county their example in the half century before 1334 must have rubbed off on other lay and ecclesiastical landlords. Indeed, if we had a complementary map of clerical wealth north-east Kent might appear even richer by comparison with the rest of the county. More than anywhere else in Kent this area was concerned with producing food for markets, and if as Willard suggests the movable goods taxed represented saleable surplus it is not surprising to find such high assessments in this part of the county.

[21] R. A. Pelham, 'Fourteenth-century England,' being Chapter VI of H. C. Darby, ed. *An Historical Geography of England before 1800* (1936) (Fig. 33).
[22] Ann Smith, *op. cit.*, 40.
[23] R. A. L. Smith, *op. cit.*, 128-145, and R. A. L. Smith, 'The Benedictine contribution to medieval agriculture,' in *Collected Papers* (1947), 103-16.
[24] R. A. L. Smith, *op. cit.* (1943), 140-1.

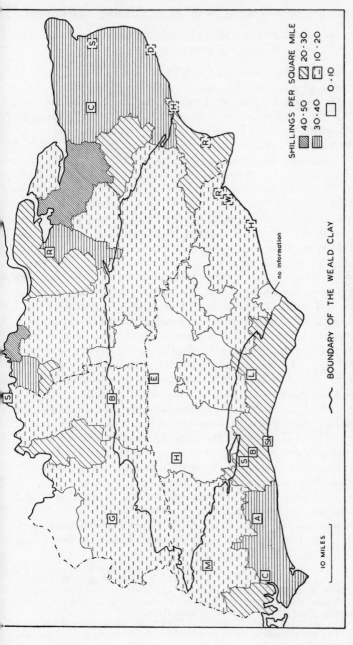

SHILLINGS PER SQUARE MILE

▨ 40·50   ▧ 20·30
▨ 30·40   ▦ 10·20
          ☐ 0·10

⌒ BOUNDARY OF THE WEALD CLAY

FIG. 2. The 1334 assessment in Kent, Surrey and Sussex.

The quotas of all cities and boroughs denoted by initial letters are excluded from the calculations.

Kent   Canterbury and Rochester.
Surrey   Bletchingley, Guildford and Southwark.
Sussex   Chichester, Arundel, Bramber, East Grinstead, Horsham, Lewes, Midhurst, Shoreham and Steyning.

The Cinque Ports, for which there is no 1334 data, are also marked by initial letters, from north to south, Sandwich, Dover, Hythe, New Romney, Rye, Winchelsea and Hastings. There is no information for the Lowey of Pevensey.

10 MILES

81

The Wealth of Kent by Comparison with Elsewhere and Particularly with Surrey and Sussex

By multiplying the assessments at a Tenth and Fifteenth, the total taxable wealth of Kent in 1334 was £27,803 14s. 0¾d. This was the fourth highest county total in England, ranking behind Norfolk (£50,827 7s. 6d.), Lincolnshire (£46,062 15s. 8¼d.), and Yorkshire (£34,709 7s. 0½d.).[25] Kent's impressive total was largely due to its size, for in terms of taxable wealth per square mile Kent's figure of £17 17s. 0d. ranks only eighth behind Oxfordshire (£26 12s. 0d.), Norfolk (£24 17s. 0d.), Rutland (£23 8s. 0d.), Bedfordshire (£21 8s. 0d.), Berkshire (£20 7s. 0d.), Middlesex (£18 11s. 0d.), and Gloucestershire (£18 4s. 0d.). Kent's figure was lowered by the comparatively low assessments in the Weald and along the ridge of the Downs. By contrast, north-east Kent on account of its position, fertility, and agricultural organization, was the largest continuous area assessed at over 20s per square mile in south-east England. Only the Thames valley and the Sussex coastal plain were in any way comparable. The assessment of north-east Kent was one of the highest figures in the country in 1334 and comparable to that of much of Oxfordshire, Norfolk, and central Cambridgeshire, all very rich agricultural areas.

By contrast to its immediate neighbours, Surrey and Sussex, Kent was a rich county. Compared with Kent's taxable wealth per square mile of £17 17s. 0d. Sussex averaged only £11 2s. 0d., and Surrey £11 1s. 0d.[26] The assessment for the three counties is shown in Fig. 2.

Almost all of Surrey was assessed at between 10 and 20s. per square mile. Only along the Thames valley near Kingston and Richmond was the assessment above 20s., the same sort of figure as in Kent west of Rochester. At the other end of the scale the Bagshot region was very poor and the only comparable figure in Kent was that for the Wealden hundred of Somerden in the south-west of the county, where the subsidy suggests that the population was very low.

Sussex, like Kent, had a considerable variety of movable wealth ranging from 4s. per square mile in the central Weald to over 30s. on the west Sussex coastal plain. As in Kent the pattern of wealth shows a very clear relationship to topography and soils. In the Weald

[25] Chalklin's statement (*op. cit.*, 67) that the total wealth of Kent was second only to that of Norfolk is not correct, as in the list by W. G. Hoskins to which he refers the historic divisions of Lincolnshire and the Ridings of Yorkshire are listed separately. When added together they show that both Lincolnshire and Yorkshire had far greater total assessments than Kent.

[26] The 1334 assessments for Surrey and Sussex are already published, viz. W. Hudson, 'The assessments of the hundreds of Sussex to the King's tax in 1334,' *Sussex Archæological Collections*, 50 (1907); *Surrey Taxation Returns*, Part B (1932), for transcription of 1336 roll. The 1334 quotas for Surrey are also listed by H. E. Malden in *Victoria County History, Surrey*, 1 (1902), 441-4.

assessments were low, generally between 4 and 15s. per square mile, with the lowest values on the Weald Clay and the sands east of Horsham. The assessments were slightly higher along the coastal fringe of the Weald between Pevensey and Rye, but in common with the chalk and Lower Greensand around Midhurst in the west, the value of movable property was only moderate. On the other hand, the chalk east of Worthing carried greater wealth probably due to the good agricultural land on the Clay-with-flints and also to the proximity of the coastal settlements. The greatest wealth, comparable to Thanet, was on the fertile and densely settled coastal plain south of Chichester where the assessments averaged between 30 and 33s. per square mile. The map of the 1334 assessment in Sussex substantiates Hudson's view that 'the wealth of the county was derived from its maritime agricultural districts.'[27] The 1334 pattern has also been verified by Pelham in his detailed studies of the 1327 subsidy and the Nonae Rolls of 1341 for the county.[28] Not only has he shown that the wealth per capita was greatest on the chalk and along the coast, but from the Nonae he has shown that this was due to the overwhelming importance of corn growing in Sussex, especially wheat.

In conclusion much the same could be said of Kent. The prosperity of the coastal fringe of south-east England, outside the Weald, was due not only to its fertility, but also to its nearness to markets at home and on the continent, and the sea transport whereby to carry produce. In terms of movable wealth in 1334 these advantages seem to have been enjoyed over a greater area of Kent than of Sussex and Hampshire, and together they made north-east Kent one of the richest parts of fourteenth century England.

[27] Hudson, *op. cit.*, 163.

[28] R. A. Pelham, 'Studies in the historical geography of medieval Sussex,' *Sussex Archæological Collections*, 72 (1931), 157-84, and 'Some Medieval sources for the study of historical geography,' *Geography*, 17 (1932), 32-8.

SOCIAL INSTITUTIONS IN KENT, 1480-1660

by Professor W. K. Jordan

I. BRIEF NOTES ON THE COUNTY

KENT ranks ninth in size among the counties of England. During the whole of our period it was economically and politically one of the most important of all the counties of the realm, possessing a particular significance because of its nearness to London and its situation athwart the principal lines of communication between the capital and the Continent. It enjoyed a special esteem because it was the seat of two cathedral cities. At Canterbury, until the Reformation swept away the rich monastic establishments clustering around the cathedral church, was to be found as well the richest concentration of monastic wealth and activity in any one community in the realm.

The county likewise possessed natural resources sufficient in our period to make it one of the most prosperous in all England. A fertile and varied soil and terrain made it a famous agricultural region, where farm lands and parks were much prized as investments by London merchants, whose steady purchases produced an almost continuous inflation in the value of the land. As early as the beginning of our period specialized fruit farming had begun, with very heavy and certainly very profitable capital outlays, which by the close of the sixteenth century had made its orchards renowned throughout Europe. Kent's agricultural prosperity grew as London's population rapidly increased, since its geographical position and relatively good network of roads gave it a most important competitive advantage in the London markets.

The Kentish gentry were at once numerous and rich, though Lambarde thought them not for the most part of ancient stock or so firmly seated in this county as elsewhere. This shrewd Elizabethan observer very correctly suggests that the gentry was a fluid class, being recruited from London, " (as it were from a certeine riche and wealthy seed plot) courtiers, lawyers and marchants " continually taking their place by the sanction of purchase among the rural aristocracy of the county.[1] At the same time, Kent was remarkable for the number, the independence, and the wealth of its yeomanry. This class remained prosperous and important throughout our period, giving to the county a stable system of small and independent holdings derived rather more

---

[1] Lambarde, William, *A Perambulation of Kent* (Chatham, 1826), 6. Lambarde wrote this account in 1570. A recent writer on the subject suggests that this generalization does not hold for all of Kent. He believes that the infiltration of merchant wealth was largely confined to the area nearest London, while in eastern Kent and the Weald the gentry were principally sprung from indigenous stock (Everitt, A. M., " The County Committee of Kent in the Civil War ", University College of Leicester, *Occasional Papers*, IX [1957], 8).

from the fertility of the region, the proximity to London and the Cinque Ports, and the opportunities for the employment of younger sons in the numerous small industrial towns than from the peculiar merits of Kent's traditional system of landholding.[1]

Of these industries, the clothmaking trade was by far the most important and widely dispersed. Its renascence in Kent dates from the fourteenth century, when Flemish craftsmen and masters laid the basis for the high reputation which Kentish cloths were to possess for a full three centuries. The weaving industry became centred on Cranbrook in the course of the fifteenth century, and the whole clothmaking trade was by the close of that century becoming specialized, with some ten towns gaining a more than local reputation for particular products. The entire industry received a saving competitive impetus during the sixteenth century when in three successive waves skilled Protestant weavers from the Low Countries found refuge in various communities within the county. Sandwich became famous for its " bays and says " and attained a great new prosperity based on the skill and energy of these refugee families, who as late as 1600 outnumbered the native-born inhabitants of this ancient town. Canterbury, which had suffered serious economic damage from the ruin of its great monastic houses, became a thriving manufacturing town with its new-found prosperity resting on its woollen industries and its probably unrivalled skill in the manufacture of silk.[2] Maidstone rapidly acquired what was almost a monopoly in the manufacture of thread, an industry giving employment to some hundreds of persons.[3] The woollen industry supported a large and wealthy group of clothiers throughout the sixteenth century, the rich landholders of the Weald often combining the direction of their estates with this profitable commercial activity.[4] The cloth trade began to languish in the seventeenth century, but it remained throughout our age an important element in the balanced economy of this fortunate and prosperous shire.[5]

The county likewise retained during the whole course of our period some importance as an iron-manufacturing region. In the mid-Elizabethan era it possessed six forges and eight furnaces, all centred in the Weald, which was still thought to provide inexhaustible resources of wood for smelting. A considerable works was set up at Brenchley

---

[1] Lambarde's comments on the yeomanry of the county are most perceptive (*Perambulation*, 7-8).

[2] Hasted reports that in 1665 there were 126 master weavers in the city and that the silk industry gave employment or support to as many as 2,000 persons (Hasted, Edward, *History of Kent* [Canterbury, 1797-1801, 12 vols.], XI, 94.)

[3] *Ibid.*, IV, 267 ; *VCH, Kent*, III, 408.

[4] *Ibid.*, III, 409.

[5] For a particularly helpful account of the economic history of Kent in our period, *vide* Jessup, F. W., *A History of Kent* (L., 1958), 98-109.

in the early seventeenth century by John Browne, who in 1619 employed as many as 200 workmen in the production of ordnance. In 1637 Browne built an even larger works at a cost of about £1,700, though by this date Kent, Sussex, and Surrey were becoming marginal producers of iron, and the industry was shortly to languish in this whole region.[1] But other specialized industries were rising to replace the iron foundries, such as the large mill established at Dartford early in the Elizabethan period by John Spilman, a jeweller to the Queen, which employed some hundreds of workmen in the manufacture of white paper, the glass works successfully established in several centres, and at least locally famous breweries in various towns.

Kent was an old, a stable, and throughout our period a relatively populous county. No persuasively accurate estimate of its population at any time during the era under consideration can be advanced, though certain at least roughly drawn suggestions may be made. Of all the southern counties, Kent ranked next after Gloucestershire in the number of men who might be mustered out for the defence of the realm in the great year of the Armada. Usher believed, on the basis of his study of subsidy returns and certain other data, that its population density was of the order of 82 to 101 per square mile in 1570 and that the number of its inhabitants had increased to 93 to 112 per square mile a generation later. If we may average the extremes of these estimates, we should have a population in the neighbourhood of 140,000 in 1570 and of perhaps 160,000 in 1600.[2] There is, however, evidence to suggest that the lower of these estimates is more nearly accurate, which would give us a population of something like 145,000 in 1600.[3]

We may be even more certain of the fact that Kent was relatively one of the most urban of all the English counties. There was no single dominating urban complex in the county, as was so frequently the case, but there were throughout the two centuries of our study a considerable number of prosperous and economically significant towns with a fair degree of corporate life and identity which were much larger than the village so typical in the English scene of this age. Our own totals of the amount provided locally for charitable uses, unusually full returns of numbers of communicants, and other scattered evidence would suggest that there were in 1600 as many as ten or twelve such towns in the county with populations of 1,000 or more. Canterbury, which

---

[1] *Arch. Cant.*, XXI (1895), 308-314 ; *VCH, Kent*, III, 386-387 ; Jessup, *Kent*, 105-106 ; Furley, Robert, *History of the Weald of Kent* (L., 1871, 1874, 2 vols.), II, ii, 483-487.

[2] Usher, A. P., *An Introduction to the Industrial History of England* (Boston, 1920), 97-98.

[3] Dr. Felix Hull, the Kent County Archivist, has suggested in private correspondence on the point that the population of Kent may not have exceeded 150,000 in the Restoration period.

Usher estimates as having had a population of slightly more than 4,000 as early as 1377,[1] had grown steadily, after a severe depression in the years following the Reformation, and numbered 5,000 to 5,500 in 1600, being by far the largest town in the county. Greenwich, Rochester, Sandwich, and possibly Cranbrook would seem in the same year to have had populations ranging from 2,000 to 3,000, though Sandwich by this date was beginning to decline. The larger group of towns with populations of the order of 1,000 to 2,000 included Maidstone, Faversham, Dover, Dartford, Deptford, and possibly Gravesend, Folkestone, and Tonbridge.[2] The total population of these essentially urban communities we have estimated at 21,900, which would mean that in 1600 Kent possessed a relatively very high urban population of something like 15 per cent. of the whole.

This fact bears importantly and immediately on the relative wealth of the county and on the size and structure of its charities. The total of its charitable benefactions exceeded that noted in any other rural county save Yorkshire, even if adjustments are made for the very large gifts made by London donors in this, their favourite county. Rogers and Buckatzsch, in their study of the several subsidy rolls, would seem to agree in ranking the county as the eighth or ninth in England in wealth in terms of the average over the whole course of our period, whereas our evidence suggests that it may well have ranked fourth or fifth in the realm in terms of its disposable wealth.[3]

[1] Usher, *Industrial History of England*, 106.
[2] Jessup (*Kent*, 90-97, 104) treats this question with care.
[3] Rogers, J. E. T., *History of Agriculture and Prices in England* (Oxford, 1866-1902, 7 vols.), V, 104-113 ; Buckatzsch, E. J., " The Geographical Distribution of Wealth in England, 1086-1843 ", *Economic History Review*, 2nd ser., III (1950), 180-202.

A SEVENTEENTH-CENTURY MARKET TOWN : TONBRIDGE

By C. W. CHALKLIN, M.A., B.Litt.

THE Kentish towns of the seventeenth century could be described in more than one sense as country towns. By modern standards their size was minute. The largest, Canterbury, had about 6,000 people, and Rochester, Maidstone, and Dover about 3,000 inhabitants. There were about a dozen more, such as Dartford, Ashford, and Sandwich, with a population of between 1,000 and 2,500 people, and finally a group of about six very small towns with between 500 and 800 people, including Tonbridge and West Malling. With usually no more than one or two main streets the fields lay almost at the back door of most of the houses. Not far from the centre there were detached houses with large gardens, barns, stables and orchards. The streets were often tree lined, and only partly paved. All this suggests that the atmosphere of the towns can hardly have differed from that of the surrounding country-side. They were largely non-industrial, and apart from the innkeepers who served the road traffic, most people gained a livelihood from serving the needs of the neighbouring farmers. Nearly all held a weekly market. Some of the more substantial tradesmen on the outskirts were also farmers, keeping some cattle or cultivating a few acres. Most townspeople were connected by blood with the local yeomen and husbandmen. In the case of the unincorporated towns yet another link with the neighbouring rural district was provided by the fact that the parish was the unit of administration, and usually included a large rural area as well as the town.

Of the smaller towns, Tonbridge, with some 600 to 800 inhabitants, may be taken as an example. It was unincorporated, and lay in the largest parish in Kent. Almost from the Norman Conquest there had been a town on the site. It lay on a main road from London to Hastings, Rye and Winchelsea, on the only important river crossing, that of the Medway. During the reign of William I this road had become a principal route to Normandy. To protect it a castle had been built at Tonbridge, and the town arose near its walls. Its strategic position made it a natural centre for the neighbouring villages, and by the beginning of the fourteenth century it was serving the surrounding area with a market.

From the bank of the Medway the land rises gently northwards, forming a well-drained site for the town. The ground determined that it should lie along a single highway, and not at the junction of several roads. The main road from Rye joined another highway from Sussex just to the south of the Medway, so as to use a single river crossing. Further, the clay, sand and gravel on which the town lies are bounded on the west side for nearly half a mile north of the River by low lying alluvial ground. Thus the London road from the west stayed on higher ground, and joined the Wrotham road (from due north) about half a mile north of the old market place, the centre of the town. Between this junction and the River only one lateral road, from Maidstone, of secondary importance, enters the High Street. It was natural that the tradespeople should build their houses and shops beside this one main road.

In the seventeenth century, from the Great Bridge over the northern-most arm of the Medway houses were contiguous on both sides of the road for about 100 yards, up to the market cross. There the street widened, to accommodate the market place, the cross being merely a roof supported on posts, open at all sides. The houses probably remained contiguous up the High Street for another 100 yards, as far as the junction with Church Lane ; above this point, on the east side, there were perhaps half a dozen more houses ; then, after a gap filled by the Bull Inn, with its barns and stables, garden and orchard sur-rounding it, came a toll house and bar and causeway across the town ditch ; beyond on both sides of the road lay a few more houses, generally well spaced ; those on the west side included the School, a long, stone, two storey building with a frontage of 160 feet. There were a few contiguous buildings on Dry Hill near the junction with the London road ; none lay beyond it.

A few other buildings lay in the two streets leading off the market place, and in Church Lane. To the south of the Great Bridge the low lying land between the five arms of the River was frequently flooded, preventing any large scale extension of the town. Besides the Great Bridge of three arches, three bridges each of one arch spanned minor streams within a space of 50 yards ; a short distance to the south lay the fifth bridge of two arches, crossing the other main arm of the Medway. There were only a few houses strung along both sides of the road as far south as the junction of the Rye and Frant roads. This was nearly three quarters of a mile from the top of the town.[1]

The two largest buildings in the town were the Church and the Castle. The Church was large, with two aisles, including a twelfth-century chancel, and thirteenth-century nave and tower. The grave-yard lay on the north, and the vicarage and its land on the south. The castle stood on a spur overlooking the River, on the west of the High Street ; it comprised a motte, with a small shell keep on top, a bailey

[1] This description of the town is based on the evidence of contemporary deeds, wills and lawsuits, on old prints, and surviving buildings.

with a fine thirteenth-century gatehouse, and walls interspersed with towers. A moat separated it from the barbican on the north, and another moat lay beyond the barbican. The fact that various parts of the grounds were let by the owner suggests that it was not garrisoned. It was taken over by Parliamentary forces in 1643, and finally dismantled in 1646.

The Castle, Church, and School were the only stone buildings, timber frame construction being normal. All the surviving houses of the period have more than one floor, two storeys and a garret in the gables appearing to be the usual type, such as the Chequers premises in the market place, or the Port Reeves House in East Lane. Shops would seem to have been usually in or near the market place : some, at least, had pent-houses with an open frontage for the display of goods. The shops probably filled the narrow frontage of the houses that were contiguous, the hall and kitchen lying behind, and the chambers and storerooms above.

Between 1600 and 1700 the population of the town probably increased by at least 20 to 30 per cent. To house the additional people there may have been some building on the verge of the town, possibly below the Great Bridge, or on Dry Hill at the north end of the town, or down the side lanes. A deed of 1625 mentioned cottages built on the waste lands of the manor of Tonbridge, probably on the western side of the High Street opposite the Church. One instance, however, is known of the erection of a house in a back garden : in the will of Thomas Johnson, mercer, 1634, he left his son Thomas the messuage in which he had lived, and his other son Abraham the house he had set up in his backyard.[1] Sometimes messuages were rebuilt and divided : thus about 1610–20 Henry Allen, land surveyor, bought from his father-in-law, John Walter, cutler, part of his messuage on the west side of the market place, rebuilt it, divided it, and lived in half himself.[2] But probably most often a new household was provided for by the splitting-up of an existing building. A deed of 1645 refers to " the messuage now divided into divers, several dwellings called the sign of the George ", at the north corner of Church Lane and the High Street.[3]

Nearly all the houses had a close or yard behind them. Some of the tightly packed houses in the market place, like the four tenements owned by John Brightling, blacksmith, in 1648, between the market place and the Castle moat, may have had to share a close. Other houses had stables and gardens of a quarter or half an acre. Thus in 1590 Thomas Harris, butcher, whose house fronted on the High Street and backed

---

[1] Kent Archives Office : Rochester Consistory will registers : DRb/Pwr 22 f. 84.

[2] Tonbridge Urban District Council Archives : deed of 1640.

[3] *K.A.O.*, Weller Poley MSS. U38 T7.

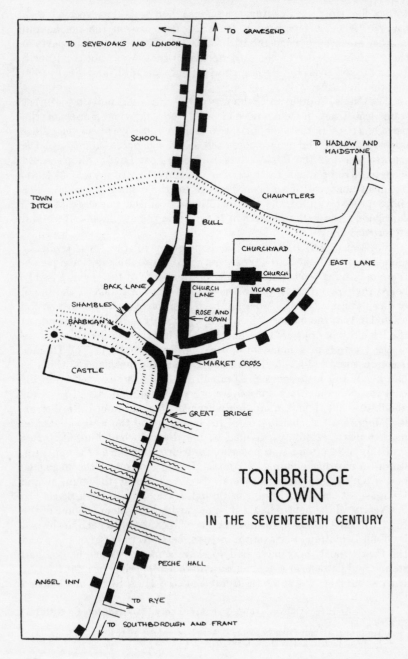

TO GRAVESEND

TO SEVENOAKS AND LONDON

SCHOOL

TO HADLOW AND MAIDSTONE

TOWN DITCH

CHAUNTLERS

BULL

EAST LANE

CHURCHYARD

CHURCH

BACK LANE

CHURCH LANE

VICARAGE

SHAMBLES

BARBICAN

ROSE AND CROWN

CASTLE

MARKET CROSS

GREAT BRIDGE

TONBRIDGE TOWN

IN THE SEVENTEENTH CENTURY

PECHE HALL

ANGEL INN

TO RYE

TO SOUTHBOROUGH AND FRANT

on the shambles, had little plots of ground on the north and south of his house, a close and a little garden adjoining, and a stable. The detached houses on the outskirts naturally had more land attached to them. Thus the messuage on the south-east corner of the Great Bridge had barns, stables, closes of two acres, gardens, and an orchard.

Many houses had their own wells, such as the house of John Hooper, parish clerk, d. 1641, on the verge of the town. Others, as in the centre near the market place, shared a well between two or more tenements. There was at least one common well for the use of the poor. Thus in 1558 Clement Haytt, saddler, left 40/– " to the repairing of the well at the north end of the town for the easement of the poor there dwelling that be not able to pay for the repairing thereof ".[1] The cleanliness of the well was of course all-important, and when Thomas How leased a messuage at the north end of the town in 1655, one of the conditions was that he cleanse and scour it, and " amend the staving thereof " once a year.[2] Judging from the evidence of the well of a timber-framed house pulled down in the 1930's, the water came from pure and plentiful springs, and the overflow ran by underground channels to the River 200 yards to the south.

For washing animals and carts and watering horses there was a horsewash at the Great Bridge, a bay of the Medway between the castle wall and the north end of the bridge. Another was made by the fifth bridge, protected from the main flow of the river by a stone wall.

A watercourse, presumably open, ran down the High Street from the toll bar to the Great Bridge. Probably much unhealthy garbage travelled along it. Other not uncommon nuisances in the High Street were straying pigs and the overflow of sewage from individual houses. But most offensive of all were the carcases and other butchers' refuse thrown out from the slaughterhouse in the shambles. All these nuisances were, however, common at this period, and on the whole the town was perhaps kept cleaner than most by the fact that the sloping site did allow an opportunity for the refuse to be washed away.

Part of the High Street, between Church Lane and the market cross, was paved at least from about 1580. In 1633 Thomas Roades of Maidstone deposed that part of the town had been paved 50 years or more, and that formerly it had been done with small stone, but lately with larger. The pavement, only six yards wide, ran down the centre of the street, and there were " divers ancient pavements " before the doors of several inhabitants, leading to the main pavement. Largely because of the heavy carriages of iron travelling from the Wealden iron works to Chatham and London, the five bridges were often in an almost ruinous condition. There was marshy ground between the fourth

[1] *K.A.O.*, DRb/Pwr 12 f. 345.
[2] *K.A.O.*, Knocker Collection, U55 T438.

and fifth bridges. Wooden clappers, 100 feet long and three feet wide, were regularly maintained at this spot. Owing to the treacherous nature of the ground, and the frequent flooding, passage through the town on horse or even foot might have been impossible in winter without them.[1]

The livelihood of the town was only to a small extent dependent on industry. By the early seventeenth century the cloth and iron industries of the Weald of Kent had passed the peak of their prosperity, but were still important features of the economy of the area. Since ironworks required not a strategic position such as was offered by the town, but the presence of streams convenient for damming, and a ready supply of ore and timber for charcoal, they did not lie in the towns. The nearest of the two furnaces and two forges in Tonbridge parish was a mile from the market place. The cloth industry, however, was closely linked with the town. For most of the century there were two or three clothiers living on the outskirts. A messuage on the south side of the Great Bridge seems to have remained a clothier's house through several changes of ownership : in 1612 Edward Oxley, clothier, sold it to Thomas Busse, of Pembury, clothier, when it was occupied by John Couchman, another clothier. In 1627 John Dunck, clothier, was in occupation, and in 1648 Robert Day of Tudeley sold it to William Farrant of Tonbridge, both parties being clothiers.[2] It is probable that these sites on the edge of the town were chosen because the town was a strategic centre for the parish ; this made it a convenient place for deposit and collection by the carders, spinners and weavers, and for final dispatch to London. On the verge of the town there was enough room for the erection of workhouses, where many of the finishing processes were done. The house that Thomas How, clothier, leased in 1655 at the north end of the town had a copper in the workhouse, and a hurdle, " tainter ", planks and joists in the workshop, suggesting that cloth was both dyed and stretched on the premises.[3] There were several weavers, and one or two dyers in the town. The simpler processes of spinning and carding were probably a part-time occupation of the cottagers, their wives and children. Yet these crafts were as much carried on in the country as in the town.

The traffic along the main road brought a livelihood to a small number of people. It was much used by travellers to and from the Continent going *via* Dieppe and Le Havre. Following the outbreak of the Civil War in 1642 Thomas Weller, the chief parliamentary supporter in Tonbridge, was ordered to arrest all suspected persons ; for many

---

[1] *K.A.O.*, Gordon Ward Collection, U442 Q7 (Town Wardens accounts 1579–1742).
[2] *T.U.D.C. Archives :* deeds, 1612–48.
[3] *K.A.O.*, U55 T438.

"have resorted lately from beyond the seas to England and have landed at Rye, and have disposed themselves into diverse parts of the Kingdom".[1] Much of London's and especially the King's fish came from Rye, for which reason it was known as the "Rippiers Way". Further, though some of the textiles from the Goudhurst and Cranbrook district may have gone by road to Maidstone, and thence by water to London, much was sent through Tonbridge. The ironmasters of the Tonbridge area, and of north east Sussex, were the other great users of the road.

Two classes of tradesmen in the town served the road traffic, the innkeepers and the carriers. There were probably about half a dozen inns. The Bull at the north end, the Rose and Crown and the Swan in the market place, and the Angel at the bottom of the town would seem to have existed through most of the period. There were carriers in the town probably keeping up a regular communication with London on the one hand and Rye on the other. Goods might be carried either by packhorse or waggon, and single travellers could probably hire horses to be left at the next convenient inn on the route.

The town was chiefly important as a commercial centre for the neighbouring parishes. About the market almost no information has survived : like most other markets in the county nothing is known about its customs and regulations. It was held weekly, on Friday. In 1671 the town was granted the right to hold a monthly cattle market, reflecting the importance of cattle breeding for the farmers of the Weald of Kent.

Most of the townspeople were engaged in non-industrial trades and crafts, such as the production and sale of food and drink, clothing, building and agricultural trades, and general services. It is possible to gain a rough picture of the number of people in each occupation from the Parish Clerk's Register for the 1660's. In the decade 1661–71, 125 tradesmen and professional people are mentioned, probably a majority of the adult male inhabitants. Their occupations are arranged in the Table (see p. 159).

One is impressed, first, by the small number in the food and drink category, apart from the butchers. There was probably only one baker in the town at a time, reflecting the fact that home baking was usual : for the same reason only one brewer appears, and there are no grocers, for a garden was appendant to almost every house. As the large number of butchers suggests, only meat was in high demand from the average householder ; for the cottager with only an acre or two of land, and all but a few townsmen would have needed meat for most of the year:

[1] Camden Miscellany, Vol. III, *Papers relating to Proceedings in the County of Kent*, London, 1854, p. 1.

95

TABLE

The Distribution of the Trades in Tonbridge Town[1]

Food and Drink		Clothing		Agricultural Trades	
Butcher	9	Tailor	10	Wheelwright	1
Victualler	2	Shoemaker	7	Blacksmith	7
Miller	2	Mercer	3	Girthmaker	1
Baker	1	Glover	3	Awlblademaker	2
Brewer	1	Cordwainer	2	Saddletreemaker	1
Maltman	1	Sheerman	2		
	16		27		12

Building, etc.		Textiles		General Services	
Sawyer	1	Clothier	3	Locksmith	1
Carpenter	6	Weaver	4	Midwife	1
Joiner	2	Dyer	1	Turner	1
Nailer	2	Flaxdresser	1	Carrier	3
		Hempdresser	2	Cooper	2
				Sexton	1
				Currier	1
	11		11		10

Professionals		Labourers		Miscellaneous	
Scrivener	1	Labourer	25	Soldier	1
Schoolmaster	1	Servant	4	Translator (?)	1
Doctor and chirurgeon	3				
Parish clerk	2				
	7		29		2

Almost all those in the clothing trade were shoemakers and tailors, the group in general suggesting the lack of specialists, such as hat- or dress-makers. These were usually found only in the larger towns. The glovers were an exception : they were to be found in the rural as well as the urban part of the parish, and in the neighbouring rural parishes, and may represent a modest local in dustry.

The strength of the carpenters and joiners in the building trade reflect the fact that almost all building was of wood : naturally there were no bricklayers and the only reference to a mason in the period is one referred to as being engaged on the Earl of Clanricard's stone mansion of Somerhill, a mile to the south-east of the town, in 1611.

Some of the rest it was natural to find in any rural society like the blacksmiths, wheelwrights, and toolmakers. There was probably at least one saddler and turner in the town throughout the period. The remainder any society, urban as well as rural, would have possessed, such as the locksmith and the midwife. On the whole trades were

[1] Church of St. Peter and St. Paul, Tonbridge, Parish Clerk's Register, 1660–81.

restricted to the necessities of life, there being an absence of specialized or luxury trades. It is probably not an untypical picture of a small market town largely dependent for its livelihood on the local farmers.

At the head of the urban society were a handful of gentry and professional men. There were one or two gentlemen living in the large detached houses on the verge of the town, such as John Skeffington, Esq., d. 1639 on Dry Hill, owner of nearly 500 acres in Hildenborough.[1] There was a master and usher at the School and the Church was served by the vicar and his curate. The other professional people were a lawyer and scrivener, a land surveyor, and two or three chirurgeons.

Despite the small size of the town, and the unspecialized nature of its economy, wealth was very unevenly distributed. Poverty loomed large in the lives of a large number of the inhabitants. The seriousness of the problem is shown by the Hearth Tax of 1664. An act of 1662 had exempted from payment of the tax all householders who were normally excused from paying parish rates, that is, those whose house was worth under £1 per annum, or possessed property or goods valued at less than £10. These people lived either just on the subsistence level, or were paupers. In the assessment of 1664, 51 per cent. of the inhabitants were non-chargeable. Old age or infirmity naturally accounted for some of the poverty : there were nine widows among those exempt, and some of the male householders would have been disabled or old. A comparison with the overseers accounts of the parish for the 1670's show that these people received most of the poor relief. Yet the fact remains that a large proportion of the inhabitants were able bodied poor, barely able to make ends meet. While many were of course labourers, most of the trades would seem to have had members living on the subsistence level.

Other inland Kentish towns, such as Ashford, Cranbrook, Maidstone, Sevenoaks and Westerham, had comparable poverty figures. It was to some extent a reflection of the decline of the cloth trade in the latter half of the seventeenth century. Thus Cranbrook, the centre of the industry, had the highest poverty rate of any Kentish town. Yet a study of the figures for the smaller towns of other parts of southern England, in Surrey and Hampshire, shows that this poverty was a national problem, not a local one based on the decline of a regional industry.[2]

Few records survive of these poorer inhabitants, for most had no real property and little personal estate. On the other hand there are a group of probate inventories at the end of the century which throw light

[1] *P.R.O.* Wards 7/94/263.
[2] Kent Hearth Tax, 1664, *K.A.O.* Q/Rth ; ed. *C.A.F.* Meetings, *Surrey Record Society*, Vol. 17. (*Surrey Hearth Tax, 1664*), 1940 ; Hampshire Hearth Tax, 1664, *P.R.O.* E179/176/565.

on the wealth and standard of living of the more substantial tradesmen.[1] Naturally the majority were men with moderate personal estates, under £50. Most of the property of these people consisted of household goods, with £2 or £3 of ready money or of debts owing to them, and stock in trade of quite small value. James Sharelock, sawyer, *d.* 1688, had £3 in ready money, £1 in debts, saws, a grindstone, wood and tools worth £1/17/–, and clothes valued at £2 ; the remainder of his inventory estimated altogether at £35/10/–, consisted of household goods.

There were also a significant number of tradesmen with substantial personal estates, including large stocks in trade and sums lent out on bond. Thomas Castell, chirurgeon, at his death in 1696, had debts owing to him worth £80, " bottles and salves and other things belonging to chirurgery " in his shop valued at £30, and only £12/10/– of household furniture. Finally, there were one or two very wealthy tradesmen, such as Joseph Puxty, *d.* 1702, whose personal estate was valued at £580/10/–. He was a tanner on a very large scale, his stock including " 220 backs " worth £242, 142 hides valued at £113/8/–, " 64 calves skins and one hogskin " worth £8/16/–, " ten loads of bark " at £12/10/–.

It would perhaps be possible to divide the inhabitants into four groups according to wealth. Half the population were " the poor ", with personal estates of under £10 in value. These consisted of labourers, and depressed artisans and craftsmen. Another 30 per cent. of the inhabitants, with estates worth between £10 and £50, were the smaller tradesmen. The more substantial tradesmen, with personal estates of between £50 and £200 in value, comprised perhaps another 15 per cent. Above them were the handful of rich townsmen with goods and money worth over £200.

The houses of the wealthier half of the population of the inhabitants represented in the inventories were normally of two storeys with garrets under the roof, and perhaps with cellars. On the ground floor there may have been a shop, facing the street, perhaps a hall, still often the main room of the house, a kitchen, parlour or buttery, and possibly a brewhouse, wash-house, or bakehouse at the back. Above were the bedchambers, usually described by the rooms over which they lay, like " the parlour chamber " or " the brewhouse chamber ". Typical of the larger house was that occupied by Giles Roberts, barber, *d.* 1691, with a shop, hall, parlour, butteries, wash-house and brewhouse on the ground floor, and above a " hall chamber ", " shop chamber ", " buttery chamber ", " parlour chamber ", " brewhouse chamber ", " closet next the shop chamber ", and " chamber over the entry ", as well as garrets and a cellar. The house of John Willard, tailor, *d.* 1687, was far smaller, with a shop, hall and buttery, and a " chamber next the street ", and a " backward chamber ".

[1] *K.A.O.*, Rochester Probate inventories, DRb/Pl.

The furniture of the hall or parlour consisted of a large table with forms, stools or chairs, perhaps an oval or drawing table, a cupboard, some cushions, hangings or glassware. The hall of James Sharelock, sawyer, *d.* 1688, had a table, six stools, a little table, a little form, a cupboard, glass cage and settle. There were no carpets, and only sometimes curtains. In the kitchen or buttery were the cooking utensils, the brassware and pewter, drinking vessels and glassware. The bed, with its hangings, mattress and bolster and blankets, was often the most valuable item of furniture in the house. John Skinner, cooper, *d.* 1688, had a canopied bedstead, with hangings, a flock mattress, blue curtains, a counterpane and cloth of printed linsey woolsey, with a buckram ceiling and three blankets worth £7/3/6. Often the bedroom was filled up with chairs, stools, a table or two, a chest of drawers, and perhaps a looking-glass. Yet by our standards the houses were draughty and cheerless.

Finally, the Kentish town of the seventeenth century differed from many modern towns in the pace of its growth. It is its comparative stability at this time that has enabled us to study Tonbridge over a period of 100 years. We have seen that the population only rose by 20 to 30 per cent., and that the plan of the town hardly altered. Although there may have been some increase in the standard of living, one cannot detect any change in the distribution of trades and occupations. Not until after 1740, when the Medway became navigable up to Tonbridge and Tonbridge became the " port " of the western part of the Weald of Kent, did the town begin to grow quickly. Within 100 years the population quadrupled, and the face of the town was transformed. Since then the town's growth has never been arrested.

PEOPLE AND HOMES IN THE MEDWAY TOWNS :
1687-1783

By A. J. F. DULLEY, M.A.

AMONG the records of the diocese of Rochester now preserved in the
Kent Archives Office are over five hundred probate inventories for the
City of Rochester itself and the neighbouring parishes of Chatham,
Strood and St. Margaret's.[1] For the comparatively short period that
they cover (the main series begins in 1687 and there is only a handful
from the years after 1740), they are an extremely valuable source for
the economic and social history of the Medway Towns, not least because
they give a comparable sample of the inhabitants of each of the four
urban parishes. The City archives, which otherwise might be useful,
for example, in showing, through the registers of freemen and apprentices, the various trades followed in the town and their relative importance, unfortunately only concern themselves with the inhabitants
of the medieval city, which by this time had so far outgrown its boundaries that more than half of the urban population lived outside the
city limits. The inventories list the household goods and other personal
property of the deceased including wages and other moneys due to him.
Often they specify his occupation, and where they do not, it can usually
be deduced from the contents of the inventory. They have one grave
shortcoming, however, from the point of view of the social historian,
in that they do not give a fair sample of the population : neither the
rich nor the poor are well represented, the latter because they had not
enough property to bequeath to justify making a will, the former because the wills of the gentry and professions and probably the wealthier
tradesmen too were generally proved in the Archbishop's Prerogative
Court, and not in the courts of the diocese. But the ordinary traders
and craftsmen of the town and their social peers are represented by a
considerable quantity of documents.

But before proceeding to analyse their contents, it will be well to
describe the town from which they came. Already in the Middle Ages
Rochester had outgrown its walls, and the parish churches of St.
Margaret's and Strood were founded in the eleventh century for the
suburban population, but Chatham remained distinct and rather
remote until the rapid expansion following the development of the

[1] K.A.O. DRb/Pi 1667/1-1669/1 ; 1/1-58/17 (Consistory Court : 1667-9 and
1687-1783), and DRa/Pi 1/1-26/9 (Archdeaconry Court : 1719-1778). I should
like to record my gratitude to the staff of the Archives Office for their help while
pursuing these researches.

Dockyard in the seventeenth century. By the end of that century the stranger could hardly tell where Rochester ended and Chatham began : only the bridge and a small area of marshland broke the line of houses along the Dover Road from Strood church to the foot of Chatham Hill, but there was as yet little building off the main thoroughfare. The Hearth Tax Assessments show that in the 1660s and 1670s the largest houses, and hence presumably the wealth of the town, were concentrated in a small area round the cathedral. Here was the commercial centre, along the High Street, and to the south the homes of such fashionable society as the town could boast. Elsewhere off the main street the average of hearths per household drops rapidly to the level of the surrounding rural area, but while in the countryside spartan housing did not necessarily mean poverty, in the town it probably did, as the lists of persons exempted from the 1664 (Lady Day) Assessment show.[1]

The population of the town is difficult to calculate with any accuracy. In 1664, 1,232 households were assessed, of which 317 were exempted from the tax, but six years later those chargeable numbered 1,416.[2] The Compton Return gives the number of inhabitants over 16 in 1676 as 3,810.[3] Even assuming that these figures were accurate, any method of calculating the total population from them must be arbitrary and imprecise. The most that can be said is that there were probably between seven and eight thousand inhabitants in the four parishes in 1670. At that period the population in Chatham at least, to judge from the baptisms recorded in the parish registers,[4] was increasing rapidly and continued to do so until about 1710, after which it remained steady till 1750. The other parishes, less dependent on the Dockyard with its fluctuations of activity, seem to have had a relatively stable population, but, with a high proportion of nonconformists recorded in the Compton Return, parish registers cannot be regarded as a complete index to population changes.

One of the facts that emerges most clearly from the inventories is the importance of the Navy to the town. The vast majority of its seamen were too poor to make a will and hence do not figure in the record, but even so there are nearly thirty inventories of naval or ex-naval personnel. Two of them, a captain who died on active service in the West Indies and a retired ship's carpenter, were well-to-do, with property worth £718 and £305 respectively, but in general, as might be expected, the seamen are the poorest group in the whole series, their chief, and sometimes their only, asset being the arrears of pay outstanding to them, usually for at least six months. Their standard pay

[1] K.A.O. Q/RTh.
[2] P.R.O. E179/129/746.
[3] " A Seventeenth Century Miscellany " (*Kent Records*, Vol. XVII (1960), pp. 153-74).
[4] K.A.O. P85/1/2.

of 23s. a month *c.* 1690 compared favourably with a domestic servant's 20s. at the same period, but the tardiness of the Navy as a paymaster forced them to live expensively on credit. A typical case is that of Benjamin Stevens, purser's steward on H.M.S. *Cornwall,* who died owed £15 in back pay, but with " insufficient other goods left to pay his arrears of rent ". Even so some managed to amass a little capital. A former midshipman had made enough profit by loaning small sums to his shipmates to set himself up in a tavern, where he continued his money-lending activities. Two of the three surgeons whose inventories survive were retired naval men who had set up in practice in the town.

Inventories of Dockyard workers are much more numerous and make up a fifth of the total. Unlike the seamen, who lived all over the town, the Dockyard workers lived mainly in Chatham, close to their employment. There one in three worked in the Yard, to judge from the inventories. In St. Margaret's, which included the houses newly built on the "Banks" joining Rochester to Chatham, the proportion was one in six, in St. Nicholas' one in eleven, while there was none at all in Strood. All the principal shipbuilding crafts are represented, although the proportion of skilled to unskilled workers is distorted, the more so because shipwrights tend to be named as such in their inventories long after the mentioning of trades had fallen out of fashion in the community at large. Clearly they were felt to be something of an aristocracy among the Dockyard employees, a position that their wages and property reflect, although even so only a few were even moderately well-to-do. In general the workers in the Yard were second only to the naval seamen in their poverty, which was due mainly to the same cause : a constantly recurring item in their inventories is their arrears of pay. More than three-quarters were owed greater or lesser sums, commonly amounting to more than half the total value of their inventories, and of the rest most if not all are to be accounted for by retirement and by the fact that many Dockyard workers sold their rights to their pay for ready cash.

Although not all the shipwrights are explicitly stated to have been employed in the Dockyard, there is no clear evidence in the inventories of any civilian shipbuilding. The nearest approach is the detailed description of the tackle of a rope-walk, but even this seems to have been a part-time business since its owner was owed wages from the Yard. It required comparatively little capital to set up a rope-walk— especially when the raw material could be obtained at His Majesty's expense—but very few Dockyard employees had managed to save even that little amount. When they could do so, they were likely to invest it in retail trade or in opening a tavern, probably run by their wives while the husbands worked in the Yard. The furnishing of their

103

houses reflects their general poverty. Very few had money to spare for luxuries and items for display like the silver plate which was common in tradesmen's houses. Most owned only the bare necessities, and there was a considerable number who were mere lodgers with no household goods of their own.

Naval and Dockyard personnel make up about a quarter of the total of those whose inventories are preserved, but they do not exhaust the number of those who gained their living by the sea. The port of Rochester was of some importance with an extensive coastal trade,[1] and much of this was carried on in local vessels. The Customs Accounts, in which the nature and direction of this trade can be traced, do not differentiate between the various quays within the Medway estuary for which Rochester served as the Customs port, although they can often be identified from the home-ports of the vessels serving them. Apart from a very small overseas trade, exporting oysters and importing wine and linen for civilian use and naval stores for the Dockyard, the principal types of trade were three : the import of coal and salt from Newcastle and Sunderland, the export of fuller's earth to the textile centres of eastern England, especially to Colchester, and a general trade with London in which agricultural products, paper and some leather as outward cargoes were balanced by inward shipments of groceries and manufactured goods. The fuller's earth seems to have been shipped from Aylesford or its neighbourhood, close to the pits from which it was dug. During a specimen twelve months in 1698-9[2] there were no Rochester ships engaged in this trade. The shipment of farm produce, chiefly oats and hops, was mainly from Maidstone, which had six ships plying regularly to London, making seventy-one journeys in the twelve months. Five Rochester ships and one from Chatham also sailed to London but their trips were fewer : only twenty including twelve by Gravesend boats sailing for a Rochester merchant. None of them carried hops or paper ; oats was the main cargo, with some wheat and barley. This disparity between Rochester and Maidstone reflects the importance of the Maidstone corn market, of which Defoe remarked : " From this town and the neighbouring parts, London is supplied with more particulars than from any single market town in England."[3] Lying as it did at the head of effective navigation of the Medway, Maidstone was the natural focus for trade for a wide area in the Weald, whereas for the district north of the Downs there were many quays and creeks from which produce could be shipped as conveniently as from Rochester.

[1] Willan, T. S. : *English Coasting Trade: 1600-1750* (1938), p. 139.
[2] P.R.O. E190/676/10, 12.
[3] " A Tour through England and Wales " (1722) (Everyman edn.), Vol. I, p. 113.

The balance of inward shipments was very different, however. Maidstone vessels brought forty cargoes, all from London ; from the same source Rochester and Chatham vessels brought forty-two and others seven. All contained a miscellany of manufactured goods, foreign imports principally wine and tobacco, and also dairy products. Local agriculture concentrated on arable farming with the emphasis on cash crops for the London market, while dairying was neglected ; and the Medway Towns represented a considerable retail market for food-stuffs no less than for manufactures.

But for local seamen and shipowners the coal trade was more important. Ten ships from Rochester and two from Chatham were engaged in it in 1698-9, but none from other places within the Customs port. In all 2,741 chaldrons of coal were imported, about half in local vessels. Comparable figures for 1683 and 1731 are 2,494 and 2,742 chaldrons respectively, giving the port sixth place among coal-importing towns in the former year and eighth in the latter.[1] A distinctive feature of the coal trade was that the collier skippers invariably acted as merchants as well as carriers of their cargoes, whereas in the London trade the merchants were not usually local men at all.

One inventory survives of a collier captain, John Jones, of the *Richard and Margaret*. He owned a share in the ship, worth some £12 or £13, but the total value of his inventory amounts to only £37. The six hoymen, whose vessels no doubt shared in the London trade, and in one case fared as far as St. Sebastian, were all wealthier men, their goods being valued at between £51 and £716. The hoys themselves varied widely in value. The *Henry and Mary* was capable of sailing to Calais and Ostend in 1698, but in 1703 a three-quarter share in her was worth only £20 " being old ". The same owner, however, held a half-share in the *Thomas and Mary*, which was worth £80, and the whole of the *Dorothy and Anne*, worth £100. Both these last were trading to London in 1698-9. Another owner had two hoys, three had one, and one, probably retired, had none. Three of them kept shops, one of which contained £12-worth of groceries and spirits, but as has been said, the hoymen were principally carriers rather than traders on their own behalf.

There were other boats on the river whose voyages were more local and therefore are not reflected in the Customs Accounts. A shipwright owned a lighter worth £40 and was owed £30 16s. 8d. for ten shipments of ballast to Chatham and Sheerness Dockyards. Another lighter-owner, a relative of one of the hoymen, had two lighters and a half-share in a third, worth £85 including a smaller boat, as well as a shop with worsted and yarn valued at £8. Also fairly prosperous was the barge-owner who leased a chalk wharf at Frindsbury and no doubt

[1] Willan, *op. cit.*, p. 210.

used his barge to ship the chalk and lime produced. In a very different class of wealth was the vintner who owned two sailing lighters and two rowing lighters, worth together with a brickyard some £120. He was an importer and wholesaler of substance, with a total inventory value of £1,034.

Fishermen were more numerous but on average less prosperous than either hoymen or lightermen and, unlike them, lived mainly in Strood. Their boats, which in most cases were worth as much as all the rest of their possessions put together, varied widely in value, the two most valuable being worth, with their tackle, as much as a large hoy, while others were only estimated at £5 or £7. Most fishermen had a small cock-boat or stoe-boat as well as the larger smack. Dredges and dredge-ropes are mentioned several times, and it is to be assumed that most if not all the fishermen were engaged in the oyster fishery, which supplied not only the local market but also a modest foreign trade, seventeen shipments totalling 508 wash of oysters being sent to Holland in 1699.[1] A few fishermen were fairly well-to-do—one held leases worth £150 in addition to a boat valued at £125 and was worth over £300 in all—but most managed a rather bare subsistence reflected in their modest household possessions and their lack of savings, whether in cash, plate or loans. It is significant of their economic and social status that of eight pauper children apprenticed in the 1680s four were apprenticed to fishermen.[2]

The other occupations followed by the townsmen were such as might be expected in any market town of the period. Apart from the Dockyard there was no large-scale manufacture in the town, although there was a good number and variety of craftsmen supplying local needs. But as the Customs Accounts show, many manufactured goods were imported, especially textiles and hardware. Only two weavers have left inventories, and one of these was primarily a pawnbroker and the other had no loom. There are also two inventories for successive generations of a family of thread-twisters, an industry that had its centre at Maidstone. The elder James Dadson ran his business on the " putting out " system, only dyeing the yarn himself. In this he was an exception among the town's craftsmen, most of whom were their own masters and employed no labour apart from an occasional apprentice. Their chief asset was their skill rather than their capital or their business organization. Such men were the twelve cordwainers and shoemakers whose inventories remain to us. Nine had stocks of leather and ready-made shoes, six had shops, and only three were worth more than £200.

But there were some trades that demanded greater capital and

[1] P.R.O. E190/676/7.
[2] City of Rochester : Enrolled Apprenticeship Indentures.

employed some wage-labour. Among them were the tanners and curriers, from whom the cordwainers drew their raw material. One glove-maker tanned his own skins, but generally these trades were carried on separately and on a fair scale. The sole currier to figure among the inventories had property worth £710, and two others of his trade were elected Mayor between 1701 and 1760. The only other craftsmen to attain to the office were four carpenters and a single wheelwright. The former, no doubt, like the more prosperous of the carpenters who have left inventories, were the town's building contractors : the bricklayers, who were also tilers, were less substantial men. Both trades had a steady employment as the towns struggled to accommodate the influx of population of the late seventeenth century. Although the wealthier townsmen were building handsome brick houses for themselves, some of which survive mutilated in the modern High Street, timber and weatherboarding or lath-and-plaster, hastily run up at minimum cost, served for the poor, so that it is not surprising that carpenters dominated the building trade.

Those who had the wealth and social importance to reach the mayoralty were more likely to be tradesmen than craftsmen. This is above all true of food trades : three bakers, three grocers, a butcher and a cheesemonger became Mayor between 1701 and 1760. The same group of trades produced twenty-five inventories, one in three totalling £300 or more. Drapers and tailors were their equals in wealth, even if only the latter became Mayors. Apart from the bakers, all of these carried an extensive stock, much of it imported from abroad like the silks and linens of the drapers or the sugar, tobacco and spices of the grocers, or else originating in distant parts of the kingdom, as did the Wensleydale and Cheshire cheeses and the woollen cloth from East Anglia or the West Country. It is clear both from the Customs Accounts and from the occasional naming of Londoners as compilers of inventories that London merchants were the main intermediaries in this commerce. One seems to have maintained an office in Rochester, where he died worth £967 in personal property, more than all but a handful of the regular inhabitants. The only other purely wholesale merchant was the vintner already mentioned, who was of comparable wealth. The other traders were primarily, if not entirely, retailers, meeting the day-to-day needs of the townsfolk and the country round about within a radius of ten miles or so, to judge from the few inventories where book-debts are listed in detail. Other assets mentioned in the inventories lie mainly within the same radius, from which came also half the apprentices other than sons of townsfolk whose indentures were enrolled both in the 1680s and in the 1730s.

It is interesting to compare the picture of commerce in the Medway Towns given by the inventories with that compiled from similar sources for a purely market town. At Petworth[1] over a comparable period much the same trades are represented, but the average of wealth is higher and the vast bulk of the trade was in durable goods especially clothing, not in foodstuffs : butchers are quite numerous but there are no grocers and only one tallow-chandler. The clothing trades were much less specialized than in Rochester and Chatham, where retailers often dealt mainly in hats or lace or ready-made clothes, for the last of which there seems to have been no demand at Petworth. There most of the trade would appear to have been a market-day one, done with the inhabitants of a largely self-sufficient rural area. In the Medway Towns on the other hand the shopkeepers for the most part were selling the day-to-day necessities to their fellow-townsmen.

Another contrast between the two towns becomes apparent if one considers the number and wealth of the victuallers, vintners and inn-holders in each. In both places they make up about a tenth of those whose trades are traceable, but in Rochester and Chatham there were fewer inns by comparison, despite the amount of traffic on the Dover Road, but more ale-houses, some at least mainly patronized by sailors. The keepers of both were a good deal more prosperous there than at Petworth ; they made the most of their opportunity to do a profitable business in discounting seamen's sick tickets and lending money to the more impecunious among the Dockyard employees in addition to their more normal trade. Few of them brewed their own liquor although about one in every five households brewed on a domestic scale. At least one victualler was a client of Best's brewery, and another commercial brewer has left an inventory. Brewing, like malting and distilling, was a trade often carried on on a sufficient scale to make those who practised it eligible for the mayoralty. A brewer and a distiller each became Mayor between 1701 and 1760 and Thomas Best the brewer was one of the " chief inhabitants " of Chatham with whom the City authorities discussed possible boundary changes in 1711.[2] The maltsters, however, despite their wealth, seem not to have held civic office. They often farmed on considerable scale and belonged to rural rather than urban society.

They, with the miller and the butchers and carriers who grazed their animals on the Common or on other marsh pastures, form a link between the purely urban life of the majority of the population, few of whom even kept a backyard pig, and the farmers and smallholders of the surrounding countryside. Outside the built-up area there were some 7,000 acres of farmland in the four town parishes, and the men who tilled them are well represented in the inventories, where they

---

[1] Kenyon, G. H., " Petworth Town and Trades " 1610-1760. *Sussex A.C.*, Vol. XCVI, pp. 33 ff., and *Ibid.*, Vol. XCVIII, pp. 71 ff.

[2] K.A.O. U38/Z1.

form the wealthiest single category. They give a very varied picture of local farming, both as to farm size and farming methods. The fourteen farms for which an arable acreage can be calculated with some certainty had a mean area of 49 acres under crops. The maximum was 273 and the minimum nine, and there was no standard size of holding. Nor was there any standard rotation of crops that can be traced. Wheat, barley and oats were grown in approximately equal proportions although there were some notable differences from farm to farm. Small quantities of peas and more rarely of beans were also grown. Fodder crops, clover and sainfoin, appear in the earliest inventories but were not generally grown until about 1720, though Maidstone had been shipping small quantities of clover seed to London 30 years earlier. By 1720 the larger and more progressive farmers were experimenting with turnips, hitherto only a garden crop. Livestock held a subordinate place in the farm economy, but all save the smallest of smallholders kept a few cattle and often a small flock of sheep besides the horses necessary for working the farm. The smallholders are often described as " gardener " rather than " husbandman ", but the name does not necessarily imply market-gardening in the modern sense. Only at the very end of the inventory series, in 1778, is there a description, a very full one, of a market garden and nursery in which were to be found most of the vegetables and fruit-trees to be expected in its modern counterpart. Fruit-trees probably occupied some acreage on most farms but are rarely mentioned since the trees, unlike growing crops, were regarded as fixtures and not as movable property. Hops receive an occasional notice, more often after 1730 than before. Hop-poles and firewood were among the products of the extensive coppice-woods which covered the poorer soils on the clay-with-flints towards the south of Chatham and St. Margaret's parishes. The profits not uncommonly formed a sizable proportion of farmers' incomes in those parishes.

The other occupations that are mentioned in the inventories fall into no neat classification. Some were wage-earners : the servant and the four labourers, one of them employed at the bridge. Others approached professional status, the surgeons, for example, or the scrivener. There were two schoolmistresses, one of them a bo'sun's widow, a school-master, a salaried official of the waterworks, and two Sergeants-at-Mace, one of whom was described as " gentleman ". Their duties included charge of the City gaol. What was described as " The Best Prisoners Room " according to one inventory, contained furniture worth £1 7s., comparable with the average apprentice's garret. The less favoured inmates, one assumes, made do with a bare cell.

The deceased is described as " gentleman " in eight of the inventories altogether. Two of them were officials of the Dockyard, one being a member of the Pett family which figures so prominently in its seventeenth-century history. One was a grocer, one a tallow-chandler, one a maltster, all occupations demanding a fair amount of wealth in those that followed them. Another was the Sergeant-at-Mace already mentioned, and the other two had no occupation that can be traced. In all probability these are not a representative sample of the gentry of the town, being more typical of that stock figure, the younger son apprenticed to trade, than of the heads of their families. They were not significantly wealthier than most of their fellow-citizens, although they managed to maintain something of the decencies of the life to which they had been brought up. The tallow-chandler's house, for example, is the earliest of the few private houses described as having a dining-room. But there is evidence from elsewhere that the gentry did not form as large or as important an element in the Medway Towns as in some others. They were too far from the metropolis to form part of the fashionable fringe that already included Greenwich and Eltham, and yet not far enough away to be able to aspire to the status of a provincial capital. So far as Kent was concerned that position was held about 1700 by Canterbury, where Celia Fiennes mentions the " fine walks and seates and places for the musick to make it acceptable and comodious to the Company ".[1] In Rochester she found nothing of note except the bridge and the castle—" a pretty little thing "—and in Chatham the Dockyard on which she expatiates in patriotic pride. Defoe twenty-five years later paints a similar picture, though he had a keener eye for the economic than the social scene. He notes the paucity of gentry in Thames-side Kent and gives as the reason that " it is marshy and unhealthy, by its situation among the waters : so that it is embarrassed with business, such as shipbuilders, fisher-men, seafaring-men and husband-men, or such as depend upon them, and very few families of note are found among them ".[2]

The clergy were no more prominent in the life of the town than the gentry despite the fact that Rochester was a Cathedral city. The bishop was non-resident and the canons had been very ill-served by Henry VIII in his reorganization of the cathedral in 1542, when he took the best of the old priory buildings to make a palace for himself. This was no sooner finished than pulled down, and much of the remainder of the precinct was left to become a rabbit-warren of tumbledown tenements. Only with the building of the Archdeaconry in 1661 and of Minor Canon Row at the beginning of the next century did something of the atmosphere of a Cathedral close gradually develop, and it is not to be wondered at that the clergy of the years following the Restoration tended to be absentees and pluralists and that nonconformity flourished

[1] Diary (Cresset Press edn., p. 123) : she was in Kent in 1697.
[2] *Op. cit.*, Vol. I, p. 114.

in default of their ministrations. The Compton Returns estimate that there were 504 dissenters over the age of 16 in the four parishes as against 3,810 conformists. The frequency with which Bibles are mentioned in the inventories, especially the early ones which tend to be more detailed, emphasizes the strength of this legacy from the Puritans. Often a Bible was the only book in the house, and where the titles of others are given, devotional works are the most common. Bibles bulk large in the stock valued in the bookseller's inventory, and even workers in the Dockyard commonly owned one when they had few other possessions.

More worldly wealth and security were sought in a variety of ways, some of which can be traced from the inventories, which, as has been said, give details of leases, bonds and debts owing as well as such tangible investments as plate, jewellery and cash. Few kept large quantities of money in the house. Only ninety-three inventories include sums above £10, and in only thirty-six of these does cash account for more than a quarter of the total value. By contrast 247 show debts owed to the deceased, in 63 cases amounting to £100 or more. It is only occasionally possible to interpret the meaning of these entries in detail, and from the way in which the compilers often included debts as an afterthought it is probable that some have been overlooked, especially in the earlier and less professional inventories. The importance of tradesmen and victuallers as suppliers of credit, particularly to the seamen and Dockyard workers, has already been described. Twenty-eight of the inventories list book-debts separately, the totals ranging from £5 to £487. This latter figure was for a Londoner, not a regular resident, and is scarcely typical since the mean amount of book-debt is £25. Good and bad debts are listed separately in 30 cases ; the mean ratio of the one to the other is 8 : 3 but the larger the total amount involved the smaller is the proportion of bad debt. Twenty-six persons were owed money on bonds of an average value of £33, and 29 on bills, which were usually for lesser amounts. Another 15 held notes, usually notes of hand but in one case bank notes. A parcel of tallies, a lottery prize, £100 invested under the Million Act, and some South Sea Annuities are also recorded in various inventories, but in general the townsfolk invested their money locally rather than in the capital.

Land, and more especially house property, whether freehold or on lease, was a favourite long-term investment and a common way of providing for widows. Only leaseholds are directly mentioned in the inventories, but in a town where many of the freeholds were owned by corporate bodies such as the Cathedral Chapter, the Bridge-wardens or the City Corporation, who normally let on long lease, leaseholds were widely owned and seem more often to represent a rent-yielding investment than a dwelling-house occupied by the deceased. There are a number of other cases where rents are mentioned but no leases, so that in all it would appear that at least one person in ten within the inventory range was receiving some income from this source. The mean rent of those specified was £6 per annum, but it is not possible to tell what size or type of house was being let.

A fairly clear picture of local housing, however, emerges from other sections of the inventories themselves, for it was the compilers' normal practice to list and value household goods room by room, so that, leaving aside the chance that some rooms might be empty or let unfurnished, one can usually gather some idea of the layout of a house as well as its contents. However, as both house-size and the use and nomenclature of the rooms were very varied, it is difficult to describe the typical town house of the period. Nevertheless there are a number of patterns and tendencies that can be traced. One appears rather earlier than the period of the inventories, from a consideration of the Hearth Tax Assessments. In the Lady Day Assessment for 1664, Rochester averaged 3·63 hearths per household, Chatham 3·31, and Strood 3·20. These figures are typical of the towns of Thames-side Kent but substantially higher than those for the surrounding rural parishes. In the Weald, apart from Maidstone (3·26), the averages are lower, as low as 2·03 at Cranbrook, and the gulf between town and country was much less there. Outside Kent comparable statistics are available for Exeter (2·59)[1] and Leicester (2·4) ;[2] there households with a single hearth made up 45 per cent and 52 per cent of the population respectively, but in the Medway Towns they were only 9 per cent of the total. The reason for the disparity was probably not a difference in wealth but a difference in social habits, partly a result of the general tendency for living standards to be higher near the capital, partly a consequence of the relative availability of fuel, which was scarcer and dearer in the Midlands or even in Devon than in well-wooded Kent with its easy communications with the Newcastle coalfield. Hence it was normal for even pauper households to possess a second hearth, even though it might not have been in regular use. Chambers commonly had fire-irons in them according to the inventories, although fires were probably seldom lit there except in time of illness.

Houses were normally of two storeys with garrets in the roof. Single-storey houses were very rare and probably were confined to the outskirts of the town, while only a few three-storeyed houses figure in the inventories. Typically the house stood end-on to the street, with one room front and back and a lean-to wash-house at the rear, but many of the smaller houses were only a single room deep, even though they

[1] Hoskins, W. G., *Industry, Trade and People in Exeter: 1688-1800.*
[2] Smith, C. T., in *Victoria County History, Leicestershire*, Vol. IV, pp. 156 ff.

might have two storeys, a garret in the roof and a cellar below ground. There were good reasons for crowding the houses on to narrow sites since so many of the inhabitants needed to live within an easy walk of their work in the Dockyard.

There seems to have been no agreement among the inhabitants what the various living-rooms should be called. The obsolescent term " hall " was still in use for the main room, although less frequently as time wore on and then mainly in farm-houses. Many of these were probably of the traditional " yeoman's house " type, with the open central hall now subdivided by a floor so that the " hall chamber " provided additional storage space for seed corn and other perishable goods that were rarely needed. An increasing number of houses on the other hand contained at least one parlour, the proportion rising from 28 per cent before 1700 to 71 per cent after 1740. Parlours tended to be rather sparsely furnished and often lacked fire-irons in the hearth. In most houses clearly they were kept for occasional use, while the regular family living-room was the kitchen. Here or in the buttery adjoining the compilers found most of the articles that were in daily household use—pots and pans, pewter tableware and the like—while such occasional domestic activities as washing or brewing were normally relegated to an outhouse or cellar, together with the coppers and tubs that were used in them. More valuable, however, were the goods upstairs. Not only were beds with their mattresses and hangings the most expensive items in the average inventory, but the best chamber also often contained turkey leather chairs, walnut cabinets and tables and other furniture more elegant than that downstairs, as well as the chest that contained the household linen. The other chambers often held nothing more than a bed, but some, especially in the houses of craftsmen, were used as storage for raw materials, tools and partly finished goods. Only the wealthier as a rule possessed a separate workshop ; the poorer artizan tended to use his front room as a shop and the chamber over it as a store-room.

The inventories give some idea of the spread of luxuries and new fashions in furnishing, although the later inventories are rarely detailed enough to be of much help in this. Clocks seem to have been something of a rarity before 1700, but are quite common after that. Wallpaper earns an occasional mention in the 1700s, at a time when painted hangings, though still sometimes found, were declining in popularity. More householders decorated their wall with pictures, usually prints, to judge from their description as " paper pictures ". For relaxation and social intercourse Rochester possessed at least one coffee house by 1711, in addition to the many taverns. The wealthier citizens were beginning to drink tea and coffee in their own homes, but beer remained the staple drink of the poor.

A further indication of the growing sophistication of the Medway Towns during the eighteenth century is provided by a comparison of the probate inventories for the first half of that period with the particulars of tradesmen and other inhabitants given by Finch in his *Directory*. By 1803 not only had a greater diversity of shops appeared—confectioners, fruiterers and fishmongers besides the butchers and bakers of the inventories, mantua-makers and milliners, straw-hat men and umbrella-makers in addition to tailors and linen-drapers—but the town could also boast a theatre and assembly rooms to cater for the entertainment of its growing middle class and the officers of the garrison. Renewed naval activity in the later years of the eighteenth century had been followed by renewed growth, especially in the new terraces fronting the New Road and in Troy Town. These areas and the outer fringes of the town generally had become the fashionable residential districts in place of the ancient centre around the cathedral. But although there had been growth and change in the outward appearance of the town during the century and a half since the earliest inventories were compiled, the basic pattern of its economic life, with its dualism between ancient cathedral city and modern industrial town, still endured as it was to continue to do right down to the present day.

TABLE 1

TOTAL VALUE OF GOODS AND EFFECTS
GIVEN IN INVENTORIES

Period	£1-£3	£4-£10	£11-£30	£31-£100	£101-£300	£301-£1,000	Over £1,000	?	Total
Up to 1700	2	21	77	67	24	13	–	1	205
1701-10	–	2	16	21	33	20	1	–	93
1711-20	–	–	11	27	16	11	–	2	67
1721-30	–	–	4	20	18	16	2	1	61
1731-40	–	1	8	19	20	4	–	–	52
1741-83	1	1	2	12	9	11	3	–	39
Total	3	25	118	166	120	75	6	4	517

TABLE 2

OCCUPATION OF DECEASED

Dockyard	Total	Worth £300+
Caulker	5	–
Gentleman	2	–
Gunner (at Upnor Castle)	1	–
Joiner	2	1
Labourer	9	–
Master Boatbuilder	1	–
Rigger	1	–
Ropemaker	7	1
Sailmaker	2	–
Sawyer	2	–

	Total	Worth £300+
Scavelman	1	–
Servant	1	–
Shipwright	29	3
Unspecified	42	3
	105	8
Agriculture		
Gardener	6	–
Husbandman	4	–
Maltster	4	3
Miller	1	1
Yeoman	7	5
Unspecified	33	13
	55	22
Seamen (a) Civilian		
Bargeman	1	–
Boatswain	1	–
Fisherman	14	2
Hoyman	6	2
Lighterman	1	–
Mariner	2	–
Wherryman	1	–
(b) Naval		
Captain	1	1
Carpenter	1	1
Purser's Steward	1	–
Shipwright	1	–
Others	19	–
	49	6
Drink Trades		
Brewer	1	–
Innholder	1	1
Spirits-seller	2	–
Victualler	15	1
Vintner (retail)	3	2
Vintner (wholesale)	1	1
Wine-cooper	1	–
Unspecified	23	2
	47	7
Clothing Trades		
Chapman	1	–
Cordwainer	11	–
Draper (or linen-draper)	6	4
Glover	1	–
Haberdasher (or ditto of hats)	6	–
Sailsman	1	1
Shoemaker	1	–
Tailor	6	2
Threadtwister	2	–
Weaver	2	1
	37	8

115

PEOPLE AND HOMES IN THE MEDWAY TOWNS : 1687-1783

	Total	Worth £300+
Building and Furnishing		
Bricklayer	6	–
Brickmaker	1	–
Carpenter	11	3
Glazier	2	–
Joiner	7	2
Turner	1	–
Upholsterer	1	1
	29	6
Food Trades		
Baker	5	2
Butcher	7	1
Cheesemonger	2	2
Grocer	7	1
Tallow-chandler	2	2
Mealman	2	–
	25	8
Other Retailers		
Apothecary	1	–
Barber and bookseller	1	1
Ironmonger	1	–
Tobacconist	3	2
Unspecified	21	4
	27	7
Miscellaneous Crafts		
Basketmaker	1	–
Blacksmith	7	1
Broom-maker	1	–
Cooper	2	–
Currier	1	1
Gunsmith	1	–
Hoopshaver	1	–
Nailor	1	–
Pipemaker	1	–
Saddler	1	–
Tanner	1	–
Wheelwright	6	1
Unspecified	6	1
	30	4
Professions, etc.		
Schoolmaster	1	–
Schoolmistress	2	–
Scrivener	1	–
Sergeant-at-Mace	2	1
Surgeon	3	–
Waterworks official	1	1
	10	2

PEOPLE AND HOMES IN THE MEDWAY TOWNS : 1687-1783

	Total	*Worth £300+*
Labourers and Servants		
Labourer	4	–
Servant	1	–
	5	–
Land Transport		
Carrier	2	–
Coachman	1	–
	3	–
No Occupation Traceable		
Gentleman	2	–
Widow	43	1
Others	50	2
	95	3

Note.—The following occupations are mentioned in other sources for the period (viz. as compilers of inventories, freemen, masters and fathers of apprentices) :

Brazier, carver, clockmaker, collarmaker, cook, distiller, dredgerman, fellmonger, goldsmith, hempdresser, locksmith, milliner, paviour, plasterer, plumber, pumpmaker, purser, tinplate-worker, waterman.

TABLE 3

OCCUPATIONS OF MAYORS OF ROCHESTER : 1701-60

Apothecary	1	Grocer	3
Baker	3	Labourer	1
Brewer	1	Surgeon	3
Butcher	1	Tailor	3
Carpenter	4	Vintner	2
Cheesemonger	1	Wheelwright	1
Currier	2	Wine-cooper	1
Distiller	1	Not traceable	1
Esquire	1		—
Fisherman	1		34
Gentleman	3		—

THE THANET SEAPORTS, 1650-1750

By JOHN H. ANDREWS

NEITHER Margate, Broadstairs nor Ramsgate was recognized as a fully-fledged port by the Customs Commissioners during the period covered by this article. Waiters and Searchers of the Customs Service were stationed at all three ports to supervise the loading and discharging of goods ; but there were no legal quays for the transaction of foreign trade, and no cargo could be handled in Thanet without documents obtained from the Customs Collector at Sandwich.[1] In 1731 the inhabitants of Margate complained of the inconveniences arising from this position, but without success.[2] Certainly their complaint had some foundation, for Margate had a thriving trade, and in the past several smaller Kentish ports, such as Hythe and Folkestone, had enjoyed greater privileges. For the historian the most serious consequence of this dependent status is the almost complete absence of commercial statistics for the Thanet ports. Their trade and shipping were recorded with those of the port of Sandwich, and it is a difficult and often an impossible task to distinguish between the different ports. Thus T. S. Willan, in his *English Coasting Trade*, 1600-1750, treats the Sandwich Port Books as if they related only to the port of Sandwich, and makes no mention of Thanet, although he discusses quite insignificant ports like Folkestone, Hythe and Romney.

THE HARBOURS AND SHIPS OF THANET

The harbours of Margate, Broadstairs and Ramsgate were all of the same type : a single curved pier excluding winds and waves from the most dangerous direction, the north-east.

The wooden pier at Margate, as shown on a crude plan of 1646,[3] resembled the present structure in shape and position, following a semi-circular course from south-east to north-west. A breakwater called the New Work ran northwards from the pier head. The space within the harbour was dry at low water, and at all times it had to be entered with care, for a long ledge of rock ran out from the West Cliff across the harbour mouth. The history of Margate harbour was more eventful than that of the other Thanet ports. Situated on a

---

[1] The stations of Customs Officers from 1675 onwards are to be found in P.R.O. Customs Registers, Series I, and the legal quays and port limits of Kent in P.R.O. Exchequer Special Commissions 6266. The latter document places Margate in the port of Faversham, but all the other evidence is against this.

[2] P.R.O. Treasury Board Papers 278/4.

[3] British Museum Harleian MS. 7598.

coast particularly exposed to erosion, its chief problem was the danger of destruction by storm waves. The pier, the road connecting it to the town, the sea-wall and the houses it was intended to protect all suffered in this way in the period 1650-90, and the estimated cost of repair had reached £2,500 by 1690.[1] Like many other harbours protected by piers, Margate lacked sufficient financial resources of its own to maintain its harbour facilities in good repair. In 1662 not even the normal harbour dues were forthcoming, for masters were refusing to pay them, and pier-wardens were not being appointed to collect them.[2] This abuse seems to have been remedied, and pier-wardens were regularly appointed after 1679,[3] but in 1690 they were £200 in debt, and a new schedule of harbour dues was requested. This request seems to have been refused, for a list of dues chargeable in 1694 states that these had been the rates for " time out of mind."[4] Finally the harbour was repaired, perhaps only partially, with money granted by the Exchequer. No further complaint was made until 1723, when Lewis wrote : " By the sea's falling so heavy on the northern part of the island the harbour of Margate has gone very much to decay, and the masters of ships which used to live there are almost all removed to London."[5] By this time the payment of harbour dues was again in dispute, but in the following year the whole matter was regularized by Act of Parliament (11 Geo. I c 3), and no further complaints were made; by the end of the period the harbour was regularly used by vessels of a hundred tons burden.

At Ramsgate a curved pier projecting from under the East Cliff to the south and west had existed at least since the sixteenth century. In 1715 the pier was lengthened, and most surviving descriptions seem to refer to its subsequent condition. Unlike Dover, Ramsgate Harbour seems to have suffered little from the reduction of its depth by drifting sand and shingle. Between 1715 and 1750 a bar was cast up, but it was nowhere more than $2\frac{1}{2}$ ft. thick. The chief difficulty was the maintenance of the pier itself and its protection from erosion, a difficult matter in a port with very little trade and therefore very little revenue. It was on this account that Ramsgate masters were exempted from the Dover Harbour dues, but no other financial aid was granted, although

---

[1] The history of this period may be extracted from Calendars of State Papers, Domestic, 1650, p. 173 ; 1682, p. 127 ; 1690-1, p. 434 ; and P.R.O. Privy Council Registers 2/73, p. 417.

[2] E. Hasted, *The History and Topographical Survey of the County of Kent*, 1779, Vol. 10, p. 317.

[3] Margate Public Library, MS. List of Pier Wardens.

[4] *Orders, Decrees and Rates Time out of Mind Used by the Inhabitants of Margate and St. Johns . . . For and Towards the Perpetual Maintenance of the Pier and Harbour of Margate*, 1694.

[5] J. Lewis, *The History and Antiquities of the Isle of Thanet*, 1723, p. 22. See also House of Commons Journals, Vol. 20, pp. 352, 361.

the town submitted a petition to the Commons in 1736, asking for a Bill to finance the construction of a second pier and the preservation of the first, which had become beyond their means.[1]

Historians tend to belittle the old harbour of Ramsgate in comparing it with the modern structure begun in 1749.[2] It was dry at low water, and too small to be a valuable refuge when a serious storm swept the Downs, but it could accommodate forty vessels of between 20 and 300 tons, and a ship of 700 tons had once repaired there.[3]

Little is known of Broadstairs Harbour. Its appearance on contemporary small-scale maps suggests that the shape and position of the pier were as at present.

The most remarkable feature of the Thanet ports during this period was not the trade passing through them, but the number of ships belonging to them. As Willan has shown (op. cit., Appendix 6), a ship " belonged " to the place of residence of its owners. The following table is from a list which seems to have been previously unknown.[4]

SHIPS BELONGING TO THE PORTS OF KENT, 1701

	Ships	Tonnage	Men		Ships	Tonnage	Men
Ramsgate	45	4,100	388	Milton ..	34	807	53
Margate ..	37	2,909	138	Broadstairs	17	731	90
Sandwich	21	1,146	104	Whitstable	33	701	46
Rochester	22	1,054	70	Dover ..	7	415	44
Faversham	32	888	47	Deal ..	1	50	5

In this list, Ramsgate ranks fifteenth among all the ports of England. Thanet ships played an especially prominent part in the coal trade and in the trade in timber and naval stores. J. Brand's *History of Newcastle* (1789, Vol. II, p. 677) has a table showing vessels employed in the Newcastle coal trade in 1702-4. The figures for Kent are as follows :

	Ships	Chaldrons of Coal
Ramsgate ..	42	2,147
Margate ..	24	1,001
Rochester ..	21	808
Sandwich ..	17	554
Broadstairs ..	12	241
Dover ..	8	232
Faversham ..	2	59

[1] House of Commons Journals, Vol. 22, p. 591.

[2] Lewis, op. cit., 1736 edition, has a plan of Ramsgate. The old and new harbours are shown on one plan in *Gentleman's Magazine*, 1752, p. 18.

[3] For the history of Ramsgate Harbour, see Lewis, op. cit., J. Smeaton, *An Historical Report on Ramsgate Harbour*, 1791, and *A Brief History of Dover and Ramsgate Harbours, by a Naval Officer*, 1837.

[4] P.R.O. Admiralty, Correspondence from Customs Commissioners, 29th January, 1702.

The tables of ships passing through the Sound to and from the Baltic are another neglected source of information. Between 1680 and 1730 an annual average of more than twenty Ramsgate ships made this voyage. In the last decade of the seventeenth century the average was nearly 50, and in 1700 Ramsgate sent more ships through the Sound than any English port except London. The average for Margate was more than ten between 1671 and 1710. None of the other Kent ports achieved an average of more than three ships per year. After 1730 this traffic greatly diminished.[1] These ships are scarcely ever mentioned in the Sandwich Port Books. Presumably they left Thanet in ballast and returned laden with hemp and timber to the Dockyards of Chatham, Woolwich and Deptford. From the early 1680's the Rochester Port Books list many Ramsgate ships, from the Baltic, Norway and New England.

The importance of the Thanet ports as shipping centres is probably to be explained by their position at the lower end of the Thames Estuary, the most convenient place for ships to gather while awaiting dispatch on what were mainly seasonal trades. Ramsgate derived most benefit from this position because of the relatively superior quality of its harbour facilities.

THE MARITIME TRADE OF THANET

The character and volume of the maritime trade of English seaports in the period 1650-1750 is best studied in the Exchequer (K.R.) Port Books. There are a few other statistical sources, but none of these gives separate totals for the smaller ports. The trade of Thanet was recorded in the books of the Port of Sandwich,[2] usually without being distinguished from that of Sandwich. Only in the case of the inward coastwise trade, and then only in eight years between 1676 and 1686, do the books specify the port concerned. The outward coastwise trade of the various ports can also be distinguished, if it is assumed that Margate ships traded from Margate, Sandwich ships from Sandwich, and so on. In most cases such an assumption would be quite false, but in Kent there are certain special reasons for accepting it. In March, 1702, it was ordered that all Kent ports west of the North Foreland should henceforth be permitted to send agricultural produce coastwise to London without using the cocquet, the normal means of authorizing

---

[1] N. E. Bang, *Tabeller over Skibsfart og Varetransport gennem Oresund*, 1497-1660, 3 vols., 1906-33 ; N. E. Bang and K. Korst, *Tabeller over Skibsfart og Varetransport gennem Oresund*, 1661-1783, 1930.

[2] A document attached to a Sandwich book for 1730 (P.R.O. Exchequer K.R. Port Books 706/6) explicitly orders that the books shall contain " a true entry of all . . . goods . . . as well coming into the Port of Sandwich and all creeks and places thereunto belonging as going out of the same."

coastwise trade. At exactly the same time, all records of such traffic cease in the Port Books of Rochester, Milton and Faversham. Up to this time Margate ships are frequently mentioned in the Sandwich books. In 1702 these mentions abruptly cease. Unless we postulate some catastrophic change in the disposition of trade or shipping, it must be assumed that Margate ships had been trading from within the North Foreland. This matter has been explained at some length because it affects the interpretation of the Port Books of all North Kent and much of Essex. Willan (op. cit., pp. 139-40) infers that the trade of this region had declined in the eighteenth century, whereas it had merely ceased to be recorded.

There are thus records of the inward coasting trade of Thanet from 1676 to 1686, and of the outward coasting trade from 1650 to 1701. The rest of the trade, including all foreign trade, is either not recorded at all or indistinguishable from the trade of Sandwich.

The distribution of the coastwise trade is shown in the following table.

NUMBER OF COASTWISE CARGOES PER YEAR, 1676-86

		Outwards	Inwards	Total
Margate ..	..	93	21	114
Broadstairs	..	2	6	8
Ramsgate	..	2	11	13
Sandwich	..	108	81	189

The outward coastwise trade of Thanet consisted almost entirely of corn, almost all of which was exported from Margate. Corn was shipped in small cargoes of two or three hundred quarters each. Such cargoes could be handled by Margate Harbour as easily as by Ramsgate, and Margate had the advantage of closer proximity to London, the market for almost all the corn shipped from the island. Most travellers and topographers, from Camden to Defoe, were impressed by the fertility and productivity of the Isle of Thanet, and the Port Books prove that this impression was correct. In the period for which records are available Thanet exported 7,000 quarters of malt, 3,500 quarters of wheat and 500 quarters of barley per year to other English ports. Among the ports of Kent, it ranked second in exports of malt and barley, and third in exports of wheat. Other coastwise exports were of very small importance. Shipments of wool, herrings, and kelp were frequently recorded, but only in very small quantities. There are no detailed records of the coastwise trade in the first half of the eighteenth century, but the available evidence suggests that its volume was maintained, despite Lewis's implication to the contrary. In 1719

Harris stated that 20,000 quarters of barley were shipped every year to London,[1] and many writers mention a weekly hoy service from Margate to London.[2] In 1724 the Margate harbour dues were reported to yield from £140 to £150 annually, a sum which compared favourably with those collected at Dover and Sandwich.[3] There is also a complete record of the coastwise trade of Thanet and Sandwich in the last nine months of 1741 : during this period 109 Margate ships, one Ramsgate ship and one Broadstairs ship left the coast within the limits of the Port of Sandwich.

During the period for which records are available, Newcastle coal was the cargo of seven out of every eight ships entering the ports of Thanet. The average annual imports in 1676-86 were : Sandwich, 1,710 chaldrons ; Margate, 579 chaldrons ; Ramsgate, 427 chaldrons ; Broadstairs, 190 chaldrons. These amounts seem small, but by contemporary standards they were not inconsiderable for ports of this size. No port in Sussex imported as much coal as Margate during this period. Certainly Thanet was more than usually dependent on imported coal, owing to the timber shortage in the island. In 1672, when enemy privateers confined the Thanet ships to harbour, the inhabitants protested : " If speedy care not be taken our people will starve for want of fuel in the winter."[4] Such reports suggest the relative costs of land and sea transport ; plentiful supplies of wood were available a few miles to the west of Thanet.

There is no means of distinguishing the foreign trade of Thanet from that of Sandwich. The Sandwich Port Books of this period record a foreign export trade in corn and herrings, and an import trade in wine, Norwegian timber, and general cargoes from Rotterdam and Ostend. According to the law, only the corn, fish and timber trades could be carried on at ports without legal quays, but at least before 1732 some wine, linen and fruit were allowed to be directly imported to Margate, where the yearly Customs receipts amounted to £2,000.[5] But the chief foreign trade of the Thanet ports was almost certainly the export of fish. Throughout the period 1650-1750 there are many references to the Thanet fishing fleets, but no records of fishing boats belonging to Sandwich. There is only one statistical record distinguishing the fishing vessels of the different ports : the lists of Cinque Port vessels visiting the Yarmouth Free Fair.[6] Between 1648 and 1660 the usual

---

[1] J. Harris, *The History of Kent*, 1719, p. 314.

[2] Lewis, op. cit., 1736, p. 134 ; *A Brief Director for All Those that Would Send Their Letters to any Parts of England, Scotland or Ireland*, 1710.

[3] House of Commons Journals, Vol. 20, p. 361.

[4] Calendar of State Papers, Domestic, 1672, p. 387.

[5] P.R.O. Treasury Board Papers 278/4.

[6] Town Hall, New Romney, Cinque Port Records, 8.

numbers were nine from St. Peters, one from St. Johns, and none from Sandwich. It seems safe to assume that all the exports of fish recorded in the Port Books of Sandwich came from the Thanet ports. Foreign exports of herrings appear only in 1695, and reached a maximum in the period 1712-33, when the average annual export was nearly 1,500 barrels. After this the trade rapidly declined, but exports of Icelandic codfish begin to appear in the 1740's. Over the whole period, Thanet exported more fish than any other port in Kent or Sussex except Dover. About half the exports went to the Mediterranean.

In the early eighteenth century the Port of Sandwich exported about 4,000 quarters of corn per year to foreign ports ; some of this doubtless came from Thanet, but it is impossible to say how much. The same is true of the large import of Norwegian deals and fir timber, and the cargoes of linen, pantiles, bricks, earthenware and bullrushes imported from Rotterdam.

There is some evidence of the use of the Thanet ports by travellers to the continent. In 1678 troops and horses were carried from Margate to Ostend and Antwerp,[1] and in 1691 two vessels were appointed to ply between Margate and Ostend carrying intelligence.[2] Among the celebrities who travelled through Margate were William III, George I, George II, Queen Caroline, and the Duke of Marlborough.[3] A regular passenger service would have been a natural development, for Margate lay closer to Ostend than did Dover, but in fact there was no regular peace-time traffic. Although passengers were not listed in the Port Books, it would be possible to trace passenger traffic, if it existed, from references to passengers' belongings, especially their horses.

THE HARBOUR OF REFUGE AT RAMSGATE

The period discussed in this article was brought to an end by the construction of Ramsgate New Harbour. The history of this structure has often been told, but a few new facts are included in the following brief account.

Ramsgate, rather than Margate, was chosen as the site of the new harbour because of its proximity to the Downs, an important but not altogether safe anchorage. The earliest suggestion for a harbour to relieve ships caught in the Downs by a storm seems to have come from the Corporation of Sandwich, three years after the great storm of 1703. A detailed scheme for a harbour at Sandwich appeared in 1736, and in the following year the Corporation spent more than £345 " on endeavouring to get a new haven." Unfortunately this money was wasted,

[1] Calendar of State Papers, Domestic, 1678, pp. 261, 375.
[2] Ibid., 1690-1, p. 313.
[3] A Description of the Isle of Thanet, 1763, p. 10.

for although the plan was approved by a Commons committee in 1745, the ultimate decision in 1749 was in favour of Ramsgate.[1]

In an undated petition, the City of London, the East India Company and nearly 800 merchants of ports ranging from Scarborough to Falmouth recommended Ramsgate as the more suitable site.[2] Ramsgate had several advantages over Sandwich. It lay on a cleaner shore, for beach material did not normally drift north of the Stour ; the chalk rock of Thanet provided a firm foundation for the piers, and an easily available building material, both of which were lacking at Sandwich ; ships could leave Ramsgate Harbour in an east wind, which was not possible at the rival site ; the tidal currents ran directly into the harbour mouth, instead of across it, thereby cleansing the harbour of silt and facilitating the entry and departure of ships ; there would be no expense of digging, and experiments had proved that the chalk would not damage a round-bottomed ship settling upon it.[3] These were the circumstances which determined that of all the places within the old limits of the port of Sandwich, only Ramsgate should still deserve the name of port.

MAPS OF THE THANET PORTS

The oldest harbour plan of Thanet appears to be a very crude sketch of Margate made in 1646 as part of a scheme for building a sea-wall (British Museum : Harleian MS. 7598). The 1736 edition of J. Lewis's *History and Antiquities of the Isle of Thanet* contains a view of Margate Harbour and a detailed plan of the town of Ramsgate, showing the pier and harbour. The projected harbour at Sandwich is shown on Labelye's map of the Downs, printed in the 1738 edition of Grenville Collins' *Great Britain's Coasting Pilot*. The position of the old harbour of Ramsgate in relation to the modern works is well shown on a small plan published in the *Gentleman's Magazine*, Vol. 22 (1752), p. 18.

[1] Smeaton, op. cit., p. 1 ; Sandwich Guildhall, Water Treasurers' Accounts, 1706, 1736.

[2] House of Commons Journals, Vol. 24, pp. 772, 861 ; Vol. 25, pp. 721, 745. The petition is in British Museum, Additional MS. 33061, ff. 157-180.

[3] The arguments in the controversy between Ramsgate and Sandwich are given in *The Gentleman's Magazine*, 1745, p. 95 ; 1749, p. 103 ; *The London Magazine*, 1749, p. 68 ; D. Defoe, *A Tour through the Whole Island of Great Britain*, 1748, Vol. 1, pp. 174-184.

THE TRADE OF THE PORT OF FAVERSHAM, 1650-1750

By J. H. ANDREWS

IN the value of its trade, the size and number of its ships, and the geographical extent of its commercial connections the port of Faversham has never achieved more than minor importance, but in the seventeenth and eighteenth centuries the total volume of its traffic placed it among the leading ports of Kent, and in certain branches of the coasting trade it had few rivals anywhere in England. In the following paragraphs an attempt is made to trace the development of Faversham in the period 1650-1750, using the series of Port Books in the Public Record Office.[1] These documents, although they contain very detailed lists of vessels and cargoes entering and leaving the port, cannot be accepted at their face value as a comprehensive record of the trade of Faversham Creek; and before describing their contents it will be necessary to ascertain whether any other landing places besides Faversham itself were included in the books, and whether there were any kinds of maritime trade which were omitted from them.

The Customs port of Faversham, as delimited by an Exchequer Commission of 1676,[2] included a considerable portion of the Kentish coast, stretching from Milton in the west to the North Foreland in the east, but not all this coast was covered by the Faversham port books. The trade of Margate was always recorded in the Sandwich books[3] and the Commissioners were almost certainly mistaken in extending the limits of Faversham as far east as the Foreland, while Milton, which seems to have been an independent Customs port at least until 1670,[4] continued for another century to keep a separate set of port books, recording not only its own trade but also that of Conyer, Upchurch, Rainham and Otterham. Four places remained within the limits of the port of Faversham—Reculver, Herne, Whitstable and Faversham itself. Of these the last two were well-known landing places of some importance, but the status of the others is uncertain. Hasted's description of Herne in 1772 as the centre of a flourishing coastwise trade seems to have been true of earlier times, for ships belonging to Herne

---

[1] Exch. K.R. Port Books, 661-728.
[2] Exch. K.R. Special Commissions 6266.
[3] See J. H. Andrews, " The Thanet Seaports, 1650-1750," *Arch. Cant.*, Vol. LXVI, pp. 37-44.
[4] Milton had its own Collector of Customs in 1670 (Calendar of Treasury Books, 1669-72, p. 585).

were frequently recorded in the Faversham port books and in 1702 its farmers, hoymen and fishermen considered their bay important enough to need guns for protection against the French.[1] Reculver was described as a " seatown, well frequented by hoymen and fishermen,"[2] but neither its trade nor its shipping was mentioned in any of the Kent port books of this period. Unfortunately the Faversham books hardly ever distinguish between the trade of these various places. One book of coastwise exports for the first nine months of 1656 gives separate lists for Whitstable and Faversham,[3] and the five coast books covering the period 1676-80 specify incoming ships landing their cargoes at Whitstable, but otherwise the ports can be distinguished only by assuming that ships belonging to Whitstable traded from Whitstable and that ships belonging to Herne traded from Herne. In the case of outgoing coasters, at least, this seems a warrantable assumption, but in many port books the ships are not described as belonging to *any* port, while much of the inward traffic was carried in ships belonging to places outside Kent altogether. Despite these difficulties, it is at least certain that the port of Faversham, in the technical sense of the word, was by no means identical with the town and harbour of the same name; it included three ports in the topographical sense of the term—Faversham, Whitstable and Herne.

It seems certain that some branches of the coasting trade escaped notice in the Faversham port books. In 1702 it was enacted that Customs officers should no longer enforce the system of cocquets and bonds for vessels carrying farm produce, other than wool, to London from places within the North Foreland;[4] as cargoes authorized by cocquet were the only cargoes listed in the North Kent port books of this period, all traffic covered by the Act immediately disappeared from the books of Faversham, Milton and Rochester. Thus nearly all the coastwise exports of Faversham passed unrecorded throughout the eighteenth century, except for one brief interval between April and December, 1741, when the old method of authorizing the coasting trade of the Thames Estuary was temporarily restored. In addition to these changes, it appears that some Faversham trades were never recorded at all during the century under review. There is known to have been a substantial traffic in fruit and faggots to London from Faversham, Milton and Rochester, but these commodities were hardly ever mentioned in the port books. The merchants handling them claimed exemption from the tonnage duty on coasters imposed in 1694, appar-

[1] State Papers, Domestic, Anne, 1/35.
[2] G. Miège, *The New State of England under their Majesties King William and Queen Mary*, 1702, p. 117.
[3] Exch. K.R. Customs Accounts 232/18.
[4] 1 Anne c. 26. This Act seems soon to have been taken to apply to almost all the coastwise trade of North Kent except in coal and wool.

ently because of the very small size of the boats employed and the short distances involved;[1] and it seems likely that they were exempted on similar grounds from cocquet fees and therefore omitted from the port books.

With these omissions and limitations in mind, we may now examine the contents of the Faversham trade statistics. Perhaps their most striking feature was the inconsiderable volume of foreign commerce. Faversham was a fully-fledged Customs port, with two legal quays for the unloading of foreign merchandise, but almost all its small foreign trade was contributed by the local oyster fishery. Kentish oysters were reported in 1709 to be produced in an area twenty miles long and seven miles wide, stretching from the North Foreland to Sheerness,[2] but most of the fishing was done among the creeks west of Faversham in a region quite distinct from the modern oyster beds at Whitstable. The oyster trade was measured in terms of the "wash," which seems to have been equivalent to twenty bushels. Exports from Faversham increased rapidly from less than two hundred wash per year in the mid-seventeenth century to nearly a thousand in the eighteenth. Throughout this period Holland, and especially the port of Zieriksee, was the chief destination, taking more than four-fifths of the total, although a small trade to the North Sea ports of Germany developed after 1700. Apart from the Dutch wars of the seventeenth century, frost was the most serious enemy of the oyster fishery; in the 1740s, for example, exports dropped almost to nothing and the beds had to be restocked with oysters imported from Cancale in France.

Apart from the export of oysters, Faversham's foreign trade was very small, and grew even smaller during the period under review; in the late seventeenth century a little wine was imported from France or Spain and the Dutch oyster boats sometimes returned with cargoes of pantiles or bullrushes, but by the middle of the following century one or two shipments of Norwegian timber usually comprised a whole year's foreign import trade. This lack of overseas commerce was chiefly due to the close proximity of London. Whatever farm produce from North Kent found its way overseas did so only after being shipped first to the capital, and the position of Faversham on one of the principal highways of the kingdom enabled the town to obtain foreign commodities easily by road; in 1737, for example, a local farmer starting an experimental vineyard imported his vine cuttings not through the port of Faversham but by way of Calais and Dover.[3]

Although London drained away most of Faversham's foreign trade,

---

[1] Hargrave MS. 222, f. 274.
[2] Journals, House of Commons, Vol. 16, p. 356.
[3] Isaac Minet's Inland Letter Book, 1737-41, 21st November, 1737. Access to this volume was kindly granted by Miss Susan Minet.

its coasting trade was greatly stimulated by proximity to the metropolitan market. In the second half of the seventeenth century about three hundred coasters left the port each year, and of these usually less than ten were bound for ports other than London. In 1683 London imported 316 cargoes from Faversham, more than were imported from any other English port except Newcastle.[1] The eighteenth-century port books, as we have seen, are incomplete, but one record has survived for 1728,[2] when only Newcastle, Sunderland and Ipswich sent more ships to London than Faversham. The figures for the Kent ports were as follows:

Shipments to London, 1728

Rochester	135	Deal	34
Milton	132	Dover	65
Faversham	353	Folkestone	10
Sandwich	238	Hythe	9

The individual contributions of Faversham, Whitstable and Herne to the coasting trade cannot be established with certainty. In 1701 32 ships, totalling 888 tons, belonged to Faversham, and 33, totalling 701 tons, to Whitstable and Herne.[3] Of the 289 shipments exported annually in the last decade of the seventeenth century, 56 were carried in Whitstable ships and 48 in Herne ships; in 1741, the only year after 1702 for which there are full records, there were 44 Herne ships and 40 Whitstable ships in a total of 237.

As might be expected from Faversham's location in the belt of fertile loams and brickearths which lies along the northern edge of the North Downs, corn was the principal constituent of its outward coasting trade. In the second half of the seventeenth century average annual exports of corn and malt amounted to nearly 15,000 quarters, of which more than 6,000 quarters were wheat, about 4,000 quarters oats and the rest barley and malt; exports of beans and peas amounted to more than 2,000 quarters a year. It is interesting to notice that ships belonging to Herne, which presumably served the region of heavier clay soils in the neighbourhood of the Blean Forest, carried very much smaller quantities of barley and malt than the ships of Faversham. Almost all these corn exports went to London.

The Faversham hop trade affords an interesting confirmation of Defoe's account of the Canterbury hop grounds. "The great wealth and increase of the city of Canterbury," he wrote, "is from the surprising increase of hop grounds all round the place; it is within the memory of many of the inhabitants now living, and that none of the

---

[1] T. S. Willan, *The English Coasting Trade, 1600-1750*, 1938, Appendix 2.
[2] W. Maitland, *The History of London from its Foundation to the Present Time*, 1756, Vol. II, p. 1263.
[3] Admiralty: Letters from Customs Commissioners, 29th January, 1702.

oldest neither, that there was not an acre of ground planted with hops in the whole neighbourhood, or so few as not to be worth naming."[1] Faversham's exports in 1656-85 were little more than 100 bags per year, only a small fraction of the amount shipped from Maidstone in the same period. By 1689-1701, however, exports had risen to 750 bags per year, and in the nine recorded months of 1741 they exceeded 2,000 bags. The whole of this trade was with London: the port books do not confirm Defoe's statement that Kentish hops were sent straight to Stourbridge Fair in Cambridgeshire without passing through London.[2]

Raw wool, the third important agricultural export of North Kent, was produced in large quantities on the rich alluvial pastures along the coast, and in the case of Faversham these supplies were supplemented by wool brought from as far afield as Romney Marsh.[3] Like the export of hops, this trade enjoyed a substantial increase in the late seventeenth century, until Faversham, with an average annual export of nearly 2,000 bags, had become the chief wool-exporting port of England. After about 1715, however, the trade stagnated and even declined: by the 1730s the English wool trade was dominated by Rye, in Sussex, whose exports had grown to nearly double those of Faversham.[4] It is interesting to notice that this shift in the centre of the legitimate wool trade corresponded with an opposite movement in the overseas " owling " of wool. By the second decade of the eighteenth century, dragoons and Riding Officers had done much to suppress the smuggling trade of Romney Marsh, but along the coast between the Swale and the North Foreland illegal trade was still on the increase and in 1718 the most notorious of the wool smugglers was a resident of Herne Bay.[5] Between eighty and ninety per cent. of Faversham's legitimate wool exports were shipped to London; the rest went chiefly to Colchester until 1729, after which Exeter began to take about an eighth part of the total.

Two local industries, copperas and gunpowder, contributed to Faversham's coasting trade. The Whitstable copperas works, well-known from late eighteenth-century records, seem to have been in operation throughout the century preceding 1750. In the first nine months of 1656 Whitstable shipped 225 tons of copperas, Faversham

---

[1] D. Defoe, *A Tour through England and Wales*, 1724 (Everyman's Library), Vol. I, p. 118. The estimate of 6,000 acres under hops quoted by Defoe was exaggerated. In 1724-32 the average area of hops in the Canterbury district was 3,700 acres (Treasury Board Papers 271/23).

[2] Defoe, *op. cit.*, Vol. I, p. 82.

[3] W. Symonds, *A New Year's Gift to the Parliament, or England's Golden Fleece Preserved*, 1702, p. 28.

[4] Lists of English ports exporting wool, 1715-19 (Colonial Office C.O. 390/8c) and 1739-43 (Treasury Various (T.64) 278, 280, 281).

[5] Journal of the Commissioners for Trade and Plantations, 1715-18, p. 417. See also Defoe, *op. cit.*, Vol. I, pp. 112, 123.

only 27 tons; total exports in 1656-1701 averaged 375 tons per year, most of which were carried in Whitstable ships, but in 1741 only 181 tons were exported. Shipments of gunpowder often exceeded a thousand barrels per year, but it seems that this traffic was not always fully recorded, for in 1673 the Faversham Customs officers protested that "great quantities of powder are also weekly exported hence without cocquet or security under pretence of His Majesty's goods, but whose it is or where it goes we are not able to give any account."[1] Faversham's export trade owed little to the manufactures of Canterbury, which despatched most of its woollens, worsteds, silk and paper to London by road.

Coastwise imports to Faversham were of three kinds—the coal trade, the trade in butter and cheese, and the London trade in general merchandise. Imports of coal from Newcastle and Sunderland steadily increased, except in the wartime years of 1689-1713, from 1,053 chaldrons per year in 1671-80 to 2,498 chaldrons in 1741-50. In 1676-80, which unfortunately is the only period for which separate records are available, about a third of the total coal imports were landed at Whitstable. Butter and cheese were supplied by the Suffolk ports of Aldeburgh, Woodbridge and Ipswich; in the second half of the seventeenth century average annual imports amounted to nearly 800 firkins of butter and more than 5,000 cheeses. Faversham imported an annual average of 68 cargoes from London in the period 1656-88 —more than any other Kentish port. Nearly every London cargo included a great variety of manufactured goods of both foreign and English origin, especially wine, sugar, linen, leather, glass, metal manufactures, groceries, spirits and oil, but the largest single item was combed wool for the Canterbury worsted industry, which amounted to several hundred bags a year in the peak period of the 1670s and in one or two years even exceeded the export of raw wool. In the eighteenth century imports were smaller—less than 200 bags per year—and after 1738 they ceased altogether.

Whitstable, as the nearest harbour to Canterbury, was the natural port for this inward traffic in wool and general merchandise, but it seems to have remained unimportant until the eighteenth century. Richard Blome, writing in 1673, described it as "the best port town (next to Faversham) for Canterbury,"[2] but in 1676-80 only 13 cargoes a year were landed there, most of them Newcastle coal, while Faversham imported no less than 93 cargoes annually. Fifty years later, however, Defoe described the trade of Canterbury without mentioning Faversham: at the time of his visit, coal and timber were brought to

---

[1] Calendar of State Papers, Domestic, 1673, p. 277.

[2] R. Blome, *Britannia, or a Geographical Description of the Kingdoms of England, Scotland and Ireland*, 1673, p. 131.

the city via Sandwich and Fordwich, heavy goods from London via Whitstable.[1] In 1726 at least one hoy began to make regular weekly voyages between Whitstable and London, the hoyman collecting goods at Canterbury and presumably unloading his return cargoes there.[2] The increase in the traffic between Canterbury and Whitstable which seems to have occurred at this time may have hastened the deterioration of the road joining the two places, which was seriously in need of repair in 1736.[3]

Herne seems to have taken no part in the Canterbury trade: almost all its traffic was composed of exported agricultural products.

[1] Defoe, *op. cit.*, Vol. I, p. 119.
[2] *Kentisn Post*, 31st August-3rd September, 1726.
[3] Journals, House of Commons, Vol. 22, pp. 544, 549.   9 Geo. II. c.10.

EXTRACTS FROM THE LETTER-BOOK OF A DOVER MERCHANT, 1737—1741.

BY WILLIAM MINET, M.A., F.S.A.

THE glory of the Cinque Ports and of their satellites, " Antient Towns " and " Members " as they were named, has departed. Hastings, Winchelsea, Rye, Romney, and Sandwich may interest the historian, but have no touch with modern commerce. As a port Dover alone survives; nor does it owe this to any exemption from the causes which ruined its early rivals, for the never ceasing eastward sweep of sand or shingle which has blocked their havens has played equally upon it. If Dover remains an important harbour to-day, it owes it to its proximity to the French coast, and to the lavish expenditure of money which has been made on it, in order to keep open communication with the continent.

Eliminating the continental traffic, Dover was a far more important and a far more necessary port in the old days than it is now. Steam conquers wind and has no need to take shelter in a harbour until a favourable breeze shall enable it to work its way out from the narrow seas to the wider ocean. Sailing-ships bound through the channel had but little room to manœuvre, and, waiting a fair wind, perforce sought shelter; this they could find but in three spots on the south-eastern coast: under the slight promontory of Dungeness, in the Downs, or in Dover Harbour. In the latter alone could they take refuge when needing repair from damage, for the two former were useless for such a purpose.

Sailing-ships still to some extent survive, but even where they do, thanks to the help afforded them by steam tugs, they do not often need to put into Dover to repair, or to await a fair wind. Dover's chief occupation is now gone, and only the necessities of the continental traffic and the demand for a naval harbour, have saved it from extinction.

The purpose of this paper is to look back on Dover in the eighteenth century, and to see what work the harbour then did, and how it was fitted to do it. First, let us realize of what the harbour then consisted. The two jetties stood where they now are, and gave access to a tidal basin, though this was then considerably smaller, for the land on which formerly stood the York Hotel and the Amherst Battery was not thrown into it until 1838. It is through this addition that the entrance to the Wellington Dock now passes; before 1838 this entrance did not exist. The sides of this tidal basin were not formed of quay walls as now, but were mud-flats, uncovered at low tides. Somewhere about 1661, however, the back part of this outer basin had been cut off by a cross wall, which is still there, and in this, at a later date, were fixed gates, thus forming an inner floating basin, now the Granville Dock.

This wall had not been built with any intention of forming an inner harbour, its original object having been one of the many devices adopted to throw the stream of water which came from the Pent, now the Wellington Dock, more directly upon the mouth of the harbour, and so help to sweep away the bar of shingle which was ever forming at that point. At its north-western angle this inner basin was connected with the Pent by a sluice-gate, but this gate was not made available for the passage of ships until about 1760, before which date the Pent cannot be regarded as part of Dover Harbour.*

At the north-eastern angle of this harbour was a ship-builder's yard where certainly small ships could be built—we know of the "Expedition" of 60 tons built there in 1738—and damaged ships repaired, by being floated at spring-tides on to a grid. Ships of considerable size could be thus dealt with, for in 1740 we have mention of a Dutch ship of

---

* The harbour in this state is well shewn in Buck's panoramic view of 1739.

400 to 500 tons, with masts and timber for Toulon, which put into Dover leaky; but as she was flat-bottomed they could not come to the leak.

Lining the inner side of the inner basin ran what is now known as Custom-house quay; on this stood many houses and warehouses belonging to Dover merchants. Among these was one known as Pier House, where lived Isaac Minet;* here he carried on his business, and from here were written the letters which form the authority for what follows.

Isaac Minet had been born in Calais in 1660, and escaped to England on the Revocation of the Edict of Nantes in 1685. A younger brother, Stephen, had preceded him, and had succeeded in getting together some small trade in Dover. Stephen died early in 1691, and Isaac, who had started in business in London, returned thence to Dover and took over and continued his brother's more promising venture. At first this was what we should call that of a ship's provision merchant; but it developed gradually, and by 1737 had become a general merchant's and ship-agency business. In later days it grew into a bank, well known in Dover as the house of Minet and Fector; but here we deal with it in its earlier and far more picturesque stage.

In those days office facilities were unknown, and every letter written was laboriously copied into a letter-book. Of these the business kept two series, one inland and one foreign. Volume 20 of the first series, extending from August 1737 to April 1741, has survived, and is now in my possession; its copies are all in the hand of the principal himself, and are all beautifully written, and carefully indexed under the names of the correspondents. They deal, as would be expected, with an infinite variety of matters, but all centring round Dover Harbour, and all having to do with ships and their cargoes. Let us begin with the cross-channel traffic which, while not relatively so important as now, even then formed no small part of Dover interests.

* The house was rebuilt in 1749, and remained till 1871, when it was pulled down. Its site is now occupied by Lukey's Ale Stores.

First there were the mail-packets sailing to Calais and Ostend; these were Government boats, carrying only mails and passengers, and they are sometimes complained of as competitors by Isaac Minet, who himself owned and employed boats crossing to Calais, Boulogne, and occasionally to Ostend. Of these there were four, the "Isaac and Mary," Captain Beale Jones; the "Jacob," Captain Boyket; the "Prince William," Captain Causey; and the "Expedition," Captain Sampson. The "Expedition" got too old for the service, and was followed, in 1738, by a new "Expedition" built at Dover. One disaster only is chronicled during these years, when the "Prince William" unfortunately ran on a sand-bank at Calais and filled, breaking her mast and boltsprit—"It is a loss we must bear with patience." No mast could be found at Dover, and one had to be sent for from London. These boats carried goods and horses when passengers were lacking, nor was this infrequent. They were all sloops of sixty tons, manned by a captain and six sailors; built at Dover, they cost about £700, as appears from the account of the new "Expedition," launched in 1738. A really good passage, with a fair wind, took four hours; but not infrequently the boats were unable to make their harbour, and sailing for Calais would perforce enter Boulogne; or, returning, run for shelter to the Downs, instead of making Dover. The boats could only leave or enter the harbour at high water, or a little before or after, according to the tides, as also to the momentary state of the bar, which was ever changing; more often than not they lay outside the harbour, and the passengers embarked by means of small boats from the beach, "which is usually effected without inconvenience, as the boatmen are extremely expert and careful, and have always displayed an intrepidity upon occasions of danger worthy of all praise."*

There was no regular day or time of sailing; they went as occasion offered, and as tide and wind permitted. Still less was there any connecting service with London, and the

---

* This was written in 1807, but was no doubt equally true in 1737.

following letter, addressed to M. de Bussy, London, 7th Feb. 1741, shews what delays were met with on the road :—

> "Il est arrivé que le cheval que votre courier a eu à Canterbury n'a pu fournir la moitié du chemin, et celui du postillion ne valant pas grand' chose a causé qu'il est arrivé ici après le départ du paquet boat et un de mes vaisseaux, de sorte qui'il est parti d'ici à 7 heures dans une petite barque moyenant 2½ guinées, que j'ai prié M. Pigault [a Calais merchant] de payer."

Another courier, travelling for the French Ambassador, seems to have missed the boat through his own fault, as appears from a letter to M. de Vismes of the French Embassy, 14th Dec. 1739 :—

> "M'estant informé du sujet du retardement du courier de son Excellence le Conte de Cambis, j'apprends que ledit courier estant ici, et le paquet boat avec la malle estant pret à partir, les gens dudit paquet boat lui demandèrent une guinée pour son passage et il leur dit ne vouloir payer qu'une demie guinée, estant le prix ordinaire lors qu'ils portent la malle. Sur quoy ledit courier estant retourné à son logement pour prendre sa selle ou bagage, ledit paquet boat mis à la voile et partit avant qu'il put étre de retour, et il ne lui fut pas possible de s'embarquer, et il ne partit aucun vaisseau depuis, à cause du gros vent. Ledit courier ayant fait ses plaintes à M. Hall, agent des paquet boats, celui ci a appellé le Cap. Balderstone qui commande ledit paquet boat mais qui ce voyage est resté à terre. Il le réprimande fortement en presence du courier, et dit qu'il étoit fort faché de son retardement. Le contre-maitre du paquet boat qui a laissé le courier se nomme Henry Styles. Je suis faché de cette imprudence qui n'est pas excusable."

The communications on the French side were equally liable to delay. There were three main roads from Calais to Paris : one by Boulogne, Abbeville, and Beauvais ; one by

St. Omer and Amiens; and a third by St. Omer, Arras, and
Péronne; and the time taken was about fifty hours. On the
19th December 1740 we read :—

> "The Lord Mayor [of London] arrived here last
> night. The wind is contrary to come out of Calais and
> very thick weather. I told him I had writ to his lady
> and offered a bed at my house which he takes very
> kindly. The Lord Mayor is gone back, having heard
> by a messenger come over that the roads from Paris to
> Calais are full of water and not fit to travel. He was
> four days coming from Paris to Calais."

On the 26th the Lord Mayor again came to Dover :—

> "Having writ me to have Sampson or Causey to be
> at Calais to bring his lady over and they have been
> there several tides expecting her coming. I believe the
> Lady Mayoress will be here this evening."

The lady finally disembarked at Deal, instead of Dover,
at 4 a.m. on the 27th; not a comfortable voyage.

Illustrious passengers often took a boat to themselves,
and here the usual price was five guineas; the humbler
traveller, taking his luck with others, seems to have paid
about half a guinea. Constantly, we learn from these letters,
prospective passengers came recommended to the firm; but,
as an amusing account shews, did not always adopt the
recommendation :—

> "There arrived at the 'Ship'* Messrs. Walner,
> Gartner & Vianna. Causey [captain of one of the
> packets], who was there at their arrivall, told 'em he
> belonged to me and was to go the first opportunity.
> They gave no ear to him, but to the Master of Mr. Hall's
> boat.† They going by my kay, where I was, I asked
> them if they knew Mr. Meyer, they said yes, and telling
> 'em that my name was Minet, one said he had a letter

---

* A famous Dover inn.
† Superintendent of the Government mail packets.

for me and gave it. I then desired them to go with Causey who belonged to me and was a much bigger vessell, and it should not cost 'em more, and that it would oblige Mr. Meyer and myself ; yet nothing would do. I had told 'em that Causey was to carry seven horses, at which they made no objection, but left me unresolved, and are gone by the small vessell. I own it vexed me to find they had so little regard for me and the recommendation. I do not remember to have met persons so little civil."

There was also evidently a good deal of what one must call touting employed to influence intending passengers to take passage on the firm's boats. This appears from a letter written to the landlord of one of the Canterbury inns :—

" I am sorry to have occasion of complaining of James Walker, your coachman, who I have been told several times hath taken upon him to speak ill of Mrs. Austin's house* and hindering her all he can and also passengers from making use of my vessells, and last night Captain Westfield's† mate being at Mr. Jennings' door about speaking with some of my friends which are gone with him, the fellow took the liberty to ask him what business he had to come there, that he might go to the King's Head, and that if it was in his power he should not come there, etc., and I am well persuaded that he hath more than once endeavoured to persuade passengers not to go in my vessells. I would not put hardship upon a poor man, but I cannot suffer such usage, and I desire you'l please to prevent it."

Special difficulties beset the Channel-service in those days. War with Spain had been declared in 1738, and both in that year and again in 1740 the Government decreed an embargo, which meant that no vessel was permitted to leave any English port for foreign parts. This difficulty was to some extent met, for the packet-boats, so long as the

---

* A Dover inn.   † Captain of one of the firm's boats.

weather allowed, never entered the harbour at Dover, but
lay outside in the roads, or sheltered in the Downs, and so
appear to have conformed with the letter of the law.*

Press-gangs were also busy, a danger which was partly
guarded against by obtaining protection for the seamen
employed. Of the work of the press-gangs we have glimpses
in two letters, 31 July 1738 :—

> " Friday last came in three boats of press-gangs,
> one rowed on board Westfield [one of the Channel-
> service captains] and took two men ; the others found
> none ; when they boarded, the pier men soon got
> together. The boat with my two men rowed out of the
> harbour, but having got a constable, he brought the
> other two Lieutenants in my counting house, Mr. Gay
> Matson, deputy mayor, and Hollingbury came and
> threatening to secure them, they sent to the other
> Lieutenant and the two men were released. They said
> they had order to have no regard to protections, which
> I could not believe, but find by your letter it was so.
> On that noise all our men remained at Calais ; eleven
> of them are come back in a French boat last night, we
> make shift with old men, and Boyket went yesterday
> morning with eight horses, and Causey last night
> with Mr. Singleton. Westfield is expected with Lord
> Rockingham."

Thus it would appear that the interruption to the
Channel-service was not very serious on this occasion. On
the 7th June 1739 :—

> " The pier is in great consternation, all the men of
> the fishing boats were pressed early this morning, and

---

* A letter written to George Ouchterlony in London, whose vessel was lying
wanting a crew in Dover, may be quoted in illustration of this embargo
(7 Feb. 1740) :—

> " I observe that you have obtained a protection for the seamen who are
> to go in your ship 'Triton,' which men you would send down here if the
> ship is not detained by the embargo, which you desire to know. In answer
> the said ship is detained as well as 23 Hollanders who came in this harbour
> by contrary winds. I have writ to the Holland Embassador for an order
> to permit their sailing."

The " Triton " was bound to Rotterdam, and sailed in the middle of March.

none left but the Master and boys; when they could have got something it is very great damage to them. They all come in and cannot find men, and our vessells . are in the same condition, so that there must be protection got for them so soon as any are granted, for the men are not willing to go without protection."

The next year the question was again serious, and Isaac writes :—

"That a petition may be made to the King and Council shewing that having at a great expense established four passage vessells for the carrying over to Calais and back, by which means twenty families subsist, and said boats being navigated by old men and boys not fit for His Majesty's service, humbly pray that the said four vessells may be exempted from the embargo and have leave to go out of Dover."

By August 1740 the war had affected Dover a little more closely (28th August) :—

" Sampson [who commanded the 'Expedition '] was to have sailed next tide with several passengers, but by a boat come over express from Calais this morning I have a letter advising that about one hour after Captains Dalglish and Boyket got in, there came in a Spanish privateer rowing shallop with 60 men double armed, but that upon application made to the Commander of the Marines there was order that he should not sail till 24 hours after an English ship that was there ready to sail. I am informed that a Man-of-War is ordered to go to Calais road to convey over the Duchess of Dorset* for whom Captain Dalglish is gone to Calais. I have sent to Walmer Castle to know when said Man-of-War is to be there, for the passengers are very desirous to be gone. It is very hard we should be so insulted."

---

* A not very flattering account of the lady will be found in the *Dictionary of National Biography*, s.v. Sackville, Charles, 2nd Duke of Dorset.

By September 1st the same or another privateer was still about :—

> " Here is yet no order to protect the passage, and another Spanish Privateer come out of Dunkirk chased a market boat yesterday during three hours, so that our vessells dare not venture tho' Jones [Captain of the ' Isaac and Mary '] went out this morning. I hope he got safe over. If no ship is appointed to secure the passage I must arm and double-man two of our four vessells."

The risk seems to have continued some time longer, for on the 15th October he again writes to Messrs. J. and W. Catnach, London :—

> " Cap. Thos. Moire came and desired my advice if he might sail for Havre without fear of Spanish privateers. I did tell him that I did not think there was much danger, and that if I had a ship bound there would not think it any risk, on which he sailed out of this harbour the afternoon, and about seven at night I was told that a Spanish privateer had taken two or three vessells and that Cap. Moire was one of them, which caused me no small vexation but was very glad to hear the next morning that he was come back. I did think I was pretty cautious in giving advice, but this will make me more. It is a shame we should be insulted hereabout by such pitiful small boats and no care taken to clear the Channel of them."

A question of shipping a cargo of corn illustrates other methods of avoiding war-risks. In 1739 the firm writes to a correspondent* :—

> " Je crois qu'on pourroit trouver acheter un vaisseau de 80 a 100 tonnes à juste prix au nom de Pigault† qui pourroit le faire naviguer par des Francois sous son

---

* Many of these letters are in French, for the writer, as one would expect, had many Huguenot business relations.

† A French merchant of Calais.

nom; et on pourroit, estant à Calais [*i.e.*, the ship purchased], le charger de bleds envoyés d'icy qui seraient mis de bord à bord sans grand frais. Cela pourroit tourner à compte; le tout allant sous son nom ne seroit exposé à aucun risque d'être pris par les Espagnols. Je crois le dit Pigault brave homme et de toute confiance. Le vaisseau se pourroit payer en peu de temps par les frets qui sont à present forts. On demande à Calais 1300 l. [*circa* £54 sterling] par mois pour un dogre de 90 tonnes, 6 mois certain. Je vous marque cecy par spéculation."

Let us now turn to a few letters which will give some idea of the dangers of the harbour. In October 1738 Alexander Pigott of Winchester is written to:—

"I am sorry to advise you that Cap. F. Breton of the sloop 'Four Brothers,' from Southampton for Havre, coming into our pier by the boldness of our pilots who well know that our harbour is well nigh stopped up by the shingle occasioned by long W. and S.S.W. winds came on shore by mismanagement. I blame him for venturing in, but the pilots had persuaded him there was no risk. Tho' I call them pilots, they are not such, but common sailors or hovellers who for a premium undertake to bring ships right or wrong. However the damage was not very serious, and the ship got away again in ten days time."

The same month another disaster is recorded to F. Wynants of London:—

"The Schiper [skipper] of the 'King David' had agreed with a pilot and boat's crew to help him out, and there being a great sea, and the wind bare to sail out of the harbour, the pilot did not think fit to venture and went away, when another pilot acquainted with the Schiper told him he could get out well enough; on which he sent back for the first pilot and boat and told him he would go to sea, on which both pilots and two boats assisted, but in such a hurry that they did not take time to set the sails as should be, so that for want of way she struck on the bar and by reason of the great sea the boats and crews left her and some of the ship's men being drunk and not capable to help, and her rudder unhanged, she drove in the bay and would have been on shore and lost had not another boat ventured out and assisted her. The men of said boat set her sails, got her to sea and carried her to the Downs where they came to anchor, and did hang her rudder, and the ship proving very leaky they have this day brought her back in our harbour. The men expected £50, but having desired our Mayor and an antient pilot, and our Harbour Master, they have allowed them £20 which I have paid. I shall see the ship refitted as soon as possible."

These delays were serious, as the damage occurred on October 26th, and the "King David" did not get away until November 19th, 1739.

A similar disaster befell the "Hamilton," and is thus chronicled in a letter to H. Lascelles, London (25 December 1740) :—

" Cap. Francis Yewart in the Brigantine 'Hamilton' from Rotterdam, being in this road, designing to come in the harbour, the wind blowing very hard, and contrary to sail to the westward where he is bound, and the sea being so high that none of our boats could go out to him he sailed for the harbour : but the eddy of the sea drove the ship behind the north pier head, where she stuck fast. The night tide following, a very good cable of 12 inches that was made use of to heave her off, broke, and she drove further and higher upon the shore. It was then thought necessary to lighten her, which was done at low water, and yesterday noontide she was with good help got into the harbour, and is very tight and has very little damage."

The "Fane" was not so fortunate, as appears from a letter to Ed. Stephens of Bristol (24 January 1741) :—

"The 'Fane,' brigantine, Cap. Stephen Richman, Bristol for Rotterdam, having sprung a leak, did yesterday design to come in our harbour, and had a signal of distress out, but no boat coming to him he made for the harbour and by reason of the eddy and sea struck against the south pier head, was drove behind it and fell on her side, and the violence of the sea broke her upper deck and carried away what tobacco was between decks. I immediately sent a carpenter who scuttled her, she being bilged and not capable of being got off or repaired. By working all the night we have got most part of the goods out of her hold. I observe that you shipped 48 hogsheads of tobacco, I cannot yet tell how many came on shore, but believe some are partly dry, which I shall examine and secure the best I can, but know not what to do with what is wet. The wreck being exposed to be carried away by the sea I had it sold after publication, and was sold for £8. The anchor, sails and cable, being ashore, shall also sell if you order. The vessell I find was sufficiently ballasted, it was the great fall of sea that laid her on her side."

The tobacco and other cargo, dried we must suppose as far as might be, were reshipped on board Isaac's own sloop the "Expedition" and sailed on February 15th for Rotterdam, the freight being £41. The anchor, etc. (including the £8 brought by the hull), produced £24; and the charges for warehousing, drying, etc., came to £16 1s. 8d. "I wish for better occasion for doing you service," concludes the letter conveying this information to the owner, who was, we are glad to know, insured.

When, as in the last instance, a ship was wrecked at Dover itself, the goods were saved as far as might be ; but a wreck elsewhere was in worse case, as appears from the account forwarded to Messrs. Mello and Amsinck, London, of the wreck of the "St. John," 200 tons, of Hamburgh, which took place near Hythe on the 10th January 1738:—

> "I find that there is saved only about 9 casks beeswax and 2 bales coarse painted callicoes which contained 80 pieces each. I have had them brought here and the latter being wet and sandy I have given them to be washed and put in order. There is saved of the ship's materials the best cable and anchor, some other parts of cables, one hawser, some parts of masts and yards, the main mast being broken in half. It is a lamentable thing to see the barbarity of the people who prevented the ship's company from saving anything by shoving them away and cutting all the sails and rigging to pieces and stealing all away, insomuch that of 2 suits of sails not one piece is saved, nor of the shrouds or rigging. Although I have paid six custom officers for their service, yet I cannot get any information from them of the persons who have cut and carried away, yet I am persuaded that they must know many of them."

The Mayor of Hythe, though in a more legal fashion, participated in the plunder, for he "insists on two guineas for a consideration of his pretended right to the best cable and anchor, the ship being stranded in his Mayoralty; which, though an unjust thing, I think it is not worth disputing, it being an old custom." The Commissioners of Customs in London were appealed to to obtain a disclosure from their six officers, who had been present at the wreck, of the names of the thieves. "They must know," says Isaac in a later letter,

> "most of the offenders; but, between us, I fear that the officers will have more regard not to disoblige their neighbours than to justice. As for any hope of any information I find none is to be expected. The chief of the officers at Hythe, Mr. Thomas Clare, writes in answer to mine that although the six officers were present at the plunder and knew most of the inhabitants

about those parts, yet they knew of none that cut and carried away, and seem rather to excuse than accuse the plunderers."

A wagon-load of sails and rigging from the ship was traced into the possession of one Cherton, who sold it to Stephen Marsh of Folkestone, but no prosecution followed, seemingly for lack of any evidence that Cherton had himself stolen the property.

Another case in which actual violence was used is recorded in 1740 :—

"An Amsterdam ship of 500 or 600 tons from Cadiz ran on shore the 24th of April, with salt and brandy for Amsterdam. The Master and men came on shore here that forenoon and in the afternoon went back to her with two large boats, but found 20 English boats about her, and the English men would not suffer them to take anything out of the ship. I hear some pieces of brandy are brought ashore at Deal, Ramsgate, etc. I have sent the Schiper with Thos. Pascall to Deal to take account of what they can hear. There were 100 pipes under the salt."

But little of the 100 pipes seems to have been recovered, and the Customs were defrauded. But on another occasion they were successful :—

"Here is a ship of about 90 tons in the road, of and from Bayonne for Hamburgh, seized by Ridley [a Revenue Officer] for his having delivered half a hogshead of wine in the Folkestone road, and some broil happening by the Folkestone men getting away without paying, three of his men are kept prisoners at Folkestone; it will be a very troublesome business and hinder the voyage, if not worse."

This was in April 1740, and Isaac's fears were realized. In June he writes :—

"Le Capitaine Dulez est parti ce matin avec un vent favorable, mais foible d'hommes, il est facheux pour les trois matelots de se voir retenu prisoniers. Il m'a donné ordre en cas qu'ils soient relachés de leur payer 24 livres, qui est une guinée chacun ; mais s'ils continuent prisoniers il serait à propos de leur allouer quelque chose pour les soulager."

The men continued in jail, and Isaac did what he could for them in endeavouring to induce the owners of the ship to make them some allowance. In July he writes :—

"Les propriétaires du vaisseau le 'Sauveur' ne veulent rien payer pour les trois prisoniers ce qui est facheux pour ces pauvres misérables qui sont detenus pour avoir voulu rendre service à leur capitaine et par son ordre. Leur géollier est venu me representer qu'il n'y a rien alloué pour leur nouriture et qu'ils seraient mort de faim si il ne leur avoit assisté, ce qui est assez vraisemblable. Il me dit aussi que les prisoniers doivent être transportés à Rochester ou ils doivent être jugés. La charité demande qu'on les assiste puisqu'ils ne sont point autrement criminels."

We hear of them once again as having been taken to Maidstone on the 30th July, no doubt to the Assizes, but with what result is not reported.

The pilots were in those days an important body of men. They formed a fellowship governed by the Court of Lodemanage, one of the three courts presided over by the Lord Warden. The pilots' house, which must have been the centre of harbour life, stood where is now the Lord Warden Hotel. When the house was taken over owing to the coming of the railway in 1844, pilotage was still to some extent a necessity, and the pilots were provided for in the tower which stands over the arch under which the railway now passes down to the pier. In 1853 all pilotage became centralized under the Trinity House, and the Dover fellowship vanished, and with it the Court of Lodemanage which had governed it.

There were yearly meetings of this Court at which its business was transacted, and these the letters note on two occasions :—

"Here was a general Court of Lothmany (*sic*) yesterday, where Cap. Hammerden was chose Master of the Fellowship of the pilots of Dover, Deal, and Margate" (26 July 1738).

"The Court of Lodmanage held this day where Richard Hutson was elected Master in the room of Hamerden. Old Henry Pascall, Treasurer; old Kindness and John Earle, who were put out of their wardenship, restored, and very great rejoicing among the pilots" (29 December 1739).

Another letter of the same date mentions the fees which were paid for pilotage :—

"Here are several persons of experience who undertake to pilot ships from hence to Hambro, Bremen, etc.; as there are also several at Deal, and some of them have had £20 to 20 guineas paid them, especially in winter, and in summer about £18. As they are now most at home no need of agreeing before your ship arrives. Here is in our harbour a Dutch ship from Bordeaux for Hambro, and an English Brigantine for Bremen. The Dutch ship takes no pilot. There is at Deal Edw. Hutchens who I can recommend to you, a very good Hambro pilot."

It is evident that the business carried on by the Minet house was very large in extent, and of the most multifarious character. As local agent for the Dutch East India Company, Isaac Minet was constantly reporting to Gerard Bolwork in London on what he had done to assist the passing ships of the Company. On 28 August 1738 he writes :—

"Four Dutch East India ships are at anchor near Dungeonnest, I sent provisions to Cap. C. Kroon of the 'Adricken,' and a pilot to Cap. Cagias of the 'Knappenhof,' belonging to the Chamber of Zeeland. This morning the enclosed letter from Cap. Dirk Bosen of the 'St. Laurens' for the Directors of the Chamber of Middleburg. I have also an order from Cap. Gerit Brinkman of the 'Hofwegen' of Horn, from Batavia, to send him an ox and three sheep. The wind is now northerly and moderate. There is another Dutch East India ship arrived yesterday, so that there are now five ships."

Ships in distress were assisted and repaired, and damaged cargoes unloaded and reshipped; provisions were provided in readiness for vessels which called in on starting for some long voyage; letters, largely for America, were received and kept till some opportunity offered to put them on board some vessel for New York or Carolina, for there was much traffic in rice with the latter place. A considerable capital must have been needed for all this, as money had to be advanced both for repairs and to the captains for the expenses and wages they incurred while in port.

Owning the boats which carried on the channel-service led to what one may call a general forwarding-agency. Among the many things dealt with in this way horses came first; there was a constant stream of horses to France. On 18 June 1739 Isaac writes to Mr. Devisme, Secretary to the French Ambassador:—

"J'aprends que Mr. Butler est parti de Londres avec 38 chevaux tant Irlandois qu' Anglais qu'il doit mener en France pour sa Majesté très Chrestienne; et comme il est arrivé ici hier au soir un ordre de ne laisser sortir de ce port aucun vaisseau [*i.e.*, the embargo above referred to] je prends la liberté de vous le faire savoir pour que vous ayez la bonté de faire representer la chose au Seigneurs de la Trésorerie pour qu'un ordre soit envoyé ici pour permettre que les chevaux soient embarqués pour Calais."

There must have been great delay in obtaining the permit, for it is not until 6th July that we read :—

"Sampson [of the 'Expedition'] went out yesterday with fifteen horses, and Boyket [another Captain] is come in with passengers this morning and will carry the rest of Mr. Butler's horses."

For this purpose the two vessels came into Dover, but the writer adds :—

"I had an order for two vessels and now they will keep out as long as they can till the embargo is off."

The vessels, we are told in another place, could carry as many as twenty-four horses.

This Mr. Butler was clearly an important personage at the French Court, as having to do with the provision of horses for the royal hunt. We hear of him in this connection not long afterwards. Hughes Minet, Isaac's grandson, was in France in 1752 and writes of Louis XV :—

"I was introduced to him at the hunt at Fontainebleau by Mr. de Butler, to whom I was recommended by my uncle [William Minet of Fenchurch Street], who knew him [no doubt as having financed the buying of horses in England]. It was his province to hold the stirrup while the King mounted. The King did me the honour of speaking to me, I being handsomely dressed in green and gold, the livery of the hunt, without which no one could be there. He asked me how my grandfather at Dover dead long before [1745] did, who had sent him so many fine English horses; how I liked France, etra. He appeared affable, and his debaucheries had not ruined his countenance."

One wonders how far the King realized that only sixty-six years before the grandfather had been driven as a refugee out of France.

Amongst minor matters which were arranged for ships by the house at Dover was the payment of the light dues.

Lighthouses at this date were farmed out to private individuals, and ships arriving at Dover had to pay for the lights they had benefited by in coming up the Channel. A receipt for these dues is in my hands; on it is a charming seventeenth-century woodcut of a lighthouse; on the top of it stands a man tending an open coal fire, while a crane projecting at the side is hoisting up a basket of fuel. The receipt is a printed form, filled in in ink, and runs:—

> "Received here at *Dover* of *Charles Hughes* Master of the good ship called the '*Bosphrous*' *of London*, of the burden of *100 tons, from the Streights* bound for *this place*, the duty (*Eight shill^s & 4 pence*) due for the maintenance of one Lighthouse at Dungenness in the County of Kent.
>
> Per me *Hen. Henshaw jun.* Collector
> for the executors of the Right Hon.
> the Earl of Thanet deceased.

Received also for the lights endorsed, viz.:—

Dungenness .	.	.	.	8.	4
Portland	.	.	.	4.	2
Caskets	.	.	.	4.	2
Edystone	.	.	.	8.	4
Scilly .	.	.	.	4.	2
				1. 9.	2 "

A good instance of the work done by the firm at Dover, as also of the delay which disaster, aided by the law, could cause to a ship, is found in the story of the "Sant' Ambrogio," Captain de Limas, a Portuguese vessel from the Canaries and Lisbon. Meeting with heavy weather, she put into Dover for repairs, in order to effect which the cargo had to be landed; and the casks, being damaged, required recoopering. Seeing that we were at war with Spain, the suspicions of the local authorities caused them to arrest both vessel and cargo, the latter consisting of 57 bales of wool and 125 pipes of wine, 10 of which were found empty by damage. Isaac

Minet appealed to Christopher Gunman, the Dover collector, but in vain; so he advised the captain to go to London to see the agents there, "mais comme il n'est pas cavalier assez pour aller à cheval et qu'il ne se trouve pas de carosse ce jour" the Captain prudently waited. The intervention of the Portuguese Ambassador was invoked, but the matter was complicated by the action of one of the seamen, who gave false information as to the ownership of the cargo to the authorities. This man must have been a thorough scoundrel to judge from the following letter :—

"An Irish fellow who spoke Portuguese, whom Cap. de Limas picked up in Dover and kept on board as interpreter, is absconded and proves to be a rogue. Last night he went to Thomas Walker, the butcher who provides meat for the ship, and told him that the scrivener wanted half a guinea and desired him to send it to him and to set it in account as so much meat delivered. Walker told him he could do no such thing; the man has not been here since, and being a rogue he may have told Captain Ridley [Revenue Officer] some false stories which no doubt he will not stick to swear to. I think fit to let you know this; he is a pretty tall fellow and wears an old blew coat."

One of this man's stories was that some ingots of silver had been secretly landed and deposited in the Minet counting-house, which Isaac Minet indignantly denied.

By the 24th of October the ship was ready to sail, but the case had by that time got into the Court of Admiralty in London. Now the Cinque Ports were very jealous of their autonomy, and had their own Court of Admiralty, and the Duke of Dorset, Admiral of the Cinque Ports, was not going to allow his jurisdiction to be ousted, and sent his officers who also seized ship and cargo. The matter was now in the hands of the lawyers, and it speaks well for them that it should have been decided as early as the 5th of December that the ship might be released. The Captain came back to Dover on the 8th and arrived very much fatigued, " being come from Canterbury on horseback and not being used to ride, he had a fall from his horse and hurt his side."

The " Sant' Ambrogio " might now have sailed, but—

> " Our pilots conclude that the rivers are frozen in Holland, and it is terrible weather, and great winds, and not fit to go to sea. Two ships with rice for Amsterdam sailed hence the 13th inst., and after having been near the coast of Holland with stormy weather, were obliged to come back here, having met with much ice. The pilots say it would not be safe to carry the ship into Midlebleek, that she being a very sharp ship would run great hazard of over setting."

Finally, on the 20th of January 1741, they got out of the harbour "this noontide, but it being very dark and misty and no wind, she is come to anchor in our road." However, she must have got away, and to Amsterdam, as later letters shew. The total delay was 104 days, the costs incurred in Dover came to £420 10s. 2d. for repairs and warehousing; what may have been paid to lawyers in London and Dover we are not told. The voyage cannot have been a profitable one, but is a good example of what went on in Dover in those times.

Another curious story is that of the " Robert and Mary," which we first hear of in a letter of the 28th October 1739 :—

> " Here is by contrary wind the ' Robert and Mary,' brigantine, Cap. Robert Pomeroy, from Leghorn for Bremen with 350 chests of lemons. The Captain came to me for advice, as he hears that lemons are scarce at London, and if this easterly wind and cold weather continues he may be detained here some time and the fruit may decay, and therefore it may be well to send them to London. As you have correspondents at Bremen you may know something of the adventure, please to give the Captain advice."

By the 10th November it became evident that the Captain's anxiety about his fruit was but a cloak to conceal his unwillingness to go to Bremen.

"The 'Robert and Mary' is still here, though the Captain hath had opportunity of fair winds. I hear he leads a loose life, and that he is not inclineable to proceed to Bremen, having heard that his wife, who hath a right to the vessel, is gone there to wait his arrival. Please let this be entre nous."

The owner's agent in London agreed to the proposal to send the lemons thither, and they were accordingly transhipped and forwarded by the "John and Constant" sloop. The Captain, however, had landed 40 cases, which he claimed as his own, and sold them in Dover for £70. Of the 310 remaining only 292 could be found. With the money thus obtained the Captain went to London, leaving his ship in charge of the mate and two old seamen, whose wages he omitted to provide. On the 27th he had not reappeared, and it became known that he, had raised £100 in Leghorn on a bottomry-bond.

By the 12th January certain enquiries began to be made concerning other cargo which had been shipped, notably for six bales of Cordovan leather from Gibraltar. Two of these were found on board; it was discovered that the Captain, having put in to Portsmouth, had there sold the other four for his own account. Bills of lading for 337 pieces of eight were produced by another shipper, but these also were not forthcoming. It was evident by this time that the Captain had no intention of proceeding on his voyage to Bremen. The ship was arrested under process of the Court, it would seem by the holders of the bottomry-bond; the cargo, what was left of it, was landed and forwarded to London, the duties and charges on the two remaining bales of leather being £178 18s. 3d., and on the rest of the cargo, currants and almonds, £263 13s. 4d. On the 28th of June the ship was put up for sale, at a reserve of £100, and was bought by Isaac Minet for £115. The net proceeds, however, only amounted to £86 13s..6d., as deductions had to be made for costs, and the wages of the crew, which came as a first charge.

The French Ambassador at this date was the Count de Cambis, who seems often to have availed himself of the firm's services. On the 23rd May 1738 is a letter to him on the adventures of his courier, which goes to shew that even Ambassadors were not above smuggling :—

> "Le visiteur de notre coutume vient me prier de vous faire savoir que le sieur Coney courier d'Espagne qui arriva ici hier de Calais avait avec lui une petite caisse qu'il dit contenoit des confitures. Mais l'ayant ouvert elle se trouve contenir une coiffe et un manteau de taffeta garni de dentelles, une coiffure et manchettes de gaze, trois papiers de frange, deux colliers et deux pendants d'oreilles et une livre de tabac en poudre. Ledit visiteur dit n'avoir pu se dispenser de retenir laditte caisse, mais que sur un ordre de la part de votre Excellence elle sera envoyé à Londres."

There is, of course, the very possible explanation that the courier was bringing over this assortment of finery for his own account; if this were so one would like to hear what his master said to him when he received Isaac's letter.

On another occasion we have the same Ambassador importing horses for his own use (letter to him 29th September 1739) :—

> "J'ai recu un paquet adressé à M. des Angles Commandant à Calais que j'ai envoyé par un vaisseau parti ce matin. Je vois qu'il doit venir à Calais quelques chevaux de carosse qui ont deja été en Angleterre. Cela n'empechera pas qu'il en faille payer les droits d'entré qui est pour chaque cheval de tous pays, excepté France, 28/6, mais si ce sont des chevaux Francois ils payent £6 5s. 6d. par cheval. Si ils arrivent je ferai de mon mieux et ferai mon soumission pour les droits selon l'ordre de votre Excellence. J'ai marqué à M. Dunoquet que je suis en avance de £1 2s. 8d. pour les droits de 4

chevaux Anglais de votre Excellence; il ne m'en a pas fait raison."

It would appear from this that there was an export as well as an import duty on horses, and that the latter differentiated very heavily against France.

Isaac himself seems to have been not unwilling to assist occasionally in evading the Customs. The Earl of Ailesbury was living in Brussels, and sent over a parcel to his connection, Lady Cardigan. Concerning this we have a letter of the 29th March 1740, written to a Mr. Shuckburgh in London :—

> " The two mantelets which the Earl of Ailesbury sent for Lady Cardigan are come over, but having been informed that they are made of cloth, which is prohibited, I have been obliged to prevent their being carried to the Custom House, where they would have been stopped. I hope they will come safe to your hands next week. Pray let it remain between us that the mantelets were not carried to the Custom House."

The Earl of Ailesbury was a Jacobite nobleman who found it more convenient to live in Brussels, where he died in 1741. He had not, however, lost his taste for English delicacies, which were often forwarded to him through Dover and Ostend, collared brawns, dried neats' tongues, cakes of orange-flower, milk water, citron water, apples, cider, trees and seeds being sent at various times. On one occasion he sends some pictures home, and a letter to his agent in London gives some curious information on how the duties on works of art were appraised :—

> " I am advised by Mr. Michot of Bruges of a case with two small pictures of the Emperor. He writes the pictures cost 50 florins, which is about 4 guineas. You know, I doubt not, that all pictures, good or bad, new or old, pay, if under 2 feet square, 20/- each, if above, but under 4 feet, 40/-, and if 4 feet or bigger £3 each. Therefore please to let me know if I must send for them

and pay the duties or if you will run the risk of them, for if they cost but 50 florins, they will be dear when the duties are paid."

The pictures came over, and the duty was £2 on each.

Another letter shews a possible device for evading the duty on pictures, by which the Customs were not defrauded, though the owner of the goods might pay less than the duty. How this was possible appears from a letter to Mr. Hervart of Southampton (3rd April 1738) :—

"J'ai l'honneur de votre lettre par laquelle vous m'ordonez de payer les droits de vos trois tableaux qu'on a retenu à notre douane. Je sais fort bien quels droits ils payent, et j'aurai ce jour executé vos ordres si il ne me sembloit que vous pouriez les avoir à meilleur marché si vous trouviez à propos de les laisser où ils sont jusqu'à ils y aient esté six mois, après quoy on doit les exposer en vente au plus offrant. Je me flatte qu'alors je pourais les faire acheter pour moins de £6 de droits qu'il faut payer ; c'est pourquoy j'ai differé."

Mr. Hervart, however, declined the suggestion, preferring to pay the duties, and the pictures were forwarded to London at a total cost of £7 15s.

From Dover goods were forwarded to London by the carrier, then one Stringer, whose wagon took three days, stopping on the way at Canterbury and Rochester, and arriving at the King's Head, Southwark. A letter to one Alvaro Lopez Suaro (9th October 1738) is a good example of the use made of the carrier :—

"Captain Bandon of the 'Switzer' arrived in this road this morning. He hath left in my hands to be sent to you a bag of Barbary silver and two parcels of gold, the three bills of loading are here enclosed, and a box with two gold watches. Finding the carrier going this day for London, and it having gone free from robbers these fifty years, I did think fit to send them. You have here enclosed Stringer's receit, who is to

have 15/- for the carriage. My commission is 10/-.
I have paid Cap. Bandon £10 on his bill on you."

The absence of banking facilities must have hampered
trade much in those days. Isaac Minet's son, William, was
a merchant in London, "next the Golden Ball, Fenchurch
Street," and the course of business between them well
illustrates the gradual change by which many firms
resembling this Dover one, from being merchants became
bankers. The Dover house needed cash for advances made
to captains, as well as to pay for repairs and provisions
supplied to ships. This was obtained from London, there
being no bank in Dover, and came in the form of notes sent
down by William. The sums so advanced in Dover were
repayable by the owners of the ships, who might live anywhere. Bills were drawn on the latter by the Dover house
in favour of William, who presented them for acceptance,
and received the proceeds as and when they became due.
In this way William was repaid the advances he had made
to Dover. The profits of the Dover business thus came to
William's hands, and the accounts between the two houses
were of course adjusted from time to time.

All inland trade was carried on by this method, nor is
there any evidence of the intervention of any third party in
the form of a bill-broker or banker to discount these bills,
which were generally of short term, ten days or twenty ;
they were evidently paid from principal to principal, though
no doubt mutual indebtedness was used to cancel liabilities,
a process carried out by entries in the ledgers of the firms
concerned. Already, however, we have the beginnings of
a general banking business, as when Isaac writes to William
(1st September 1740) :—

> "Here is a bill of Mr. Gunman's on Mr. Manley
> £359 0s. 4d., of ten days date, of the 30th instant.
> I want £300 or £400 of bank bills against the arival
> of two ships from Holland."

James Gunman, Mayor in 1737, was one of a well-known
Dover family, and the transaction looks as though Isaac

161

Minet had discounted the bill, and, as its holder for value, was intending to collect it through his son in London.

These letters deal only with inland matters, but constant references to the passing of bullion between Dover and abroad more than would be necessary to adjust the balance of international trade, proves that bills arising from foreign commerce, though occasionally mentioned, were not nearly so frequent. The letter quoted just above speaks of Barbary silver and parcels of gold arriving in Dover, and constantly we have notices of bullion passing through Dover in discharge of foreign trade debts. This took many forms: guineas, louis d'or, écus, moydores, dollars, sequins; but whatever the form the metal might assume, it was never reckoned at its face-value, but always by weight, and several times we have it noted that coins were short in weight.

> " I have received a bag from Mr. J. Lasablonière [a Boulogne merchant] containing £252 6s. 6d., well told, but have sent him back five Moydors overlight which I reckon he'll send me back five others in lieu of them."

The arrival of five moydors of full weight in a fortnight's time is duly reported to London, on which account the shipment had come. Another note of the same kind gives us the value of the Moydor as £1 7s. :—

> " I have received from Calais from Mr. Dusaultoir £106 0s. 0d., but one Moydor is too light to pass, which shall be sent back to him, remains £104 13s. 0d."

The same letter shews how this bullion was sent up to London, where, it would seem, some doubts existed as to the safety of the transit:—

> " As to Stringer [the carrier] there has no misfortune happened these fifty or sixty years, and if he be careful he can secure 400 to 500 £ at all events at a time, without an iron chest, which he has not now got."

The extent of this foreign banking business, as it justly deserves to be called, was very large. To take a few instances only, occurring close together. On the 5th of January 1746 Isaac writes :—

> " I have received from Boulogne two bags, one £161, the other £61, and also from Mr. Clerq [a foreign correspondent] £422 2s. 0d., for which he orders me to send him Louis d'or of 21/-. I write him I cannot get any here and shall keep the money until further orders."

On the 15th January, again from Boulogne, three parcels of gold arrive containing £204, three bags containing £182 from Mr. Coilliot of Calais, to be exchanged for Louis d'or ; and from Mr. Clerq again £105 to be exchanged for guineas ; while reference is made to a further sum of £412 13s. recently received from abroad, with which the London house is credited. On the 22nd of January £216 11s. in gold comes from a Mr. Friocourt for the same credit. Here then, in a space of seventeen days, we find £1962 6s. in specie coming from abroad into Isaac's hands, and one may fairly say that the business only needed the addition of the idea of a running cash to become a bank.

In addition to all this shipping agency and banking business, the house carried on a considerable general trade, both on its own behalf and in conjunction with the London branch. This consisted mostly in corn, which was shipped abroad in large quantities, and in the importation from abroad of brandy, mainly it would seem in fulfilment of contracts for the supply of the British Fleet. Into the details of those transactions it would be superfluous to enter. The brandy was bought at Boulogne, Calais and Dunkirk, having come thither from Bordeaux, Cette, Nantes and la Rochelle.

Our trade with foreign countries has ever been hampered by differences in currency, measures and exchange, but in the eighteenth century the calculations due to these causes must have been even more difficult than they are to-day.

163

This can be well illustrated by a proposal for a contract for brandy to be bought at Dunkirk :—

> "Having been advised by Mr. Pigault that there were but 80 hogsheads in Calais, I made the computation that 120 butts at 130 gallons each is 15,600 gallons, which at 2/6 the gallon makes £1950. The 15,600 gallons at 3 gallons to 5 stoops makes 26,000 stoops, which at 30 sols per pott makes £1706 5s. 0d. I asked 2/7 per gallon, but said I was willing to take 2/6. I find that at 2/3 per gallon it will be £1755, and if it is to be had at 29 sols [per stoop] it will come to £1649 6s. 10d., which, considering some charges, would leave about 5 per cent. profit. At Calais or Boulogne it must pay duty out at 3 livres per hogshead [3 livres =2s. 7½d.]."

A further letter introduces us to yet other measures.

> "Mr. Coilliot writes," says Isaac Minet, " J'espère vous fournir 25 tonnes d'eau-de-vie de la Rochelle, Bordeaux, et Cette, de toute bonne qualité rendu à bord icy [Boulogne] à raison de 4s. 7d. la verge ou velte qui vous produira autour de 2 gallons. Nous avons un vaisseau venant de Cette de 100 tonnes d'eau-de-vie en gros futailles de 65 à 80 veltes préférable par leur qualité à celle de Nantes et Rochelle."

The Rotterdam velt, moreover, differed slightly from the French, 30 of the former making 32 of the latter. If we add to such a bewildering variety of measures and quotations an ever-shifting monetary exchange, we shall scarcely be surprised to read that " the brandy affair is of consequence, and demands great attention to be well managed."

The exchange with France, for most of the dealings were with that country, added not inconsiderably to the complication. French currency at that date consisted of livres, sols and deniers, which stood in the same relation to each other as do our pounds, shillings and pence, but their value was far lower. The pound sterling was generally worth somewhere

in the neighbourhood of 24 livres, but on one occasion varied
to 32 livres. Moreover, there were livres and livres, but the
only standard one was the livre Tournois, which is often
distinctly specified.

There is but little in these letters of anything but
business interests. Here and there, however, in those to his
son William a note of family matters is struck. Fifty years
had passed since Isaac had left his native land, and one
often wonders what connection these Huguenots kept up
with the relatives they must have left in the old country.
One glimpse of this we get in 1740 :—

> "Here are two women, daughters of the widow
> Minet of France, who are come to see me, a widow and
> a lusty young woman. I make them welcome, being
> the nearest relations I have in France."

Three days later he refers to them again :—

> "The two women of France will not stay long,
> I will endeavour to send them back satisfied; they
> behave modestly and well for their condition and send
> their civilities."

They left after a stay of six days, when Isaac writes
again to his son :—

> "Les deux parents de France sont partis hier par
> Causey n'y ayant autre chose à faire. Je les ai renvoyé
> fort contentes; leur visite me coute autour de 12 guineés.
> Elles sont modestes et me paroisent fort honestes and
> assez sensibles, and ne m'ont rien demandé; et, quoique
> parents de loin, ce sont les plus proches que j'ai en
> France et je benis Dieu de ce que je puis leur faire
> plaisir."

Constant little gifts of delicacies passed between the two
houses in Dover and Fenchurch Street, of which two forms
may be noted as being Dover specialities. Samphire,
a plant which grows on the cliffs round Dover, the leaves of
which were used to flavour pickles, was often sent up.

" Whitings have not been very large this season, I have
ordered a rumball to be bought when good to be had," is a
phrase which drives one to the dictionary, and here Wright
does not fail us :* " An old custom used by the fishermen
of Folkestone ; they choose eight of the largest and best
whitings out of every boat when they come from that fishery,
and sell them apart from the rest : and out of this separate
money is a feast made every Christmas eve which they call
Rumball.   Probably the word is a corruption from ' rumwold,'
and they were antiently designed as an offering for St. Rumwold, to whom a chapel, which stood between Folkestone
and Hythe, was once dedicated, but is long since demolished."
He says the word is obsolete, but it was clearly still in use
in 1740, and Isaac intended to send his son some specially
fine whitings when they were to be obtained.

The labour involved in carrying on such a business must
have been great ; one would like to know how many clerks
were employed, but Ruth Colebran is alone named of these.
Isaac himself was 77 when this series of letters begins, and
was therefore unable to do any of the travelling to neighbouring towns which was often necessary, or to go off to
ships which lay either in the Downs or off Dungeness ; we
are often told that Colebran did this.   It is during these
years that we have the first notice of one who became well
known in Dover as one of its foremost citizens, as later did
his son, John Minet Fector.   Isaac Minet's brother Thomas
had a daughter Mary, who had married one Jeremy Fector,
originally from Mulhausen, but settled in Rotterdam, where
their son Peter was born in 1723.   Sent over to Dover in
1739 at the age of 16, partly perhaps that he might learn
English, partly in the hope that his great-uncle might be
able to find some employment for him, we first hear of Peter
in a letter of February, 1740, when Isaac writes of him :—

" Le jeune Fector, qui est ici parle assez bon Anglais,
et est assez intelligent & sage et capable de servir dans

---

* *Eng. Dialect Dict.*, London, 1904 ; *s.v.* Rumbal.   The explanation he gives
is quoted from Harris's *History of Kent*.

un comptoir ; si vous lui pouvez trouver quelque place cela ferait plaisir à ses parents."

Clearly then at this date there was no intention of taking him into the Dover office, but by May of this year we find him there, probably on the advice of William, who evidently took a fatherly interest in the lad, and must have written to him, as in August Isaac writes again to his son :—

"You wrote to Peter Fector, it is very well to admonish, but as I observe he does all he can to improve and his inclination good, too much reproof is not necessary."

Peter Fector was, as his later career proved, endowed with great ability. On Isaac's death William, of London, put him in charge of the Dover business, though he was only 22, and in 1751 he married Mary Minet, his old master's granddaughter, and became a partner in the firm, which was thenceforward known as Minet and Fector. His son John Minet Fector (1754—1821) was well known, as of Kearsney Abbey. The family is now quite extinct in the male line, and survives only in the Lauries and Bayleys, who derive from the marriage of Charlotte Mary, a granddaughter of Peter Fector, with Sir E. G. Bayley.

Of general Dover matters we have but little noted. In 1739 there was question of a new organ. It does not appear for which church this was intended, but in all likelihood it would have been for St. Mary-the-Virgin. Both Isaac Minet and his son subscribed, and the former says of it :—

"The organs are to be played both by an organist and engines, and promise to be very good : to cost about £300 and about half is subscribed, I suppose parliamenting may bring the rest."

Of Dover men at this date by far the most celebrated was Philip Yorke, son of a Dover attorney, and born in Snargate Street in 1690. His success in life had been notable, and in 1737 he became Lord Chancellor under the title of Lord Hardwicke. The town was naturally anxious to mark its appreciation of such a citizen, and in 1739 comes this brief note of how this was done :—

> "Mr. Papillon got my Lord Chancellor to sit for his picture to be put up in our Court Hall."

An approaching parliamentary election, at which Mr. Revell was one of the candidates, is also referred to. He had evidently been canvassing, and Isaac Minet supported him :—

> "Mr. Revell," he writes on the 4th March 1741, "just now came to me with Mr. Matson. I made him sensible of the grumbling of some of the company which followed him at his visits, who, not finding provision when they came to the Maison Dieu, went away dissatisfied. It is true there was more people than was expected, and it was no way Mr. Revell's fault. However, as I heard that V. V. was one of them I advised Mr. Revell going to him to make apology, though I do not conceive it can hurt our cause. Things are quiet here as to parliamenteering, and I believe that Mr. Revell is very safe. My respects to him."

One little scandal is mentioned, of which we are told nothing but the fact that "Captain Ridley and Captain Hammerden boxed one another yesterday. I am told Ridley was victorious, though they were parted." Both were well known in Dover; Ridley, as Captain of a Revenue vessel, and Hammerden, as Chief of the Pilots.

Isaac himself was closely connected from early days with the civic life of Dover. In 1706 he had become a common Councillor, and in 1731 he was elected a jurat. Pressed to allow himself to become Mayor he twice refused. In 1738 he writes :—

> "Captain Dalglish was yesterday elected Mayor, cela fait plaisir à John Matson. J'ai fait en sorte de ne pas être mis en election, cela ne me convient pas."

He again refused the post at a later date, and left the honour to his grandson, Hughes, who became Mayor in 1765.

The life of the writer of these letters was a striking one. Purely French for its first twenty-six years, it became as purely English for its last fifty-nine. From such a continuous series of documents, and they number some 2500, one can gather somewhat of the business aptitudes of the writer. Thoroughness in every detail; unremitting attention—there is never once a trace of any holiday; uprightness; these seem to have been the main factors which built up his success. By 1737, the date of these letters, he was a made man, but a man who had made himself. One would wish to know something of the business side of his early life, but of this nothing has survived, and we can only reason from the known to the unknown. The qualities which kept his business at the level we find it in 1737 were the selfsame qualities which had brought him success in his first years at Dover. We have found him at this date admirably seconded in all his enterprises by his son in London, but we must not forget that, in his first struggles, he had but himself to rely on. Of Isaac in all his other relations in life this is not the place to speak; for this much material exists, material which has been put on record elsewhere.* Here I have used his letters to throw a ray of light on life in Dover 180 years ago. This slight glimpse of the story of the harbour and of its activities will perchance be of interest to those who know and love the Dover of to-day, and their number is not few.

* *The Huguenot Family of Minet*, London, 1892.

A TOUR THROUGH KENT IN 1735.

V. J. B. TORR.

INTRODUCTION.

THE following pages comprise the Kentish portion of a long tour undertaken on horseback by four Cambridge gentlemen through the greater part of England, early in the reign of George II, the record of which has fortunately been preserved (the original account having probably perished) among the valuable manuscript collections of the industrious Cambridge antiquary, the Rev. William Cole, of King's College, which are now among the Additional MSS. in the British Museum. This tour is of such varied interest in its picture of early Georgian England, that no apology need be offered for its appearance on the score of its comparatively modern date—in reality it was a long time ago and since then the great changes of the Industrial Revolution have transformed many parts of the country ; it should be remembered that the Camden Society devoted two volumes (No. 129 of series) to the publication of the English travels of Dr. Pococke, considerably later in the eighteenth century. The present tour should be read in conjunction with the well known travels of a lady, Celia Fienes, at the close of the preceding century, whose journal was printed over forty years ago under the title of *Through England on a Side-saddle*.

The travels of the four gentlemen, which we may call the " Cambridge Tour," will, it is hoped, form an interesting prelude to an earlier and more important journey through Kent of a Norwich lieutenant, exactly one hundred years before, which it is intended to print in the next volume of *Archæologia Cantiana*.

The tour of 1735, while less minute than the other in its description of notable places, is nevertheless of value for its record of collections of pictures in private houses, which

171

may in some cases have been subsequently dispersed, in part or whole ; and for its notice of industries carried on in the Midlands before the invention of steam and the extensive employment of machinery. Apart from these considerations, the human touches which enliven the narrative cannot fail to hold the modern reader—touches which Cole, to whose enormous industry in copying things of interest which came into his hands we are indebted for the narrative, dubs " mere commonplace and trite observations," an opinion with which it is difficult at this distance of time to agree.

His own preface to the tour, printed here with the rest, makes it unnecessary to treat of the persons who spent nearly three months on the road ; but the briefest indication of the route they followed through England may be acceptable. The account begins with their departure from London through Kent, as will be read hereafter, by an itinerary which is more interesting than the one followed by the lieutenant a century before. Too often, both in old days and now, travellers tend—either from considerations of safety or accommodation, or from lack of originality—to stick to the main roads only. In the present case the diversion to Tunbridge Wells and the Medway valley journey to Rochester, as well as the circuitous route from Canterbury to Dover, introduce many interesting places and observations which would have been missed had the Watling Street been followed from London.

From the point of their farewell to Kent, near Rye, the four travellers made their way through Sussex to Winchester and Dorchester, and thence by devious ways to Bristol and Bath. From Oxford they struck northwards and westwards, by Worcester, Shrewsbury and Chester to Manchester, their most northerly point. The return was made by way of the Peak District, Nottingham, Peterborough and Huntingdon, Cambridge being reached once more on October 19th, 1735.

Not a little of the interest of this long tour is derived from Cole's editorial notes which occur at intervals, though only one example will be seen in the Kentish section. These

172

paragraphs are found in quotation marks and are written in a refreshingly racy style which in its political comments is strikingly reminiscent of that of Dr. Johnson, who was, of course, Cole's contemporary. Nor are his outspoken opinions confined to politics : it will be seen from his preface to the journal that his opinion of its compiler, Whaley, was of the most unflattering description, and every now and then he rubs this in in his remarks. Thus at Stanmer in Sussex, Whaley having praised their host, a Mr. Pelham, Cole remarks : " No doubt M^r. Pelham was a Wig, & treated him with French Claret & Venaison," and attributes his omission of any account of his host's house or of the portrait of his beautiful Persian wife, who it seems was already deceased, to the fact that " his Gutts & his Brains were so full of Venison & Whiggism, that he had no Room for any Thing besides." In other places he reminds us that Whaley was an " abandoned Character " and a " Rascal." Cole's definite views were expressed, under Woodstock, to the derogation of Marlborough, and, at Belvoir Castle, he speaks of the Marquis of Granby, son of his contemporary at Eton and Trinity College, Cambridge, as having been a favourite of his, till " he spoke on the popular Side, in Favour of the factious & rebellious Americans," in May, 1775. Under Shrewsbury, it is interesting to meet a reference to Johnson himself, who said to one of two Cambridge dons conversing with him in London : " Sir ! You are a Young Man, but I have seen a great Deal of the World, & take it upon my Word & Experience, that where you see a Whig, you see a Rascal." It was feared that such bluntness might make an awkward situation, " but they laughed it off, & were very good Company." Cole does not lose the opportunity of adding : " I have lived all my Life among this Faction, & am in general much disposed to subscribe to the Doctor's Opinion, with some Softening " ; and that whatever may have been the merits of the Shrewsbury Whigs, they had at least one rascal in their company while Whaley was in that town. Cole's views were undeniably narrow in more than one respect, but it should not be forgotten that as an antiquary

173

he has left us much that is of value, and that, as before remarked, his industry was very great. He bequeathed his collections to the British Museum, fearing that if they were made over to the care of the King's College authorities, then wholly obsessed with classical studies, they might as well be thrown into a horsepond! Doubtless his own prejudices again played a part, but at least it is certain that his collections would have been less carefully preserved in Cambridge then than would be the case to-day, and the greater accessibility of the British Museum to students has probably justified his actions.

The orthography of the MS. of the tour seems to have been carefully copied by Cole, and has accordingly been equally adhered to in this transcript, with the single omission of the copious underlining which is employed, without special or consistent purpose, and which is a hindrance to the eye in reading. The MS. is paginated in Cole's hand and foliated in pencil by the Museum authorities, page 244 corresponding to folio 122b and so on : but as references occur in places of the tour to numbers of pages, it has seemed better to keep to the original arrangement.

I have included at the end an extract of the travellers' accounts while they were in Kent, as being certainly of that interest two centuries later which Cole, writing subsequently, felt posterity might find in them. These accounts form the conclusion of the tour and have no separate total for Kentish expenses : this is accordingly supplied in brackets.

ADD. MS. 5842, p. 244.

A TOUR THRO' ENGLAND IN THE YEAR 1735.

" THE following Journal was lent to me in 1775, by M^r.
" Alderman Bentham of Cambridge, who married the only
" Sister & Heir of M^r. Riste, one of the Party in the Expedition.
" It is all written in M^r. Whaley's Hand, who was the Writer of it,
" & went as Tutor & Companion to John Dodd of Swallowfield
" in Barkshire Esqr. then a Fellow-Comõner of King's College
" in Cambridge, where M^r. Whaley was then Fellow. M^r. Riste
" went as Companion & Governor to Francis Shepheard Esqr.

" Son to Francis Shepheard of Exning in Suffolk Esqr. & then a
" Fellow-Comoner of Clare-Hall, who died soon after his Return.
" Altho' a great Part of the Journal seems to be mere comon-Place
" & trite Observations, I shall nevertheless transcribe the Whole,
" as I find it : & only add, that of all the Men I ever was acquainted
" with, the Writer of this Journal was the most abandoned &
" worthless, & the most unfit to be trusted with the Education
" of a young Gentleman, whose Morals he was sure to corrupt :
" as a Scholar, I suppose, he was no ways deficient. M^r. Dodd had
" too much good natural Sense to be injured by such a Tutor,
" whose Behaviour was too gross & indecent to be suffered in his
" Family, after he was married ; & was accordingly soon after
" disgracefully sent away. M^r. Shepheard was only a natural
" Child, & of no very promising Parts, but of decent Address &
" Carriage : his Death added greatly to the enormous Fortune of
" his natural Cousin, Miss Frances Shepheard, natural Daughter
" to Samuel Shepheard of Botesham in Cambridgeshire Esqr.
" now Lady Viscountess Irwin ; a Lady of uncomon Accomplish-
" ments both by Nature & Education."

Monday July 28. 1735.

J.D.—F.S.—G.R.—J.W. set out from London, came through
Lambeth, Camberwell & Peckham to Lewisham four Miles from
thence to Dinner at Bromley, where there was a Cock-Match,
10 Miles from thence, thro' Farnbury, over Madam's Court Hill[1]
(from which is a most delightfull bounded Prospect) to Sevenoak.

Lambeth. Here we saw the Palace of the Æ^p. in which is a
stately Hall, a very pretty Library, & Pictures of most of the Æ^{ps}.
particularly one very fine one of Juxon, Successor to Laud,
taken after he was dead. Now, contrary to the Rules of the
Church, we hastned from Lambeth.

Bromley. Here is a Palace of the B^p. of Rochester, on whom
King Edgar conferred the Manor A : D : 700. Here also is an
Hospital for 20 poor Widows, who have an Allowance of 20<del>l</del>

---

[1] A corruption of Morants Court, in Chevening. This is the fine hill
where the North Downs bend northward at the break of the Darent
Valley. The old main road from London to Sevenoaks, still a by-road,
went through Pratts Bottom and Knockholt Pound. I am indebted to
the local knowledge of my friend, Capt. H. W. Knocker, for the information that the present high road, E. of Halsted, is not a by-road converted,
but an early nineteenth century work, to avoid the steeper gradient for
coach traffic.

each p A͞n. & a Chaplain, who has 50₤ p A͞n, being the Donation of the Founder, D^r. John Warner, B^p. of Rochester. Market on Saturday.

Lewisham, a Place famous for several great Meetings, viz : of the Emperor of Constantinople, by K. Henry 4. in 1413 ; of Anne of Cleves by Henry [8.] in 1539 ; of Henry 5. when he came out of France 1410 : Of the Emperor Sigismond 1416 : & K. Edward 4. 1474, by the Mayor, Aldermen & Citizens of London in their Robes ; of the Admirals of France & B^p. of Paris, by the Lord Admiral of England, & 500 Gentlemen ; & of Cardinal Campejus[1] (who came from Rome to hear a Cause of Divorce of Harry 8. from Q. Ann " sic ") by the Duke of Norfolk, & many Prelates & Gentlemen. Here are 2 Free-Schools, one for Latin, another for English, founded by M^r. Abraham Colf, formerly Mayor of this Place, of which the Company of Leather Sellers, London, are Governors.

July 29. Sevenoak,[2] is a clean, small Town, with a very pretty Free-School & Alms-House [p. 245] in it : from hence we went to Knowle 1 Mile ; to Tunbridge Town 6 Miles, & from thence to Tunbridge Wells 5 Miles. Near Sevenoak on the left Hand, in a Vale, is a pretty Brick House of David Pollhil's Esqr. at Chipstead, on the right, a good House, on a Hill, of Sir Henry Fermour's.

Knowle in Kent is the Seat of his Grace Lionel Cranfield Sackville, Duke of Dorset & Earl of Middlesex, at present Lord Lieutenant of Ireland. Next to Audley End House, it is the largest & most regular old Stone Building I have yet seen in England ; & in it, one compleat magnificent Apartment, fitted up in the modern Taste, of a Salon, a long Gallery, & a State Bed Room. In the Salon is a very fine Picture of Sir Edward Sackville, by Vandyke, who was afterwards made Earl of Dorset, but made much greater to Posterity, by his famous Duel with the Lord Bruce, whom, after a long doubtfull Struggle, he kill'd near Antwerp. In the same Room is a very good Picture of that great

[1] See the paper on Campeggio's progress through Kent at an earlier date than the divorce, in the present vol. of *Arch. Cant.*

[2] The final " s " is of comparatively modern introduction, like the " o " of Meopham and the " p " of Lympne. Note also the uniform spelling in this MS. of Tunbridge Town equally with the Wells, the contrary being again a modern distinction. Evelyn in his Diary writes Bromley also with a " u " ; the traditional pronunciation of this place seems failing nowadays, but " Teeson " (*infra*) holds its own.

Wit, & Poet, Charles Earl of Dorset, by Kneller : & another
exceeding good Peice by Wooton, representing Dover Town &
Cliff, with the Entry of the present Duke thither, to take his Oath
of Office, as Lord Warden of the Cinque Ports. In the Gallery
are copies, tho' I think, very indifferent ones, of the Cartons at
Hampton Court. A good Picture of Robert Dudley Earl of
Leicester : one of Howard, Earl of Surrey, who was beheaded in
Harry 8. Time : & one of K. James, 1. in which the Painter seems
to have taken peculiar Care to express that Mixture of Meanness
& Pedantry, of which his Soul was composed. The Park of Knowle
is exceeding fine, about 9 Miles round, cut into beautifull Ridings,
& affording, in many Places, most delightfull Prospects.

Tunbridge, or the Town of Bridges ; so called, because here
the River Medway branches itself into 5 little Streams, over each
of which is a Bridge of Stone. Here is a Free School erected by
Sir Andrew Judd of London, & a Causey in the Road to London
by M^r. John Wilfred. Five Miles South of Tunbridge are the Wells,
of which I will only say, that if by the Waters here Health may be
restored, by the Diversions Time may be perfectly lost.

July 30, in the Afternoon we left Tunbridge Wells to those,
who had less Health, or more Money than ourselves ; pitying the
first, & despising the latter. We returned to Tunbridge, from
thence went thro' 2 small Villages, Hadlow & East-Peckham, to
Mereworth, 7 Miles from Tunbridge Town. Within half a Mile of
Mereworth, on the right Hand, as wee rode along, wee saw an old
House[1] belonging to Sir W^m. Twisden, & on the left, a genteel new
House of M^r. Masters of Yote-Place, who has a Family Vault in
the Church Yard of Mereworth.

At 8 in the Evening we came in Sight of Mereworth Castle,
the Seat of Fane Lord Catherlough : as we could not see that,
& reach Maidston the same Night, rather than miss the Sight, we
resolved to hazard our Ease, for our Improvement ; & took up
with a very indifferent Inn, or rather Ale-House, within Sight of
my Lord's House. Here we seemed in the State of the rich Man,
who rolling in Hell, had a Prospect of Heaven, without being able
to enter it ; & the Bason before his Lordship's House, seemed the
great Gulf that was fixed between them. Not that our Case was
exactly parellel either of Dives, or Lazarus : for we had Victuals
& Drink enough ; but, contrary to the Proverb of Rest, but no

---

[1] Roydon Hall, the famous seat of the Twisdens, in East Peckham.

Abiding, wee here had Abiding, but no Rest. After a hearty Breakfast at the Publick House, we proceeded to the Nobleman's to feed our Eyes ; & here indeed they were well content to be kept open, where they met with a perfect Novelty ; an Italian House in England ; a British Gentleman's Dwelling, fitted to keep off Heat from the People under the Line. Notwithstanding the Variance of the House with the Climate, it is a sweet Place, situated in the Middle of a Mote : in the North Front a large Bason ; in the South a large Canal, the View terminated by a Theater of Hills & Wood ; on the West Front a View into the Country ; on the East, a very large Bowling Green ; North of that a large Kitchin Garden ; South, a fine Wood, cut into Walks, & a Cherry Orchard, & descending Terras all within the Gardens. In the North Front of the House are very good Stables, & opposite to them the Church, in which is the burying Place of the Earls of Westmerland ; a large Monument of the Baroness Despencer & Burwash, Da͞ur to the Lord Abergavenny, & Wife of Sir Tho : Fane of Badsell in Kent ; a Monument also of Sir Tho : Nevell, Councellor to K. Henry 8. who died 1514.[1] For a full Description [p. 246] of this House, See the Architecture of Colin Campbell Esq[r]. who designed it.

July 31. Our Alehouse at Mereworth we freely left, & proceeded for Maidston 7 Miles from thence. In our Way thither, we passed thro' a small, but very pleasant Village, called Wattlebury,[2] where is a tolerable good built House belonging to Sir Tho : Styles. At another Village, called Teeson, is a pretty House of Sir Philip Butler's. About 12, we got to Maidstone, where we dined. No Curiosities we saw here. It was Assize Time. This Town is a Corporation of a Mayor & 12 Jurats, sends 2 Members ; the present John Finch Esq[r]. & Horsenden Turner. One of its Members of last Parliament was John Hope, a Butcher, who, at his Election gave the Butchers who voted for him, Silver Handles to their Steels. Its Trade Hops, & Thread.

From Maidstone we came the same Evening, thro' Sandling, over Aylesford or Boxley Hills, to Rochester, 8 Miles. From Aylesford Hill is a most delightfull & extensive View of a flat, woody Country, & the River Medway. We rode between Hop

---

[1] An error for 1542. The monument in question is a brass, fortunately preserved from the earlier church at Mereworth. See Griffin and Stephenson, p. 142.

[2] Wateringbury.

Grounds & Cherry Orchards most Part of the Way from Tunbridge to Rochester, & came to the Crown Inn there in the Evening July 31.

Rochester, situated on the Banks of the Medway, over which is a very fine Stone Bridge of 11 large Arches, is still called a City, & its Church a Cathedral ; but it has Nothing but its Charter to prove the first, & its Chapter the latter. Its See was founded by Ethelbert, King of Kent A : D : 604, contains a small Part of Kent, 18[1] Parishes. The Castle is said to have been built by W^m. the Conqueror, & was formerly in the Constableship of the Arch B^p. of Canterbury. It has sent Burgesses to Parliament ever since the 26 Edw:4. is at present governed by a Mayor, 12 Aldermen, a Recorder, 12 Com̃on-Councill Men, a Town Clark, & 3 Serjeants at Mace. It's present Members are Admiral Haddock, & David Polhill Esq^{rs}. The Cathedral is very old & mean. In a Chapel dedicated to S^t. W^m. on the North Side of the Choir, are 3 Monuments ; one of John Warner, B^p. of Rochester ; one of John Lee Warner, Archdeacon of Rochester ; one of Lee Warner Esqr. his Son : as also one erected by Merton College 1598, in Honor of their Founder, Walter de Merton, Chancellor of England, & B^p. of Rochester, who died 1277. It was destroyed almost in the Rebellion, & restored by the College 1662. Here is a good handsome Town Hall : in it are the Pictures of K.W. & Q.M.[2] of Sir Jos : Williamson, Plenipotentiary at the Peace of Ryswyck ; Sir Tho : Colby ; Sir John Jennings ; Sir Cloudesley Shovel ; Sir Stafford Fairborn ; Sir Tho : Palmer, & Sir John Lake, all Members for the City. There is also a very good Picture of an old Man, whose Name was Richard Watts, & who was Town Clark of Rochester. Being at one Time apprehensive of Death, he sent for a Proctor to make his Will, who contrived it so, as to have all devised to himself : but Watts recovering, detected the Cheat, & at his Death, built an Hospital for the Poor of the Parish, & in it ordered Lodging every Night for 6 poor travelling Men, not contagiously diseased, Rogues, nor Proctors, & to have 4^d. every Morning. Here is also a Free School founded by Sir Jos : Williamson for Mathematicks.

Chatham, anciently the Seat of the illustrious Family of the Crevequers, but forfeited to the Crown by Hamon de Crevecœur,

[1] This astonishing under-estimate will fit neither the diocese nor rural deanery of Rochester, as they were then ; even " 81 " would be too little.
[2] King William III and Queen Mary II.

joyning in Rebellion with Simon de Montfort Earl of Leicester against Henry 3. The Dock for the Navy Royal was first settled here by Q. Elizabeth ; to which her Successors have made such Improvements, that it is now reckoned the most compleat Arsenal in the World. Wee here saw the Royal Sovereign, a first Rate, which can carry 110 Guns, & 1050 Men. It is by the Keel 150 Feet long, & from the Taffrill to the Outside of the Lion is 214 Feet in Length. It is 52 Feet broad, 63 Feet high, & draws 24 Feet Water. We saw the Union, a 2ᵈ. Rate, 90 Guns, 900 Men. The Nassau, a 3ᵈ. Rate, 70 Guns, 450 Men. The Cambridge, a 3ᵈ. Rate, 80 Guns. The Greenwich, a 4ᵗʰ. Rate, 50 Guns. We staid all the first Day of August at Rochester.

Aug: 2. We left Rochester, came thro' Chatham, over Chatham Hill, & had a fine [p. 247] Prospect of the River for 4 Miles. We came thro' a Village, called Raynham, the burial Place of the Tufton's, Earls of Thanet, & another, called Newington, a Roman Station, to Sittingborn, 11 Miles, where we dined ; & then came thro' a very pleasant Country, & over Bocton Hills, from whence we had a beautifull Prospect of the River & Sea, by Sheerness, to the City of Canterbury, 26 Miles from Rochester.

Aug : 3. We came to the King's Head in Canterbury, where the Cook of the Inn did us the Honour to take us for Mountabanks, George Riste being the Doctor. The old Durovernum, Canterbury, is a City of great Antiquity, & said to have been built 903 Years before Christ. It's a Town & County of itself, by Charter, 26. Hen : 3. consisting of a Mayor, Recorder, 12 Aldermen, a Sherif, 24 Com̃on Council Men, a Sword Bearer, & 4 Serjeants at Mace. It has 14 Churches, besides the Cathedral. The Cathedral is the most magnificent one I have seen, & very particular, in being composed of a Mixture of Roman & Gothic Building. The Choir is extremely neatly wainscoted. Behind it are the Tombs of Henry 4ᵗʰ. & his Queen, & Edward the Black Prince, & a great many more than can be mentioned in a Journal ; but one that cannot be passed by, which is Nicholas Wotton, first Dean of this Church, so constituted by Hen : 8. 1541. He is represented kneeling on a Tomb, praying at an Altar : the Figure is white Marble, extremely well executed, but the Head, which is said to have been done in Rome, is masterly beyond Expression ; & all the Pillars, Festoons, & other Decorations of the Altar & Tomb, are in a very charming Taste.

180

Aug : 3. Sunday, we spent at Church, & in walking about Canterbury. On Monday Aug : 4. we took a Coach & 4, & went with a very honest Clergyman[1] to his little Vicarage House in the Isle of Thanet, where we went into the Dove House, killed a Dozen Pigeons, pluckt them, spitted 'em, roasted 'em & eat them ourselves : nor did the Vicar's Wife save her Bacon : for we found a fine Ham, out of the Middle of which we cut several Slices & broiled 'em ; took a Cup of good brown Ale, & a Glass of good Florence : & thus we dined with less Grandeur, but more Freedom than a Duke.

From the Vicarage of Monkton we went to Queax, a good old Seat of M[r]. Wyatt ; a Quarter of a Mile from which, in a Walk, is an Arbour in a Tree, from which is a most delightfull View of the Sea, & the Island of Shepey. On a Hill, 2 Miles from hence, near Minster Windmill, is the most extensive Prospect of Land & Sea I ever saw. On the South is a Prospect of Sandwich, Deal, & the Downes : East[2] we see Margate, Shepey, & the Coast of Essex : over the Downes we could see the Chalk Cliffs of Calais.

" By the By, there are no Chalk Cliff[s] at Calais, which is a " flat, sandy Shore : the Cliffs of Boulogne are high & chalky. " The Altar before which Dean Wotton kneels is a Desk, or Prie- " Dieu : an Altar is a flat Table : this is a declined Desk with a " Book on it. What he says of Rochester has many Mistakes " in it, as also in other Places, which is too troublesome to " particularize. W[m]. Cole. June 23. 1775. Milton near Cam- " bridge."

Aug : 5. We went to the Races on Barham Downes, about 4 Miles from Canterbury, and lost some Hours in staring at some Hundreds of People, as idle, & foolishly employed as ourselves. In the Evening we went to the Assembly, where indeed we did not like the Room so well as the Company, which was very good : Lord Winchelsea, Sir Edward Dering, Lord Romney, Sir James Grey, Sir Tho: D'Aeth, Sir W[m]. Knatchbull, cum multis aliis. There are many French & Walloon Families in Canterbury, whose Manufacture is Silk, about 500 Looms being employed in it there.

Aug : 6. We left Canterbury, & came, thro' a Village called Littlebourn, to Wingham, in which Parish is Dean-House, the Seat of Sir George Oxendon : a good old House, & in it many

---

[1] Peter Vallavine, LL.B., Vicar of Monkton, 1729-67 (*ob.*) (Hasted, fol. ed. IV, 314).

[2] An error for " North."

good Pictures, particular-[p. 248]ly a very fine one of Christ
disputing with the Doctors, in Water Colours : & another in Oyl,
of the Roman Slave pulling a Thorn out of his Foot.   From hence
we went (in View of a good old House of Sir Tho : D'Aeth's, at
Knolton) to Waldeshare, the Seat of the Furnesse's ; a very good
House, very well furnished.   In the Hall is a capital Picture of
Liberality & Modesty, by Guido.   Had we seen nothing but this
one Picture in our Journey, our Labour had been overpaid.   There
is a fine Gallery next the Garden, very well furnished with
Pictures, with which, according to the laudable Custome of
England, the Housekeeper was quite unacquainted.   But the
Top, I think, of them, was, a Representation of the Pictures in
the Duke of Tuscany's Gallery, by David Teniers, 1651 : among
which is Esther & Ahasuerus by Paulo Veronese ; S^t. Catharine,
by Raphael ; a dead Christ, by Caracci ; 2 Women's Heads, by
Palma, vecchio ; Mary & Elizabeth, by Ditto, Woman caught in
Adultery, by Titian.   Here is a fine Park, & large Gardens.   At
the Top of the Park, is a very fine Belvidere, with a wide Prospect
both of Land & Sea.   It is a square, white Building ; its Height
80 Feet, but unfinished.   We came this Evening to the King's
Head in Dover.

Aug : 7. we passed in Dover, Dubris Portus, a very ancient
Town, & one of the Cinque Ports : it is situate on the Sea Shore,
& has a fine Harbour, in the Form of a Crescent, round which the
Town is built, under 2 very high Hills ; on the North of which is
a very eminent Castle, said to be built by Jul : Cæsar,[1] for an
Account of which D^r. Stukeley is to answer rather than me.   The
Duke of Dorset, Lord Warden of the Cinque Ports, is Constable
of it.   We there saw a Brass Canon, which was presented to
Qu : Elizabeth by the States General, which is 24 Feet, 2 Inches
long, & will carry 24 Pounds of Powder.   The Date of its Make,
Utrecht, 1544.   There is a Well in it 350 [*feet*] deep.   On the
South Side of Dover, about half a Mile distant from the Town,
is the famous Cliff, a Description of which, those who have not
seen it, but read Shakespeare's Description of it, do not want,
& those who have not read it, don't deserve.   It is a Town
corporate, & sends Members to Parliament, elected by the

---

[1] This singularly uncritical idea is the same tradition as reported
by the lieutenant a century before, and probably refers to the townsmen's
belief of the age of the actual buildings, rather than of Cæsar having been
their first founder.

Freemen. Its present Members are . . .[1] Revel, & David Papillon, Esq^rs. It had formerly 7 Churches, has now but 2, S^t. Mary's, & S^t. James's. From all Parts of it, we had a fair View of the Cliffs of Calais, & the Coast of France, but had rather have seen Dover from them.

Aug : 8. We went from Dover to Deal, thro' a Village called Ringwold, & another called Warmer, in which Parish, by the Sea Side, within a Mile of Deal, is a Castle built by Henry 8. very pleasantly situated on the Sea Shore, but, I believe, of little Use at present to any one but Lord Middlesex, who is Governor of it. There is another Castle at Deal, & another about a Mile North of it, called Sand Down, built by Henry 8. Deal is a large Town, but has nothing worth seeing about it, but its Sea, which is called the Downes, & is a Road much frequented by Merchant-Men, & Ships of War. We returned to Dover this Night, & about 2 Miles from Deal had a Prospect of Sandwich, about 4 Miles from Deal, which is another of the Cinque Ports, a Corporation, & sends Members to Parliament. Its present Members are, Sir George Oxenden, & Josiah Burchett, Esqr. Between Warmer & Deal, D^r. Stukeley thinks, is the Spot where Cæsar landed in his first Expedition.

Aug : 9. We left Dover, & came along the Sea Side to Folkstone, 7 Miles, a Market Town, & Corporation, probably the Lapis Tituli of the Romans, but the worst that ever was seen. From hence we went along the Beach, passed Sandgate Castle, built by Henry, 8. to Hithe, which is another small Corporation, the Portus Lemanus of the Romans, as also a Cinque Port : its present Members, Hercules Baker, & George Glanville, Esq^rs. 11 Miles from Dover. From hence we went thro' a Village, called Dinchurch, to New-Romney, another Corporation, & Cinque Port. Its present Members, Stephen Bisse, & David Papillon Esq^rs. It has a very large, neat Church, & an handsome Altar Peice & Organ, given by Sir Henry & Rob : Furnese. From hence we came thro' Lydd over the Sands, & cross Rye Harbour, when the Tide [p. 249] was ebbing. To Rye 33 Miles from Dover we had Dungeness Point in View from Romney to Rye.

(p. 269)

" At the End of the Book is an Account of the Expences for " the Journey, which for 4 Gentlemen, & probably 2 Servants,

---

[1] Thomas Revel, M.P. for Dover, 1734-54 (Hasted, fol. ed. IV, 95).

" at least one, with their Horses, at about 10ˢ. for each Person a
" Day, with Money given to see Places, seems to be very reason-
" able, & would not be so easy at this Time.   Whaley, who loved
" good Eating & Drinking more than any Person I remember,
" must also have inflamed the Bills considerably on his Account.
" It may be a Curiosity some Time hence, & therefore I will
" transcribe it.   It is all written in Mʳ. Riste's Hand, who was,
" probably Purse Bearer on the Journey, & paid the Bills, as he
" was an Œconomist, & a good Accountant, & being one of the
" most exact Men, made the Company sign the Accounts twice ;
" once at Judge Denton's at Hillersden, who was Mʳ. Dodd's
" Guardian, & afterwards when they came Home."

July 26. Paid for 3 Books, & a Map, for the Journey	0. 7. 6.
Paid a Coach, with the Portmanteaus to Mʳ Shep-	
heard's	0. 2. 6.
July 28. Paid the Expence of the first Day	2. 5. 9.
29. at Sevenoake & Duke of Dorset's	2. 3.10.
30. at Tunbridge Wells	4. 0. 4.
31. at Lord Catherlough's, Inn, &c.	3. 1. 3.
	12. 1. 2.

(p. 270)

	12. 1. 2.
August 1. & 2. Paid at Rochester	4. 6.10.
The same Day, being wet, at Sittingbourn, to Canter-	
bury	0.13. 4.
Aug : 3. 4. 5. & 6ᵗʰ. at Canterbury	10. 5.11.
Aug : 7. 8. & 9. at Deal, Dover & Romney	7.16.10.
	[35. 4. 1.]

[This account was settled and signed by all four gentlemen
twice, first at Hillersden near Buckingham, Sept. 17 or 18—the
account differs from the journal, whose " 18 " is probably correct
—and secondly at Cambridge, Oct. 20, 1735.]

A TOUR INTO KENT, 1759

Edited by F. Hull, B.A., Ph.D.

THE examination of accumulations of family papers not infrequently discloses journals and diaries of tours or visits to distant parts. Though these accounts may have little literary or historical merit, they serve often enough to introduce the personality of the writer or to bring once more into perspective the outlook of a particular age.

Of such a character is the little journal printed below: it adds little to our historical or topographical knowledge; its author was no Pepys or Boswell; nevertheless, through its pages we glimpse again the Kent of the expansive eighteenth century. Although it was written during the Seven Years War the writer and his friends could freely visit the dockyards at Chatham or the gun emplacements at Margate, and indeed, but for a passing reference to the French prisoners of war at Sissinghurst, nothing would give us cause to know that this is the year of Minden, Quiberon Bay, and the capture of Quebec.

The family of Mount, prosperous stationers of London, like many of their mid-eighteenth century business contemporaries, sought 'a suitable country residence and purchased Wasing Place near Aldermaston in Berkshire in the year 1760. It is from the archives formerly stored there that this diary comes. The collection was deposited in the Berkshire Record Office at Reading by the owner, Sir William Mount, Bt., in 1949, and it is through his courtesy and the co-operation of the County Archivist that the diary can now be reproduced for Kentish readers.[1]

While the journey which Mr. and Mrs. Mount and their party undertook was mainly one of pleasure, the fact that Mr. Mount owned copperas works at Whitstable was clearly an incentive for a visit to Kent. Their itinerary was simple: from London they followed the Dover road to Gravesend, Rochester, Faversham and Canterbury. A detour to Whitstable was followed by the journey from Canterbury to Margate and so to Ramsgate. There the party divided, one group going by sea and the other by land to Deal, and thence, united again, to Dover. On the return Canterbury was again visited and Ospringe also, but then the party headed for Maidstone and Tunbridge Wells, returning to London by Sevenoaks. The whole journey occupied nine days.

There is little need for editorial comment, but where it seemed

[1] Berks. R.O., D/EMt F5.

185

necessary notes have been added to the text. The occasionally odd or archaic wording, the vision of the " undeveloped " Margate and Ramsgate, with the figure of Beau Nash in the background, the suggestion of being " humbug'd " by Thomas à Becket's tomb, the roguery of landlords, the importance of the gentry and the largess of the nobility, all display the character of the age from which this whimsical account survives. Of the actual keeper of the diary nothing is known. He maintains a strict anonymity and the original is merely endorsed " For Mr. Mount." The most likely member of the party appears to be Mr. Hunt, for it is improbable that Goodwin would refer to his indispositions in quite the manner recorded, nor from a remark about feminine ingenuity is it likely that any of the ladies was responsible.

In preparing the text capitals, spelling, punctuation and the use of abbreviations with apostrophes have been retained as in the original, on the grounds that by 1759 these things were largely a matter of personal idiosyncrasy and may therefore reflect in some measure the character of the author. Standard abbreviations and abbreviations by superscript letter have been extended or transmuted to their modern form.

1759 May 14

This morning Mr. and Mrs. Mount, Mrs. and Miss Hunt, and Messrs. Hunt and Goodwin set out for a Tour into Kent from Warrington's in the Borough at 7 o'clock, Mrs. Hunt claiming the Arrival there first; Breakfasted at the Red Lyon on Shooters hill being 7 miles. Enjoyed the prospect for about an hour and then proceeded to Gravesend. A fine prospect to the Left allmost All the way of the Thames and Medway.[1] Din'd at the Falcon at Gravesend by the water side being about 13 Miles. No Conveniency for horses there. Procured a Turbot from a Dutch Vessell lying at Anchor with other Ships. Had a fine View opposit to the [——] of Tilbury Fort.[2] Before Dinner All the party but Mr. Mount walkt up to the Windmill on a high hill near the Town, where wee had a glorious View. Merry there, and procured tolerable Appetites for Dinner. Proceeded to the Bull at Rochester, 18 Miles, and before Supper walkt in the City, and had a Sight of Mr. Gordon's house.[3] More struck with the outside than with the Appartments. One might here make a moral Reflection. Fine gold, Silver and other fish there, good Tulips, at a non plus about the Aeolian Harp. Lay at Rochester. In this City is the following remarkable Inscription on the front of a very neat and handsome Inn.

------

[1] This surely is a mistake, no view of the Medway would be possible in this part of the journey and in any case not on the left-hand side.
[2] A word, possibly " walls," is missing in the original.
[3] The Gordon family resided at Boley House, see *Arch. Cant.* XVIII, p. 200.

Rochester
Richard Watts Esq. first devised 1569
This Releif for Travellers
Six poor travelling Men not contagiously
diseased, Rogues nor proctors, May have
Lodging here one night freely, and every
one fourpence in the morning

The Mayor and Citizens of this City, Dean and Chapter of the Cathedral Church and Wardens and Commonalty of the Bridge are to see this executed for ever.

Tuesday 15

After Breakfast went to Chatham about two Miles, Saw the Dock and yards. A Review there of a Number of Soldiers made a good Appearance as wee past. Was on Board the Valliant a Man of warr then building, Had many things explained to Us in the Yards by Mr. Hughes, known to Mr. Mount, and wee had the pleasure of being present in the Smith's Shop at the Instant the severall workmen were turning an Anchor of a Man of warr of 4 ton weight then in the fire; All our Attentions were engrossed, as it was a Surprizing thing, and wee were fill'd with horror at the glowing heat of the severall furnaces, and at the Appearances of the Workmen, who with great Dexterity managed the affair; Anchors are made by hammering piece upon piece. Refreshed ourselves at the Rose at Sittingborn. The Assembly is kept here, a good Room and Conveniency for the Musick.[1] Din'd at the Red Lyon at Ospring which is 18 miles. One Mr. March of Faversham joined Us, being an Acquaintance of Mr. Mounts. Made Us Laugh with his Ya-Haws etc. Politely invited Us to Tea at his house, and showed us the way to the Decoy ponds near Faversham. Were much pleased with the walk, and tho' Mr. Mount and Mrs. Hunt chose to ride, yet the party occasionally met; Were Instructed in the manner Wild Ducks are taken, and had Tea at Mr. March's at Faversham— which is a pretty clean Village. Then sat out for Canterbury which is 9 Miles. This Evening Mr. Goodwin had the Blue Devils strong upon Him, a Disorder occasion'd by Various Causes.[2] He went to bed early, had the honor of a Visit from the Ladies, and to his great mortification, put them to the Rout, by Instantly jumping out of bed to receive Them.

---

[1] The Assembly referred to was presumably the social gathering common in the eighteenth century.

[2] Blue-devils: according to *O.E.D.* can be a depression of the spirits or delirium tremens.

Wednesday 16

Took post Chaises to Whitstable about 7 Miles, to View some copperas works belonging to Mr. Mount, greatly entertained at the process. A fine View of the Medway, and of the Island of Sheppey.[1] Bought Shrimps here, and were much pleased with the wife of the Tennant, who is a perfect pattern for Industry and economy. The works were lately repaired and in good order. Returned to Canterbury to Dinner. This day wee saw the Cathedral. Were humbug'd at St. Thomas a Becket's tomb. Some fine Monuments in this Church. Walkt in the Deans Yard and about the City. Read an Inscription near our Inn recording the Benevolence of Sir Edward Hales in Conveying water from his park at St. Austin's, for the use of the City.[2] After Dinner went for Margate, and had the most pleasant ride imaginable, in the Isle of Thanet, having Corn fields perfectly clean, all most All the way which is 16 Miles. Hunt and Goodwin who had staid behind on account of the heat, found the party in the utmost Confusion at Margate, occasioned by a Scarcity of beds, and at the Aspect of the Landlord where they had applied, Goodwin proposed to leave their Quarters and try elsewhere. Happily they were better, tho' indifferently off at one Jewell's, who by the much Intreating of Mrs. Jewell, took Them in, upon the resignation of a bed by a Young Clergyman. Jewell was much how Came You So? tho' tolerably diverting by his humor. One Beale a Quaker the first Inventor of the bathing Machines, and who keeps a Lodging house, was very Civil in walking with Us about the Town. The only persons of Note arrived were Lord Vane and a Mr. Stewart, Son of Admiral Stewart.

Thursday 17

After Breakfast walkt on the Gun Fort, where are 3 Cannon mounted, Could see the North Foreland, and a fine View of the Sea. A Man of War fired a Gun to bring a Vessell too, Had a few Turns on the pier Head, and were much Entertained. Proceeded to Ramsgate, walkt with the greatest pleasure on that part of the pier which is finished. It makes a very long and beautiful walk extending out to Sea. The part done has taken up ten years performance. Saw here only one bathing Machine belonging to Beau Nash.[3] The shore not so Convenient for bathing as Margate. Regaled ourselves at a very handsome publick house commanding the Sea, and hir'd an open Vessell of about 3 ton Burthen, to sail with Mrs. Mount, and Miss Hunt and Mr. Goodwin to Deal, which is about 9 or 10 Miles. Persuaded by

---

[1] Again this view was more probably of the Swale than of the real Medway.

[2] Bagshaw's *Directory* (1847) refers to the spring in St. Augustine's as one of the sources of the City's water supply.

[3] Beau Nash, 1674-1762, by this time a mere pensioner of the City of Bath.

the rest of the party to desist from their Voyage thro' apprehension of
Danger. But laying in provisions, after a most solemn and tender
parting, They were Launcht to Sea. Expected to be Sea Sick, as they
were told by the Ramsgate people, they could not escape, the wind
blowing so fresh, and against a strong tide, and therefore the Vessell
lyable to be much tossed. Had a most agreable and safe Voyage to the
3 Kings at Deal, no accident hap'ning to marr their pleasures. Were so
delighted that they petitioned for more Such, but could not prevail on
the Boatswain who thought it would be dangerous. They experienced
in this Voyage Gunnell too.[1] Past Ash, and Sand down Castles and
had a fine View of Waldershare Tower, a seat of the Furneses'.[2] The
Rest of the party made Sandwich in their way to Deal, which is 14
Miles by Land arriving an hour or two later than the Sea folks, heartily
tired and weary by the sandy way they had travelled through. After
Dinner walkt on the Beach. Saw in the Downs opposite to where they
Din'd, the Chesterfield, on board whereof Commodore Boys was
expected to hoist his flag, A Dutch Indiamen, the Argo Man of War,
and Woolfe Sloop and other Vessells riding at Anchor. Hunt and
Goodwin ran a Race on the beach which was almost knee deep in
Stones. Gathered Sea Weed and past an hour or two in such Amuse-
ments. In the Evening went for Dover being 9 Miles. In their
Journey they left Deal and Warmer Castles on the left hand, and had a
pleasant Ride. More Merry, than Satisfyed about their Supper, the
Caterers having too much buoy'd the Company, with a Surprize of
Elegancy. Strong debates after Supper, about the Ladies riding
Habits—Setled by the Ladies, whose Sex are remarkable for Ingenuity.

Friday 18
When they had breakfasted, took post Chaises for Dover Castle, to
ease their own Voitures. Viewed everything remarkable, and from the
Tower saw a Review of about 400 of the Soldiers in Garrison, which had
a surprizing Effect from that height. Discovered the Spires of Calais,
and the hills on the Coast of France. Shakespeares Cliff and the
Devils Drop, put them in mind of his beautiful description thereof.[3]
Were showed the place on the side of one of the Cliffs, where the Lord
Warden of the Cinque ports, and the Constable of Dover Castle, (which
at present is the Duke of Dorset) is sworn in[4]; A well here of near

---

[1] Gunnell: *O.E.D.*, a small ell-shaped fish (1686).
[2] Sir Henry Furnese bought Waldershare in the late seventeenth century and
it remained in the family until 1735, when coming to coheirs it ultimately fell to
the North family, Earls of Guilford.
[3] *King Lear*, Act IV, where Edgar describes the scene to the sightless Glouces-
ter.
[4] Lionel Cranfield Sackville, first Duke of Dorset (1681-1765), was appointed
Lord Warden for life in 1757.

400 feet Deep. Returned to Dover, and then set out for the old Quarters the Red Lyon at Canterbury which is 16 miles, Refreshing by the way, and going over Barham Downs, whereon are severale fine Seats, belonging to Mr. Oxendon son of Sir George, Sir Thomas Hales, a Mrs. Rooke (mightily fond of law) Mrs. Taylor, Mr. Beckingham and Mrs. Corbet.[1] After Dinner Messrs. Mount and Goodwin paid Visits to some of their friends, and the Ladies and Mr. Hunt entertained themselves in seeing the Silk Looms. Goodwin was again at this place somewhat troubled with his former disorder. Mem: The air of Canterbury does not agree with him.

Saturday 19

After taking Dr. Ward's prescription of Milk and water, Rum Sugar and Nutmeg, they reacht Ospring to breakfast, being 9 Miles, There they were joined by Mr. and Mrs. March, the former whereof, went with the Gentlemen to Faversham, to look at some horses on sale, Mrs. Hunt and Mrs. March, in the Interim walking to one Mr. Pearse's, to see his house and Gardens, Mrs. Mount chose to stay at the Inn. Instead of purchasing, Mr. Mount sold his horse to Mr. March. Proceeded to Maidstone for Dinner, which is 18 Miles, baiting by the way at Hollingbury Hill.[2] At Maidstone were joined by Mr. Mason, who having bespoke a Regale at the Bull, made them Leave their Quarters at the Star, to partake of a much better Entertainment than the former Caterers had provided. The Roguery of the Landlord of the Star discovered by Mr. Hunt. A Large party of the Black Cuffs were quartered at this place, and are frequently attached to Sissinghurst Castle (where the French prisoners are kept) to relieve those in Garrison there.[3] After Dinner were much Surprized and pleased with the severall works and buildings, and the Art of paper making at Mr. Watman's about two Miles walk from Maidstone.[4]

Sunday 20

Mr. Mount and the Ladies while the other gentlemen were dressing, gave them the Slip, and went to the Right Place, the Gentlemen to the Wrong tho' much pleased with the Clergyman's Discourse;[5] After Dinner All were disposed for coming into the pale of the Church, and

[1] Andrews, Durey and Herbert (1769) indicates Dean, the house of the Oxendon family; Howlet Place, Sir Thomas Hales' residence, and the houses of Beckingham, Taylor and of Mrs. Rook.
[2] Hollingbury Hill, probably Hollingbourne.
[3] Sissinghurst Castle was used for prisoners of war during the Seven Years War who, according to a document in the Kent Archives Office, did more than £360 worth of damage.
[4] This refers to the Turkey Mill just south of the Ashford road.
[5] Presumably "the right place" was All Saints Church and "the wrong place" the Congregational Church in Week Street.

were politely seated in the best pews. After their Tea, they rode to the
Hon. Mr. Fairfax's at Leeds Castle, being about 6 Miles distance passing
in their way Lord Rumney's Seat, and the house of General Belfour,
and Mr. Cage.[1] Were an hour or two in the park and walks, and were
greatly pleased as both abounded with fine turf and plenty of water and
flowring shrubs. The Gardens are free for the neighbouring Gentry.
Returned to Maidstone to Supper. Mr. Mason purchased a horse of
the Landlord.

Monday 21

Breakfast at an Inn near Merriworth house, a Seat of Lord Westmor-
land's being about 8 miles. No Conveniency for Lodging at this Inn.
Were greatly Entertained for 3 hours and more, with the magnificence
of the house and gardens; Saw the Shell Room, and Birds, and the
Egyptian piramid. And were entertained at his Lordship's with a
Cold Collatian. One of his Grooms attended Them, for a shorter Cut,
thro' Esq. Masters grounds, (which were extreamly pleasant) in their
way to Tunbridge Town,[2] No way in regard to the Roads, could be
worse, than from Mr. Master's. In Hadley Lane,[3] providential Escapes
from Bone breaking. Refresht themselves at Tunbridge Town, and
reacht the Sussex Tavern at the Wells, which is 13 miles from Merriworth house to Dinner. Mr. Lindo's family, the only persons at the
Wells. In the Evening were upon the walks, and amused themselves
in the Tunbridge Ware Shops. Visited the Mounts Ephraim, and
Zion and Mount Pleasant and the Grove. About two Miles from this
place thro' a most wretched Road for Carriages, you come to a place
called the Rocks, which are of a stupendious heighth, and romantick
appearance.

Tuesday 22

Breakfast at Seven Oak which is 13 Miles, and saw the Duke of
Dorset's house and park called Knolle. In the house are above 700
Rooms, the furniture allmost as ancient as the house, but very Superb
and grand. Infinite Numbers of pictures. A very fine one of the
Ceremony of swearing in the Lord Warden of the Cinque Ports, the
back View whereof is Dover Castle and the Country round; He has been
Lord Warden upwards of 40 years. His Grace is so good natured and
polite as to give an Assembly once a Week to the Gentry residing near
this place. One of the Grooms attended them on Horseback, to show

---

[1] General Belfort resided at Grove Green, Weavering Street, and Mr. Cage at
Milgate.
[2] " Esq. Masters grounds," the Yokes estate between Mereworth and West
Peckham.
[3] For Hadley sc. Hadlow.

191

the principal Views of the park.   At this place is a good house belonging
to one Esq. Lambert.[1]   Din'd at Bromley, and about 7 o'clock set out
for London, Mr. Goodwin taking his Leave of the party, at the new
Cross Turnpike, to go for Mortlake in Surrey.

On this Expedition the Ladies and Mr. Mount occasionally rode
their led Horses, and the Ladies to the great pleasure of the Gentlemen,
Expressed the Satisfaction they had received throughout this Tour.

[1] " Esq. Lambert " probably Thomas Lambard, whose residence was just
south of Sevenoaks.

A HAND-LIST OF ENGLISH ENCLOSURE ACTS AND AWARDS.

PART 17.

OPEN FIELDS, COMMONS AND ENCLOSURES IN KENT.

BY W. E. TATE, F.R.HIST.S.

KENT, as Professor H. L. Gray's map shows,[1] lies well outside the main area recognized as having formerly been cultivated under the two- and three-field systems. Meitzen[2] considered that the differences—very obvious to even a superficial enquirer—existing between the field structure of Kent and that of the Midland counties are clear evidence of " Celtic " settlement. The difficulty in the way of accepting this theory is that Kent, as we shall see later, is probably of all the English counties the one most pre-eminently English in its settlement. Nevertheless, it is characterized by the peculiar field systems alluded to, and in general by very early enclosure. So far is this true that some very competent authorities have doubted how far either common arable fields or common pastures were ever generally prevalent here. Professor Gray found evidence of such, however, and his findings are confirmed and are amplified by the later researches of Dr. and Mrs. Orwin.[3] They have found definite evidence of the existence of open fields medievally both to the north and to the south of the Weald. They quote Dr. Muhlfeld[4] for further evidence as to the existence of four fields at Wye in 1312. Dr. Muhlfeld, however, found that these fields early disappeared. They suggest that the early disappearance of open fields in Kent as elsewhere has little to do with racial factors but may be the resultant of three forces :

(a) The existence of the Weald in the centre of the county and of extensive marshes along the North and East coasts.

(b) The geographical position of the county athwart the main route of communication between London and the Continent. They suggest, very reasonably, that this may have tended towards the development of a money economy at a much earlier date in Kent than elsewhere.

(c) The existence of gavelkind and the right it gave to tenants to buy and sell without licence from their lord. (They might have added to this the fact that in other ways gavelkind tenure was particularly hostile to common rights and favourable towards enclosure.)

Professor Gray's[5] instances of the existence of open arable fields within this county relate to : Adisham (late 13th century), Badlesmere (1338-9), Barfreston (1235-6), Bilsington (1338-9), Brabourne (1337-8),

193

Chilham (1338-9), Chislet (late 13th and 14th centuries), Eastry (*recte* Eastrey) (13th and 14th centuries), Gillingham (1452-3), "Hertesdowne" (1456-7), Hothfield (1338-9), Ickham (late 13th century), Iwade (1236-7), Lewisham (15th century), Littlebourn (late 13th century), Margate (1456-7), Monkton (late 13th century), Newchurch (early 15th century), New Canderby (14th century), Orpington (1342-3), Ringwold (*recte* Ringwould) (1338-9), Romney Marsh (early 15th century), St. Mary Cray (1342-3), St. Peters in Thanet (14th century), "Sawlyng" (1456-7), "Syankesdon" (1456-7), Throwley (1339-40), Westgate (1456-7), Whitstable (1338-9), and Wye (*c.* 1272-1307, 1311-12. and early 15th century).

The evidence of Tudor, Jacobean and even later surveys confirms the deduction drawn from medieval records that the open field system, or *an* open field system, was fairly widely spread in the county until at any rate three or four centuries ago

Hoo St. Mary's seems to have been largely open in the 16th century. Sutton at Hone, *c.* 1509-47, had its demesne entirely in severalty but its tenanted lands perhaps 25 per cent. open, Horsham Manor in Alteram, Ham, and Upchurch, and Newington were intermixed in 1589-92. Eltham was partly open in 1605. Dr. Slater[6] thinks that Eltham was clearly in common fields of a kind in 1578, and both here, in the royal manor, and in the neighbouring ecclesiastical manor of Addington he thinks that traces of the open field lay-out are to be seen quite plainly in the villages to-day. West Court *als* Sibertswold was "lately enclosed" in 1616. Guston, near Dover, was about two-thirds enclosed by 1616 (the demesne being markedly more so than the tenants' holdings), Dale *als* Court Ashe manor in Deal was almost entirely in open field in 1616-17. Sutton by Dover was largely so about the same time. St. Margarets at Cliffe was largely open until 1645.

But, as Professor Gray points out, Kentish open fields are very different affairs from those found in the Midlands. There rarely appears in them any trace of a two-, three-, or four-field grouping. The lands are not always even located in "furlongs," and Professor Gray well describes the Kentish open field parcels as situated in "a bewildering number of field divisions, bearing local names, and furnishing little clue to the husbandry employed. The only resemblance between these lands and those of the two- and three-field area was that the parcels were small and intermixed; they were not grouped in fields, much less equally divided among two or three great fields of approximately equal areas (though Ringwould had its three fields until recent years). In general there is little evidence as to whether the parcels of any individual tenant were dispersed throughout the area on any system, or congregated in any subdivision of it.

The normal Kentish tenurial unit is the *iugum* or *dola*, a more or less rectangular area—sometimes styled a *tenementum*—subdivided sometimes into four *ferthings*. Its area was anything from 25 or 60 to as much as 200 acres, with an average of perhaps 60 or 70 acres. Sometimes very confusingly the fourth of a *iugum* is styled a ferthing or a virgate. To make confusion more confounded, elsewhere and more usually in Kent a virgate is a rood—a quarter of an acre. Sometimes a larger unit—the *sulung*—persisted—without any reference to *iuga*. This was an area of perhaps 200-300 acres. The great difference between land tenure in Kent and that elsewhere is that as a rule here the holdings were relatively compact, and such discreteness as existed was not a primitive survival but a late result of the partitioning among coheirs, etc., of estates (originally consolidated) in accordance with the well-known land customs prevalent in this county. It is likely enough that, as Professor Gray suggests, some Kentish open fields in the downlands may represent comparatively late approvements from the waste, which has been apportioned with a rough and ready attempt at equity as between tenant and tenant. Even when estates lay in separate *iuga* or *dolae* they were markedly less scattered than were comparable estates in open fields in the Midlands, and lay often in adjacent *iuga* or *dolae*. *Iugum* and *dola*, says Professor Gray,[7] had become by the beginning of the 15th century rather financial units than agricultural ones, corresponding rather to the Midland virgate than the Midland furlong. The *iugum* seems to be clearly enough the old Jutish family holding, often bearing the same name as that of its occupiers (though Professor Gray thinks that often in the 13th century as e.g. at Wye (1311-12) the tenants took their name from the holding rather than *vice versa*), and the history of the *iugum* is one of continuous subdivision and re-allotment. The differences between the Kentish system and the Midlands one are many, those between the Kentish system and the " Celtic " one are less obvious, and reside mainly in the original area which was sub-divided. In " Celtic " counties this was the township, in Kent it was the smaller roughly rectangular *iugum*, presumably laid out in the first place by the Roman *agrimensores*.

Clearly such a system as this lent itself to early enclosure. There are other features, too, of Kentish husbandry which help to account for the early enclosure of the county. In Kent, pasture rights upon the fallow could not be the same deterrent to enclosure as they were in the Midlands, where they were exercised over a large compact fallow area. As a matter of fact, in the Kentish township there seems to have been little fallowing.[8] The land—at any rate the demesne, which in this county was generally an area distinct from the land in the rest of the manor—was cropped more or less continuously. Moreover in Kent, as in the " Celtic " counties, the existence of large areas of unreclaimed waste must have tended to diminish the importance of pasturage on the fallow, when there was one. The variety of tenure characteristic of Kent—gavelkind—in another way lent itself to early

195

enclosure. " It was an ancient usage respecting gavelkind lands that the lord could inclose at his discretion."[9]

As noted above, all the authorities agree that Kent is essentially a county of early enclosure. Professor Gray thinks[10] the enclosure of the county was largely complete before the 16th century. Dr. Slater[11] styles it certainly " a county of very ancient enclosure." Mr. Curtler[12] says " most of Kent was enclosed early." Miss Leonard[13] thinks the county was enclosed " before the 17th century." In 1517 Wolsey's enclosure commission visited the county. Its returns were not forthcoming at the time of Leadam's *Domesday*, and unlike those of several other counties they do not seem to have been unearthed subsequently.[14] Presumably little agrarian change was taking place locally in the early 16th century. At any rate the county was exempted from the depopulation act of 1536.[15] Not of course that the county was entirely unaffected by the movements of Tudor times. Professor Tawney[16] speaks of Kent " like the other counties mainly of small enclosure carried out by the peasantry, being little affected by the agrarian risings of Tudor times." Leland[16A] visited the county in his tours 1535-43, but has little to say of its agrarian state. The only references to it I have been able to find are : " The lordship at that tyme (Godhurste i.e. Goddard's Castle *temp.* Sir John Cutte), was partely a ground much overgrouen with thornes and busshes, and was but xx markes by the yere. Now it is clensid and the valeu much enhaunsid. And much goodly Wood is yet aboute it. . . . There is good plentie of woodde in Weste Kente. The partes of Kent beyounde Cantewarbyri hath the name of Este Kent, wher yn diverse placis is sufficient woodde. . But on the coste from Reculver to about Folkestane is but little . . . the commodities of Kent, as fertility, wood, pasture. .. . . In the isle (of Thanet) is very litle wodde. Rumeney (Romney) Marsch . . . is a mervelus rank grownd for fedying of catel . . ."

A casual reference shows, however, that in 1543[17] Boxley Park and a neighbouring wood were enclosed by Sir Thomas Wyatt. Other enclosures in this same parish were " cast open and throwen downe by the people . . . in the tyme of rebellion of comenwelthe (i.e. the 1548-50 disturbances). In 1549 the anonymous author of the *Discourse*[18] notes " the Countries wheare most Inclosures be as essex, kent, devonshire and such."

The year before this, the commons of Kent had taken the law into their own hands in the effort to stem the tide of the agrarian change which was threatening by then to submerge what little common or common field still remained. King Edward VI himself includes Kent in the counties where agrarian disturbances had developed before the issuing of Somerset's commission, and Strype, Stow and Speed all cite Kent among the earliest counties affected. Godwin in 1675[19] describes Kent as "The Fountain of this General Uproar." Five hundred villagers laid open an enclosure made by no less a person than the Lord Warden of the Cinque Ports, who, according to the grossly exaggerated account in the *Spanish Chronicle*, was reputed to have "taken in all the commons in Kent." The authorities at Canterbury had to send for artillery to deal with the rebels, who threatened to besiege the city. After the suppression of the early disturbances a commission was sent down to pacify the rebels, and it ordered the destruction of the enclosure complained of. In July 1549 the county was still uneasy, though it was reported to Russell that the commons in Kent and the neighbouring counties confessed their faults "with verie lowlye submission" and were ready to fight the western rebels. In August 1549 they "meekly confessed their folly and prayed for the King's most gracious pardon." In 1550, however, Kent was among the counties where men of the Boulogne garrison were stationed to preserve order.[20]

Lambarde in 1570 tells us of Kent that the soil is for the most part bountiful, consisting indifferently of arable, pasture, meadow, and woodland . . . wood occupying the greater portion . . . except it be towards the east which coast is more champaigne than the residue. He also repeats the statement that "no man ought to have common in lanes of gavelkind, howbeit the contrary is well known at this day, and that at many places."[21] About this time Harrison in his Description,[22] making special reference to the evil of enclosure for imparcation, alleges that there were "a hundred parks in Kent and Essex alone."

"A circuit of these enclosures contains oftentimes a wall of four or five miles. Where in times past many large and wealthy occupiers were dwelling within the compass of one park . . . there now is almost nothing kept but a sort of wild and savage beasts, cherished for pleasure and delight, and yet some owners, still desirous to enlarge these grounds, do not let daily to take in more, not sparing the very commons whereupon many townships now and then do thrive, affirming that we have already too great store of people in England . . . the 20th part of the realm is employed upon deer and conies already."

There is record evidence of as well as literary reference to the early enclosure of the county. As noted above, the demesne of Sutton at Hone[23] was enclosed *ante temp.* Henry VIII. Professor Gray[24] is satisfied that "Sondrisshe was enclosed by 1 Mary (1553-4), Nether Bilsington by 1567, and three manors in the parishes of Cranbrook, Goudhurst, and Hawkhurst, were entirely in severalty by 1587. A series of surveys of manors in and about Romney Marsh, the property of All Soul's College, 1689-93, shows nearly all the land as consolidated. Eltham was mostly enclosed by 1605, Neates Court by 1608-9. Northbourne also was enclosed by this time, and in a hundred pages of surveys of

Kentish manors or townships at this period, there is reference to but two minute scraps of open arable field, respectively at Faversham and Shoreham. As noted above,[25] Westcourt or Sibbertswold was mostly enclosed shortly before 1616. Guston, near Dover, was largely enclosed before this same year, Frith manor in the same parish was wholly enclosed, and Reach and Sutton by Dover largely so by the same time. According to Miss E. M. Leonard,[26] Farningham was (enclosed and ?) depopulated by Sir Anthony Roper in 1633.

At the end of the 16th century Kent, like its neighbours Middlesex, Surrey, and Sussex, was exempted from the last depopulation act.[27] If one may trust the statement of a contemporary "thereby noe Inconvenience in ye stat found."[28] Burton seems to confirm this, since in his *Anatomy of Melancholy*[29] he instances Essex and Kent as proofs that enclosure produces wealth, "for that which is common and every man's is no man's, the richest countries are still inclosed, as Essex, Kent, with us etc." It may or may not be with reference to this early enclosure of Kent that Thomas Fuller[30] informs us only a year or two later that "when hospitality dyed in England she gave her last groan among the yeomen of Kent." Evidently enclosure in Kent, having absorbed the common fields, early turned its attention to the reclamation of the Weald. At any rate Gervase Markham's *Inrichment of the Weald of Kent* (1625)[31] was devoted solely to improving the Kent and Sussex Wealds. It is dedicated to Sir George Rivers of Chafford. It may be a tribute to Markham's persuasive powers that John Aubrey[32] less than half a century later informs us that the Weald of Surrey is "like the Wealds of Kent and Sussex a rich deep inclosed country."

Certainly the enclosure of almost the entire County except the Weald seems to have been completed long before this. Kent is last of the thirteen counties listed by Professor Gonner[33] in order of the amount of the enclosure compositions paid 1635-8, with a total payment of but £100 compared with Lincolnshire's £19,000 and Leicestershire's £9,000. John Moore,[34] who detested enclosure, said in 1656: "I complaine not of inclosure in Kent or Essex where they have other callings and trades to maintaine their country by or of places near the sea or City, but of inclosure in the inland countreys which takes away tillage."

Richard Blome[35] in 1673, like Lambarde a century earlier, differentiates in his account of Kent between the west and the east "where it is more champain." In 1675 there appeared John Ogilby's folio road book *Britannia*, with its 100 strip maps, on which Professor Gonner[36] based his calculations as to the extent of enclosure towards the end of the 17th century. If he is right in taking the percentage of enclosed road as a fair indication of the percentage of enclosed land generally in each county, Kent was 36th of the 37 counties listed in order of open land still remaining. It had but 5 per cent. of open land, and the only county with less was Essex with 3 per cent. Leonard Meager[37] in 1697 includes Kent among the enclosed counties " where people can live happily and supply corn to the open-field counties." It is quite clear that Celia Fiennes[38] does not mean what she appears to say in describing her journey through Kent from Canterbury to Dover, c. 1695 by " a good road and a sort of Champion country."

There seems relatively little evidence as to enclosure in Kent during the latter half of the 17th century and throughout the 18th. As to Kentish agriculture the principal authorities are the Board of Agriculture's *Surveys*[39] and Marshall's *Rural Economy*.[40] These agree that at this time there were no open arable fields remaining in Kent. According to Marshall, " The greater part of the hills [of the eastern extremity of Kent] are inclosed. There is nevertheless much *open down*, especially on the sides, and lower parts of the hills, where the soil is of a chalky nature ; what may properly be called the true chalk-down soil : and this, it may be said, is everywhere kept in an open state ! While the parts, which are covered with a strong clayey soil are chiefly enclosed."

Marshall's notes are (of the Maidstone district) " the entire district appears to have been inclosed from the forest or pasture state. I observed not a trace of common field lands. (Of the Weald) " The whole is in a STATE OF INCLOSURE, and mostly divided, by wide woodland belts, into well sized fields." He, however, seems to suggest the existence of open lands in Thanet. " The whole country lies open ; excepting the immediate environs of villages." This latter is confirmed by Professor Gray who says " Eighteenth century references to open fields in Kent are rare, but do occur occasionally." He notes, e.g., one to Henhurst, where some part of the land was clearly in open field in 1770.

All three of the county reports are by John Boys,[41] who describes himself as " of Betshanger, farmer." Curtler says he was a " large " farmer. There seems to be little to our purpose in the first report which is not repeated in the second, so I content myself by giving references to the latter.

As to the lack of open fields Boys says, " There is no portion of Kent that is occupied by a community of persons, as in many other counties." Concerning enclosure generally and about the remaining commons crying out for the process, Boys says a good deal. The open part of East Kent was between Canterbury and Dover and Deal, the enclosed part from Dover to Rochester, and from the Isle of Sheppey to Lenham. Sheppey was (all) in small (and old) enclosures. West Kent was more highly enclosed than the east of the county, though there were many commons between the Hog's Back, the boundary of the Weald, and the Surrey border. There were others on the gravel near Dartford and

Blackheath. South-western Kent was the most highly enclosed of all parts of the county. The waste lands and impoverished commons of the county were overdue for enclosure. They amounted in all to some 20,000 acres, mostly on poor loams, wet clays, and gravels and sands. The commons Boys lists are " Baddlesmere Lees, Barming Heath, Blean Common, Black Heath, Bromley Common, Boxley Heath, Challock Lees, Charing Heath, Chart Leacon. Cox Heath, Dartford Brinks, Dartford Heath, East Malling Heath, Ewel Minis, Hays Common, Hotfield Heath, Ightham Heath, Langley Heath, Lenham Heath, Pinnenden Heath, Rodes Minis, Seal Chart, Stouting Common, Stelling Minis, Swingfield Minis, and Wrotham Heath." Enclosure of these·would do much. " I shall here take the liberty of suggesting to the Honourable Board of Agriculture, the propriety of recommending to the legislature a plan for a general act of enclosure, founded on the principle of Mr. Gilbert's act[42] for incorporating parishes for the support of the poor, so far as that act relates to the calling a meeting, and determining by a majority of two-thirds in number and value of the occupiers, whether their common shall be divided ; and, if determined in the affirmative, then to proceed by appointing commissioners, and expediting the business, as in cases where separate Acts of Parliament have been obtained."

Elsewhere Boys refers to the great need of a general enclosure act. " Our commons for live stock are generally much covered with furze, thorns, brakes, or heath, with a mixture of plots of poor grass-land ; the cattle and sheep feeding upon them, are of course in a half-starved state. The total destruction of all commonable rights, by a general act of parliament for inclosing, is an object, in my humble opinion, of the greatest magnitude to the interests of this kingdom in general, and to this county in particular. There have been some exertions for accomplishing a division and inclosure of an extensive common in East Kent, within these few years ; which failed for want of unanimity among the persons concerned. . . . Had the same encouragement been given by parliament, for the last fifty years, to agriculture as we have then given to manufactures, we, probably, by this time might have had many thousand acres of land, that are now desolate wastes, in a high state of cultivation. . . . The right of commonage on the barren heaths of this county is certainly an obstacle to their improvement. . . . There is scarcely an acre of (waste) land to be found in this county, but what might be converted to some valuable purpose. The gravelly and sandy heaths . . . would produce good Turnips, seeds, and corn. The cold clays and wet commons, no doubt, would also produce good corn, or make inclosed meadows and pastures."

Professor Gonner's opinion[43] is that much land in Kent was enclosed directly from the waste, that the county was in historic times "singularly devoid of common," and that probably such land as was suitable for enclosure had been taken in at a very early date. Common field he thinks very rarely existed, and where there was any as a rule it disappeared early.

SURVIVAL OF OPEN LANDS IN KENT.

At Ringwould and Kingsdown[44] there were, respectively, four fields and three which survived in some degree of completeness until the time of the tithe map. The fields of Ringwould totalled about 330 acres. At the date mentioned it was the exception for two adjoining strips to belong to the same owner, and this parish gave the best example of open field survival in this part of England. Both parishes were enclosed by non-Parliamentary means, the more prosperous owners gradually buying up the strips and enclosing piecemeal.

There are still some commons in Kent, fairly full details of which are given by Lord Eversley.[45] The principal ones are the following, regulated under the Metropolitan Commons Act of 1866 : Blackheath, 267 acres, regulated in 1871 ; Chislehurst, 182 acres ; Hayes, 200 acres ; one secured by other means, Woolwich, 187 acres ; and some others most of which apparently have received no statutory protection, but which nevertheless have survived to this day. *Plumstead Commons* occupy 170 acres. The lords of the manor are Queens College, Oxford, who acquired it in 1756. The Court Rolls exist from 1685 and reveal the existence of a curious manorial custom—that all monies arising from dealings with the waste and from amercements in the manor court should be divided equally between the lord of the manor and the poor of the parish. From 1859 to 1866 about a third of the common was enclosed by the lords. Legal proceedings followed an attempt at further enclosure and these dragged on from 1866-71. Ultimately the commoners were entirely successful and succeeded not only in retaining their common and in securing the award of costs against the lord, but also in getting several important principles of law duly established. The main common and Bostal (?) Heath, 55 acres, are now vested in the L.C.C., the former being regulated under the Metropolitan Commons Act of 1866, the latter acquired by buying out the manorial interests. At Dartford, the Heath of 120 acres escaped enclosure in 1865-74. Hothfield had a common in 1797 and Meopham, one of 6 acres. Eden refers to these and the value of the former to the poorer parishioners.[46] I have not been able to ascertain whether or not these two commons still remain. Hayes Common in Baston and West Wickham manors suffered extensive enclosure shortly before 1865. The Baston portion was regulated in 1868 under the 1866 Commons Act, the Hayes portion was saved some years later by the action of the Commons Preservation Society.

PARLIAMENTARY ENCLOSURE IN KENT.

Perhaps one should include among Kentish enclosure acts some of the earliest measures on the statute book for the embankment and reclamation of marsh lands. I refer of course to the Tudor legislation for the enclosure and maintenance of Plumstead Marsh and the embanking (and enclosure ?) of Greenwich Marshes.[47] As to later enclosures in the county the tables subjoined (A. to G.) show very much what one would expect, having in mind the considerations set forth above.

List A., Kentish enclosures by Act of lands including open field arable, is blank.   List B., enclosures by Act of lands consisting of waste, pasture, etc., alone, contains but 17 entries, all, be it noted, decidedly late in date, and all covering relatively small areas.   Clearly this indicates the enclosure in comparatively modern times of various scraps of common waste (as distinct from common fields), which had somehow or other escaped enclosure in earlier times.   The largest of these covers but 900 acres, and the average is perhaps 350 acres. Lists C. and D., enclosures respectively of open arable and of lands other than open arable, enclosed under the Acts of 1836 and 1839, show, as one would expect, complete blanks.   All open field and waste of a manor that was worth enclosure, and for which a modicum of consent to enclose could be obtained, had in general disappeared long before 1836.   Lists E. and F., the statement of enclosures carried out under the General Acts of 1845 *et seq.* also show very much what one would have expected.   Lists E. (i) and E. (ii) are complete blanks.   No open field remained in 1845 to be enclosed either by Provisional Order alone, or by Provisional Order confirmed in Annual General Act. List F., enclosures of waste by Act in the years following 1845, contains some 14 entries, averaging about 110 acres each, and clearly showing the final " mopping up " in the Victorian era of nearly all the last remaining scraps of common in the county.

List G., enclosures by private agreement duly embodied in awards enrolled among county or national records contains but two entries. Here again it seems clear that almost all open lands in Kent—mostly pasture grounds, but no doubt including small areas of open field arable— for which a concensus of agreement could be arrived at had been enclosed.   This had happened long before the days when enclosures were sanctioned by either act or formal agreement, and embodied in a formal award, duly executed and proclaimed, and finally enrolled in a court of law.

In the tables below (M) signifies Manor, C.R., County Records.

A. ENCLOSURES BY PRIVATE ACT OF LANDS INCLUDING OPEN FIELD ARABLE.

Nil.

B. ENCLOSURES BY PRIVATE ACT OF LANDS NOT INCLUDING OPEN FIELD ARABLE.

Date of Act.		Area in Act.	Date of Award.	Award enrolled.
1740	Rusthall (M)	?	?	?
1763*	Bromley	?	?	?
1805	East Malling and Teston	450	1810	C.R.
1807	River	122	?	?
1810	Lewisham	850	1819	C.R.
1810	Sellinge	72	1813	C.R.
1811	Burham	280	1815	C.R.
1812	Erith	200	1815	C.R.
1812	Crayford	170	1820	C.R.
1814	Boxley	300	1819	C.R.
1814	Coxheath in Boughton Monchelsea, Loose, Linton, East and West Farleigh, and Hunton	900	1817	C.R.
1814	Wrotham and Ightham	500	1820	C.R.
1814†	Birling	80	1815	C.R.
1819	Aldington Freight *als* (*et recte* ?), Aldington Frith	n.s.	?	?
1821	Bromley	350	1826	C.R.
1822	Brabourne, Smeeth, Bircholt and Sellinge	300	1824	C.R.
1840	Swingfield Minnis *als* (*et recte*), Folkestone	620	1844	C.R.

C. ENCLOSURES (MAINLY OF OPEN FIELD) UNDER 6 & 7 WM. IV, c. 115, 1836.

Nil.

D. ENCLOSURES (MAINLY OF LAMMAS LANDS, ETC.) UNDER 6 & 7 WM. IV, c. 115 (1836), AS EXTENDED BY 3 & 4 VIC., c. 31. 1840.

Nil.

E. ENCLOSURES OF OPEN FIELD UNDER THE GENERAL ACTS OF 1845 *et seq.*

(i) *By Provisional Order alone, not needing confirmation in Annual General Act.*

Nil.

(ii) *By Provisional Order confirmed in pursuance of Annual General Act.*

Nil.

F. ENCLOSURES OF LANDS NOT INCLUDING OPEN FIELD UNDER THE GENERAL ACTS OF 1845 *et seq.*

(i) *By Provisional order alone, not needing confirmation in Annual General Act.*

1845	Great Mead and Rye Street in Cliffe	?	1853	C.R.
1845	Postling Leeze in Postling	?	1854	C.R.
1845	Shorne Mead in Shorne	?	1853	C.R.

* Act repealed in part by act of 1877. See *Arch. Cant.*, XXXIII (1918), pp. 113-24.

† Act not 1813 as in 1904 *Blue Book.*

(ii) *By Provisional Order confirmed in pursuance of Annual General Act.*

Date of Act.		Area in Act.	Date of Award.	Award enrolled.
1845 and :				
1846	Alkham	84	1849	C.R.
1848	High Minnis and Rhodes Minnis in Lyminge	212	1855	C.R.
1849	Westwell Leacon in Westwell and Charing	96	1851	C.R.
1849	Brasted Chart in Brasted	450	1853	C.R.
1851	Aylesford	25	1854	C.R.
1852	Ditton Common in Ditton and Barming	25	1859	C.R.
1854	Queenborough	255	1856	C.R.
1856*	Langley	55	1858	C.R.
1860	Kennington Lees and Walls Green in Kennington and Boughton Aluph	50	1864	C.R.
1862	Common Saltings, etc., in Wouldham	163	1866	C.R.
1864	Barming Heath in Barming	58	1866	C.R.
1866	Charing and Lenham	66	1868	C.R.
1867	Rhodes Minnis in Elham	29	1872	C.R.
1869†	Fairbourne Heath in Harrietsham	37	1871	C.R.
1877†	Biquores Estate in Dartford	?	1880	C.R.

G. ENCLOSURES BY FORMAL WRITTEN AGREEMENT ENROLLED AMONG COUNTY OR NATIONAL RECORDS.

Date of Agreement.		Area.	Date of Award.	Award enrolled or deposited.
1820 under 29. Horsey Hill in Westerham.				
Geo. II, c. 36, 1755-6		?		(duplicate ?)
			Indenture of agreement also allots.	
1841	Broxham (M) in Chiddingstone, Hever, and Edenbridge	?	1844	C.R.
1843	Maidstone (M)	?	1854	C.R.

NOTES.—There are no acts, as far as I know, indexed under Kent but relating to places now in other counties, and none relating to places formerly in other counties, but now in Kent. There is but one amending act, for Bromley Act 1763, repealed in part in 1877.

In completing the Kentish part of my undertaking I have received help from Sir Edward Harrison, Hon. Secretary of the Kent Archaeological Society, and from Mr. W. P. D. Stebbing, F.S.A., Editor of *Archaeologia Cantiana.* I owe these gentlemen my thanks. I am much obliged to Mr. W. L. Platts, Clerk of the Peace for the County, who has given me much assistance in my undertaking. My thanks are due also to the Leverhulme Research Trustees and their Secretary, Dr. L. Haden Guest, M.P., for the interest they have taken in my work, and

* Not under 1845 act alone, as stated in 1904 *Blue Book.*

† Not entered in 1904 *Blue Book.*

the practical help they have given me in finishing this part of it. I shall be grateful to any reader who is able to help me by offering any corrections or additions to either the text or the lists.

REFERENCES.

[1] H. L. GRAY, *English Field Systems*, Cambridge Mass, U.S.A., 1915, frontispiece.

[2] *Siedelungen und Agrarwesen*, II, 122, 154, quoted by Gray, op. cit., 272.

[3] Dr. and Mrs. C. S. ORWIN, *The Open Fields*, 1938, pp. 64-6.

[4] Dr. H. E. MUHLFELD, *Survey of the Manor of Wye*, Columbia U.S.A., 1933, xxxiii.

[5] Gray, op. cit., p. 279.

[6] *The English Peasantry* . . ., 1907, p. 231.

[7] Op. cit., p. 290.

[8] Op. cit., p. 302.

[9] C. I. Elton, *Tenures of Kent*, 1867.

[10] Op. cit., p. 404.

[11] Op. cit., p. 230.

[12] *Enclosure . . . of our Land*, 1920, p. 220.

[13] Miss LEONARD in *Trans. R. Hist. S.*, N.S., XIX, 1905, p. 137.

[14] E. F. GAY in *Trans. R. Hist. S.*, N.S., XIV, 1900, p. 238.

[15] 27 Hen. VIII c. 22 (1536). Miss Leonard, op. cit., p. 124.

[16] R. H. TAWNEY, *Agrarian Problem* . . ., 1912, p. 262.

[16a] LELAND, *Itinerary* . . ., ed. Miss L. T. Smith, 5 vols., 1907-11 ; II, p. 30 ; IV, pp. 42, 57, 61, 67.

[17] E. F. GAY in *Trans. R. Hist.*, N.S., XVIII, 1904, p. 202, note 1.

[18] *Discourse of the Commonweal*, ed. Miss E. Lamond, 1893, p. 49.

[19] *Annals of England*, p. 134, quoted by E. F. GAY in *Trans. R. Hist. S.*, N.S., XVIII, 1904, 202.

[20] GAY, op. cit., p. 207.

[21] *Perambulator* . . ., 1570 (1574), pp. 3, 5, 6, 7.

[22] *Description* . . ., 1577-87, reprint of 1888, p. 206.

[23] Supra., p. 55.

[21] Op. cit., p. 273.

[25] Supra, p. 55.

[26] Op. cit., p. 133.

[27] 39 Eliz. c. 2 (1597), Slater, op. cit., App. D., p. 32.

[28] *A Consideration of the Cause in Question* . . . 1607, in Cunningham, *English Industry and Commerce*, Modern Times, II, App. II, pp. 702-3.

[29] 1621, Reprint of 1887, p. 58.

[30] *Holy State*, 1642, p. 117.

[31] *The Inrichment of the Weald of Kent*, 1625.

[32] J. AUBREY, *Natural History* . . . *of Wiltshire*, 1656-85, III, p. 48.

[33] E. K. C. GONNER, *Common Land and Inclosure*, 1912, p. 167.

[34] *Scripture Word* . . ., 1656.

[35] *Britannia*, 1673.

[36] Op. cit., p. 173.

[37] *Mystery of Husbandry*, quoted by G. E. Fussell in *Ministry of Agriculture Journal*, Jan. 1937, p. 944.

[38] *Through England on a Side Saddle* (1889), p. 103.

[39] JOHN BOYS, *General View of the Agriculture of Kent*, 1794, 1796, and 1805.

[40] WILLIAM MARSHALL, *Rural Economy of the Southern Counties*, 1798, I, 21 ; II, 364.

[41] The 1796 8vo is an expansion of the 1794 4to. The 1805 8vo I have not seen. I think it is a mere reprint of the 1796 volume. These quotations are from 1796, pp. 53, 5, 7, 17, 9, 12, 127-9, 174, 177.

[42] The act referred to is Gilbert's Act, 22 Geo. II, c. 53. " For the better relief of the Poor," 1781-2, on which see my book *The Parish Chest*, now in the Press. Boys's very reasonable suggestion was carried into effect in 1836 by 6 & 7 Wm. IV, c. 115.

[43] Op. cit., pp. 238-40.

[44] *Ex inf.* Mr. W. P. D. STEBBING, quoting the late Dr. F. W. Hardman.

[45] G. SHAW LEFEVRE, *English Commons and Forests*, 1892, pp. 178-80, 318, and 366-72.

[46] Sir F. M. EDEN, *State of the Poor*, 1797, abridged edition of 1928, pp. 210-11.

[47] T. E. SCRUTTON, *Commons and Common Fields*, 1887, p. 94, and 37 Hen. VIII c. 11 (1545), (Greenwich) and 22 Hen. VIII, c. 3 (1530), 14 Eliz. c. 15 (1572), 23 Eliz., c. 13 (1581), and 27 Eliz., c. 27 (1585), (Plumstead).

KENT HOP-TOKENS

By John W. Bridge, F.S.A.

The Hop (*Humulus lupulus*) appears to have been introduced into England for cultivation in the reign of Elizabeth I, about the year 1524, and the village of Little Chart, in Kent, claims to have " England's oldest hop-garden."

Walter Rowles, in *The Kentish Chronologer* of 1807, tells us that in 1492, before the use of hops, wormwood was used for preserving malt liquor.

The cultivation of hops was a popular industry, first because it was very profitable, and secondly because it employed labour for almost all the year, " Planting, Soiling, Houghing, Poling, Tying and Picking." About the year 1870, some 46,600 acres were under hop-cultivation in Kent, and it is obvious that as all the picking had to be done in a few weeks, many thousands of pickers were required. These came chiefly from London, for " a holiday with work and pay," and were known as " furiners."

Payment for picking was arranged through the medium of tallies and hop-tokens. These showed the number of bushels picked, and were the basis of payment after the rate was agreed upon, which sometimes took several days.

The pickers received payment on account from time to time in exchange for these tokens, but the growers kept a sufficient balance in hand to prevent loss should the pickers leave before their work was completed.

Hop-tokens were passed as money between the pickers themselves, and were also accepted by the shop-keepers and inn-keepers in the locality, who were sure that the tokens would be redeemed later by the growers who issued them.

Tally-sticks (from the Latin " talea," a rod), were used either separately or in conjunction with the tokens. They were made of wood, and were about 9 in. long and 1 in. wide, sawn down the centre to leave one piece longer than the other, with a thick piece at the top. This had a hole bored through it, to enable the tally-man to carry them by means of a cord hung over his shoulder, in order that he might have both hands free to mark the tallies. Both pieces were numbered for identification, usually with ink, the picker retaining the shorter piece. After the hops had been measured, both pieces of wood were

207

Plate I

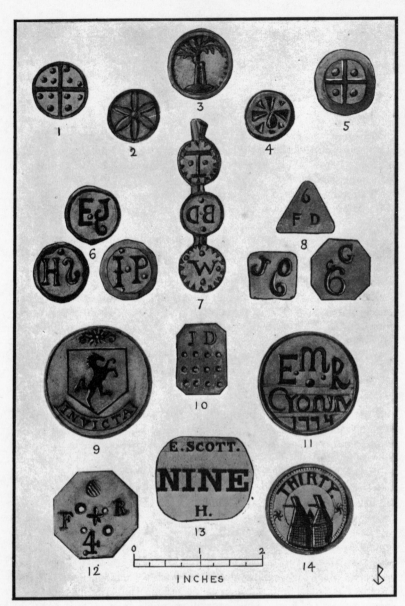

KENT HOP-TOKENS

fitted together, and notches cut across them with a knife or triangular file. A notch usually denoted five bushels, the odd bushels, if any, being marked on a different part of the tally-stick. Later, tokens, which were metal discs with a number or mark, were given to represent the odd bushels, to be exchanged later with the tally-man for additional five-bushel notches. When the notches reached the end of the tally-stick, the tally-man expected a "drink" from the picker, before commencing to mark the other side. A mark was made, usually with ink, on the tally-stick to record any money paid on account to the picker, and when the tallies were finished with, the notches were planed off in order that they could be used again for the next season.

The tally-sticks were gradually superseded by the tokens, also known as tallies, checks and medals, and these were made to represent, by combination, any number of bushels.

The earliest tokens (1-5) were made of lead, thick and crude, and it is quite possible that the medieval merchants' tokens were once used for hop-tokens, followed later by metal discs having figures to denote the number of bushels picked, and the initials of the growers, for identification and the prevention of forgery (6). The earliest dated hop-token is said to be that issued by Toke of Godinton in 1767.

As the hop-growing industry increased, many varieties of hop-tokens were made, with more or less elaborate designs, the usual metal used being lead alloyed with zinc, but brass, copper, iron, cardboard and paper were also used. Nearly all were home-made, or made in the neighbourhood of the hop-gardens in which they were used.

Most of the tokens with elaborate designs belong to Sussex, where it seemed to be fashionable for the hop-growers to compete with each other to produce pleasing pieces. This type of token was in use until about 1862, when the excise duty was taken off hops. The hop-growing industry started to decline from that date, and the later tokens were mostly plain, cut from sheet metal and punched with numbers to denote their value, and the initials of the growers, instead of being cast. The method of casting was either in strips (7) between wooden, plaster, or chalk moulds, or separately. A mould for the Bradbourne tokens, now in the Maidstone Museum, is made of brass. It is interesting to note that some of the ancient Greek coins were cast in strips, and afterwards broken apart. This method of casting was also used for the old Hebrew coins, and the Ancient British tin coins of 2,000 years ago.

Mistakes were often made in preparing the moulds by not realizing that the letters and figures should be reversed (7 and 9).

Tokens with the value of six were in some instances made in different shapes (8), triangular, square, or octagonal, to prevent confusion with the nines. The Offen tokens of Egerton have a small hole pierced on either side of the figure nine to distinguish it from the six.

Many were countermarked with initials when one grower took over a stock of tokens from another, or a son from his father (8). Sometimes the initial letter of the place where the tokens were used were placed beneath the initials of the grower or the figures (13). The letter " B," however, usually denotes bushels, and " D," dozens of bushels. Some sets of tokens are uniform in size for the different values, while others have been made progressively larger as the values increase. The numbers on the tokens vary from 1 to 200, but the lower values are the more numerous. The Kentish horse (reversed), with the motto " Invicta " appears on the 120 bushels token of Aaron Pinyon, of Boxhurst, Sandhurst (9). Perforated metal tokens were used by John Day, of Scott's Farm, Hunton. These were shaped like dominoes, the numbers being shown by the punched holes (10). There are comparatively few tokens with money values upon them. One of these sets comes from Catt's Place, Brenchley. They were issued by Edmund and Rosamund Monckton in 1774, and consist of a crown, half-crown, shilling, and sixpence (11). On the two larger pieces the initials of the husband and wife appear together. It will be realized that payment with this type of token must have been difficult and complicated, hence their scarcity. An unusual type of token from Smarden is made of copper, octagonal in shape, with the grower's initials and the figure 4 in addition to four perforations (12). E. Scott, of Hunton, used printed cards, with the six and the nine spelt out to prevent these numbers being mistaken one for the other (13).

F. W. Waters, of Frog's Farm, Newenden, issued a 30 bushel token in 1860, showing two oast-houses (14).

In East Kent, five-bushel baskets are provided for the pickers, but in the Weald the hops are measured out of the canvas bins into which the hops have been picked. Children sometimes pick into separate receptacles, such as umbrellas and odd baskets, and if they do not behave, are " given the bine," a somewhat painful form of punishment !

On your first visit to a hop-garden, you would soon be recognized as a new-comer, and would be met by one of the pickers, who would rub your shoes with a handful of hop leaves, and invite you to " pay your footing " with " shoe-money." In some cases where careless picking has resulted in leaves being included with the hops, the measurer may refuse to measure them until " the next time round," which may mean the next day. This penalizes the picker, as the hops shrink if left too long. When the measurer is seen approaching, pickers will " hover up " the hops, by inserting their arms in the bins, and lifting the hops so that they will lie as lightly as possible, and will take less to fill the measuring-basket. After the hops have been measured, they are put into long sacks called " pokes," in which they are carried to the oasts for drying over fires on which sulphur is thrown. After drying, the hops are pressed into " pockets," which are marked with the name of the grower and the date, and are ready for sale. The old method of pressing hops was for the pocket to be suspended below a hole in the cooling-room, the hops being filled in gradually with a wide canvas " hop-scuppet," while a man trod or jumped upon them until the pocket was full.

In Kent, the buildings in which the hops are dried are called oast-houses, and the hop-grounds are known as hop-gardens. In Hereford-shire and Worcestershire these are called hop-kilns and hop-yards respectively.

When the hop-pickers were finally " paid off," they would go into the nearest town to buy new clothing, etc. Their discarded garments, boots and shoes would be left in the roadways outside the shops. About 50 years ago it was not unusual for three or four cartloads to be cleared away after a Saturday's shopping in Maidstone.

The use of hop-tokens has been discontinued for many years, the the accounts now being kept in books.

" Hop-dogs," with a serrated hook at the end of a wooden handle, used for pulling poles out of the ground, are becoming rare, as the modern method is to grow the hops on coir yarn. The tokens, too, are gradually disappearing, as many were thrown away as useless or sold for old metal, although some are still used for fruit-picking and sheep-shearing tallies, and in some instances as card-counters.

It is hoped that if any are found, they will be taken or sent to the Maidstone Museum, for identification, recording, and preservation.

FRUIT GROWING IN KENT IN THE
NINETEENTH CENTURY

By David Harvey Ph.D.

The nineteenth century was a formative period for the Kentish fruit industry. At the beginning of the century fruit growing was a relatively unimportant sector of the agricultural economy of the county, but by 1900 it had achieved the status of a major industry. The reasons for this sudden transformation can only partly be understood by reference to conditions within Kent. For this reason it is essential to preface any study of the Kentish fruit industry by some general remarks about the changing demand for fruit and fruit products at the national level.

The most conspicuous factor of all, of course, was the very rapid increase in national demand during the nineteenth century. Not only was population increasing, but the population was becoming increasingly urban and industrial in composition and, more important, the standard of living of that population was rising. Fruit and fruit products are typically sensitive to such trends—particularly to the level of per capita income. As individual incomes rise so expenditure on 'luxury' foods such as fruit rises relative to expenditure on more essential foods. But the demand for fruit and fruit products was also sensitive to their cost. If fruit was expensive few would buy it, if it was cheap the demand increased. The expansion of fruit production was thus partly a function of incomes and partly a function of the cost of producing and marketing the fruit. In this latter respect the cost of transporting fruit to market was critical. In the early nineteenth century Kentish fruit was so expensive in the northern markets that it was available only to the upper income classes, but with the coming of the railways the price of Kentish fruit fell in the northern markets so as to become generally available to all except the poorest classes.

The rise in demand for Kentish fruit was thus partly a result of changes in national per capita income levels and partly a function of the declining costs of getting the fruit to distant markets. This simple relationship was, however, modified by a number of factors, such as government regulations affecting fruit imports, and the price of sugar which was critical for the jam and preserve industry. The rise in demand for Kentish fruit was not, however, a simple secular trend throughout the whole of the century—certain periods were periods of stagnation in the fruit trade, while others were periods of very rapidly increasing demand.

It is a matter of some controversy as to how far living standards changed during the early years of the nineteenth century, but even if average incomes did not increase, the natural increase of population meant a steady increase in demand for fruit. Added to this, the home industry was protected from foreign competition during the Napoleonic Wars, and although there was a brief period of depression after the end of the Wars as fruit imports from Flanders were revived, the government imposed tariff restrictions in 1819 which eliminated this uncomfortable competition. With a protected home market, a declining price of sugar and rising demand, the acreage of fruit in Kent as a whole increased during the 1820s and 1830s. The scale of this increase is difficult to judge, although one observer thought it was a seven-fold increase. This claim is probably much exaggerated. But the evidence does suggest that fruit production expanded and that expansion was most important in apple production, for this sort of fruit could be more easily transported to distant markets than the more perishable 'soft' fruits.[1]

In 1837, however, the fruit industry was plunged into a phase of crisis by the sudden reduction of the duties on foreign fruit (the tariff on apples, for example, was reduced from 4s. per bushel to a 5 per cent. *ad valorem* duty which was equivalent to between 3d. and 7d. per bushel). The effects of this change are difficult to gauge. William Harryman wrote to the *Maidstone Journal* in 1841 that 'by repealing the duty on foreign fruit, they rendered valueless the orchards which had taken all my life to raise and upon which I have expended large sums of money'.[2] The editor of the *Maidstone Gazette*, true to his free trade colours, maintained on the other hand that the 'prediction of ruin, low rents and land thrown out of cultivation' had not been borne out by events.[3] But even the *Gazette* reported in 1842 that 'the fruit growers are now scarcely able to get a market for their fruit', while Lord Torrington voiced the opinion that 'the sooner Kent is without an apple tree the better'.[4] In response to repeated requests minor adjustments were made in the duties but these had little effect. The *Gazette* claimed, however, that the real problem was the high price of sugar, for 'if sugar were at a price at which it could be bought, every sound apple that falls would be saleable at a remunerative price, instead of being, as at present, made into bad cider, or thrown into the hog tub'.[5] Certainly

[1] See 'Report from the Select Committee on the fresh fruit trade', *British Parliamentary Papers* (1839), viii.

[2] *Maidstone Journal*, 15th June, 1841.

[3] *Maidstone Gazette*, 29th June, 1841.

[4] *Maidstone Gazette*, 2nd August, 1842; Viscount Torrington, *On farm buildings, with a few observations on the state of agriculture in the county of Kent* (1845), p. 78.

[5] *Maidstone Gazette*, 12th July, 1842, and 27th August, 1844.

the rapid rise in sugar prices from 1838 to 1842, due to a national scarcity, meant that jams and preserves became very much a luxury. It is perhaps significant that the complaints from fruit growers diminished after 1846—the very time when new sugar duties meant a steady decline in sugar prices. But the impact of foreign competition cannot be ignored. In the main these imports were of hard fruit—particularly apples—whereas foreign imports of perishable soft fruits—such as cherries, plums and all small fruits—were not so important. Thus foreign competition challenged the English grower in precisely that form of production that had received the greatest attention since 1800. As a result of this many of the orchards that had been planted up between 1800 and 1835 were grubbed up. The Ministry of Agriculture returns record roughly 11,000 acres of orchard in Kent in 1872 which, even allowing for difficulties of comparison, does not match the 13,000 acres or so recorded in the tithe returns *circa* 1840.

But although orchards were affected, other forms of fruit production were not affected. Production of small fruit (raspberries, strawberries, gooseberries, currants, etc.) and production of some forms of tree fruit (particularly plums and damsons) increased very rapidly after 1850. This increase was partly a function of weak foreign competition, but the major factor was the falling cost of distribution. Even before the railways penetrated into Kent, the rail links between London (Covent Garden) and the rest of England allowed Kentish fruit to reach northern industrial markets relatively cheaply. As early as 1840 the *Maidstone Gazette* reported that cherry prices had been improved because of the 'great quantity sent by the railway to Liverpool, Manchester, and other manufacturing places'.[6] Again, in the 1850s it was noticed that improved prices in Kent were 'partly due to the increased facilities afforded by railway transit for obtaining a new market in districts to which cherries rarely penetrated in any quantities hitherto'.[7] But the increase in small fruit and soft fruit production after 1850 was not simply a function of falling costs of distribution; it was also closely related to the rise of the jam and preserve industry to importance.

During the 1850s and 1860s the price of sugar fell very substantially —and cheap sugar meant cheap jam. One commentator wrote in 1873 that 'the jam trade has, within a few years, attained a position never dreamed of years ago, when that article was considered one of the luxuries which only the rich could indulge in. So great has this trade become that small fruits, plums and damsons are not hereafter likely to go to waste for want of buyers.'[8]

The net result of all these trends was a decline in the importance of

[6] *Maidstone Gazette*, 11th August, 1840.
[7] *Southeastern Gazette*, 30th June, 1857.
[8] *Southeastern Gazette*, 16th September, 1873.

apple and pear production and a rise in the importance of soft fruits between 1840 and 1870.

But in spite of these changes the fruit industry was still not of *vital* importance to the agricultural economy of Kent by 1870. The major revolution came in the last three decades of the nineteenth century. Although accurate statistics are lacking, the increase in the fruit acreage was evidently enormous, but even an enormous increase in Kentish output could not keep pace with the phenomenal growth of national demand. The rapid rise in per capita incomes, the marked fall in transport cost, and a jam industry which developed a substantial export trade on the basis of the 'cheapest sugar in the world' were the major factors accounting for the tremendous increase in demand. Certainly the home market was capable of absorbing all the home production on an increased acreage together with vast quantities of imported fruit.[9] At the same time this was a period of general agricultural depression, and fruit farming, together with market gardening and dairying, remained one of the few consistently remunerative sectors of the agricultural economy. And in the Kentish case the depression in hop cultivation after 1878 gave an added impetus for farmers to turn over to fruit cultivation.

But the expansion of fruit cultivation in Kent as a whole was hampered by a number of features. Technical knowledge was insufficient—there were no technical research stations in those days. Undoubtedly much of the expansion in production was not accomplished with sufficient care—as one observer commented, 'the man who sticks a tree in the ground and expects, without giving proper care and attention to obtain good crops, the man who grows the wrong varieties, gathers the fruit at the wrong time, packs it in the wrong way, and sends it to market at the wrong time, will never make fruit growing pay'.[10] There was plenty of shoddy speculative planting in Kent during these years, but even the serious growers were faced with difficulties, for research, particularly in orchard culture, is a long term project which cannot be expected to yield results even in a decade or so. There were also problems of land tenure. Fruit cultivation required long term capital investment—again this is particularly true of orchard culture—and without security of tenure, and adequate compensation for improvements, no tenant would take the risk involved. Many individual landlords made adequate provision for this, but general uncertainty prevailed until the legislation of 1906.[11] Many contemporaries complained of the inadequacies of tenurial arrangements, and pointed out

[9] 'Report of the Departmental Committee on the fruit industry of Great Britain', *British Parliamentary Papers*, xx (1905), and xcvi (1906).

[10] J. Morgan, 'The fruit growing revival', *The Nineteenth Century*, xxiv (1888), pp. 881-2.

[11] See D. R. Denman, *Tenant right Valuation* (1942), chapter 5.

that this often led to farmers adopting forms of production which could yield their return within, for example, 14 or 21 years, which was the typical length of lease. Again, this placed a premium on small fruit cultivation rather than orchard cultivation. The home marketing system for fruit also proved inadequate to meet the new demand. The railways were not always co-operative in providing the special facilities for getting the fruit quickly to market, Covent Garden (the central point in the national marketing system) was congested, and the 'antique rather than time honoured' marketing system proved inadequate to the new demands being made upon it. These marketing problems only began to be solved in the twentieth century.

But in spite of these inhibiting factors, the widespread economic and social changes during the last three decades of the nineteenth century led to a marked expansion in the Kentish fruit acreage. Thus, by 1900 it was considered one of the major forms of land use in the county and contributed a great deal to the agricultural prosperity of the county. But not all parts of the county developed equally rapidly, and it is to this story of regional development within Kent that we must now turn.

REGIONAL DEVELOPMENT

It is not easy to detail the regional development of the Kentish fruit industry. The tithe awards can be used to give a general picture of the location of the industry *circa* 1840, but no other information is available until 1871 when orchard land was first recorded in the agricultural statistics. Small fruit was not recorded until 1887, however, and even until the end of the century there was considerable confusion over the definition and classification of fruit land. The map (Fig. 1) shows the location of all forms of fruit cultivation as indicated by the tithe awards and shows also the distribution of both orchards and small fruit in 1840 and 1893. Apart from the general picture that emerges from a comparison of these maps, however, we have to rely for information upon the literary sources which are sparse at the beginning of the century but fairly voluminous towards its end. To assemble this evidence as conveniently as possible, Kent had been divided into *five* districts. The definition of these districts corresponds to the divisions usually accepted by nineteenth-century agricultural writers and their approximate boundaries are shown on Fig. 2.

Mid Kent. The deep fertile ragstone soils around Maidstone—conventionally known as Mid Kent—had a long tradition of fruit cultivation and by 1800 this area was undoubtedly the main fruit producing area in the county. 'In the management of grown orchards,' wrote Marshall, 'the district far exceeds every other I have examined.'[12] Boys

[12] W. Marshall, *Rural economy of the southern counties* (1798), p. 312.

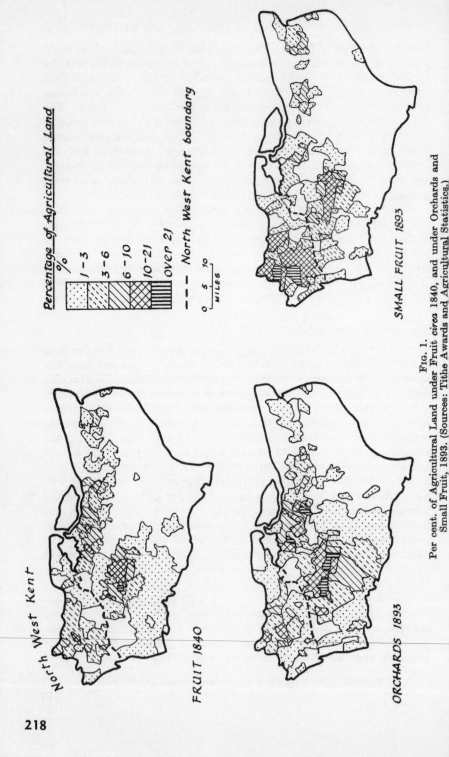

Fig. 1.
Per cent. of Agricultural Land under Fruit *circa* 1840, and under Orchards and Small Fruit, 1893. (Sources: Tithe Awards and Agricultural Statistics.)

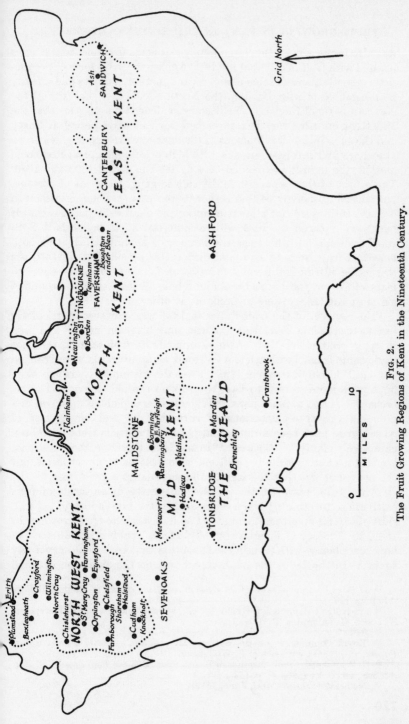

Grid North

ASH
SANDWICH
EAST KENT
CANTERBURY
ASHFORD
Boughton
under Blean
Seynham
FAVERSHAM
SITTINGBOURNE
Newington
Borden
NORTH KENT
Rainham
MAIDSTONE
Barming
E. Farleigh
Wateringbury
MID KENT
Mereworth
Yalding
Hadlow
Marden
TONBRIDGE
THE WEALD
Brenchley
Cranbrook
SEVENOAKS
Erith
Plumstead
Crayford
Wilmington
Bexleyheath
North Cray
Chislehurst
St Mary Cray
Farningham
Orpington
Eynsford
NORTH WEST KENT
Chelsfield
Farnborough
Shoreham
Halstead
Cudham
Knockholt

0   10
MILES

FIG. 2.

The Fruit Growing Regions of Kent in the Nineteenth Century.

219

was also impressed by the 'large number of fields from one to ten acres planted with fruit of different kinds'.[13] Apples, the main form of production, were sent considerable distances and market contacts had already been established with London, the North Kent coast, Essex, and the northern parts of England. The literary evidence thus suggests that the Mid Kent industry was well developed (for this early period at least), and the subsequent development of the district clearly took place on an already established base. In fact, with high prices and a protected home market, the industry expanded here during the period 1800 and 1840. The extent of this expansion is difficult to gauge in terms of acreage, but what is absolutely certain is that there was a great improvement in orchard culture so that a great many of the old derelict cider orchards had been replaced by 1835 with commercial apple orchards.[14] Both small scale specialist holdings and large scale holdings cultivating both hops and fruit, were to be found during this period. But by 1840 the marketing of fruit had become focussed on London, where the development of Covent Garden as the major wholesale market in the country, led most Kentish growers to think of 'no other market'.[15]

The revision of the fruit duties in 1837 was, however, particularly serious for the Mid Kent fruit producer since his main interest had been in apple production. Most of the complaints of depression in the fruit trade came from this district. As a result many orchards were grubbed out—as Whitehead wrote in 1881, 'it was the custom 40 years ago when hops were more certain to pay, to grub up the old cherry and apple orchards . . . and to plant hops'.[16] When fruit was planted up it was of a different variety—'plantations of currants, red and black, and of gooseberries have been formed, and plum and damson trees have been extensively planted'.[17] Between 1840 and 1870, therefore, the traditional kinds of fruit cultivation in Mid Kent were replaced by newer forms, but the net result was that the acreage did not change a great deal.

After 1878, however, the marked prosperity of all kinds of fruit cultivation, together with the depression in the hop industry, led to a shift of capital investment from the hop industry into fruit growing. In 1889, Mr. Brassey of Preston Hall, Aylesford, 'grubbed up 140 acres of hops and planted with fruit in the belief that that crop would never pay again'.[18] In the 1880s the main accent was on the extension of small

[13] J. Boys, *A general view of the agriculture of the county of Kent*, 2nd Edn. (1796), p. 113.

[14] Fresh Fruit Commission (1839), *op. cit.*, see the evidence of W. Harryman, M. Lucas, G. Langridge, R. Tassell, etc.

[15] *Ibid.*

[16] 'Royal Commission on the agricultural interests', *British Parliamentary Papers*, xvii (1881), evidence of C. Whitehead.

[17] C. Whitehead, 'Fruit farming in Kent', *Journal of the Bath and W. of Eng. Ag. Soc.*, ser. 3, xv (1883-4), p. 152.

[18] *Southeastern Gazette*, 18th June, 1889.

fruit cultivation—either on its own or as an undercrop to the orchard land—but in this Mid Kent found it difficult to compete with the better located northwest Kent fruit industry because of higher transport costs and a rather inefficient marketing organization. By the 1890s many of the Mid Kent growers had become disillusioned with small fruit cultivation—'one grower said emphatically, "bush fruit will never pay— soft fruit is done" and he added that orchard fruit and pastures paid best'.[19] Thus the 1890s saw the Mid Kent grower revert to his traditional interest of apple cultivation, although it was precisely in this branch of production that difficulties of technical knowledge and land tenure were most serious. In spite of all these difficulties, however, the Mid Kent industry changed from being a 'mere hedge against the contingencies of hop growing', to a major form of land use which during the subsequent decades of the twentieth century, was to become the leading sector in the agricultural economy of the district.

The Weald. The development of commercial fruit production in the Weald—on the river gravels and clays around Yalding and Peckham and on the varied sands and clays of the High Weald—came relatively late. Even as late as 1840 there was little commercial production. The tithe awards indicate a scattered pattern of 'home' orchards which produced apples mainly for local consumption and for cider making. But close to Mid Kent commercial production was already under way and this spread throughout the century across the Weald. A major factor here was the development of the Wealden railway (opened in 1842) and in 1851, for example, Henry Brown of Marden was recorded as being an 'owner and occupier of a fruit plantation employing twelve men'.[20] Properties classified as 'fruit holdings' began to be advertised for sale in the 1860s. Typical, is the advertisement for a property in Brenchley which drew attention to 'the facilities afforded by the railway for the obtaining of manure and for the conveyance of fruit and other produce to the London market'.[21] This extension of fruit cultivation from Mid Kent out into the Weald, became even more significant during the period of general agricultural depression after 1878. In 1887 farmers in the area were being 'urged to cultivate apples more extensively', and although there were many difficulties to be overcome, particularly in the remoter parts of the Weald, a considerable area of orchard land had been developed in the Weald by 1900.[22] Apples were the main form of production although plum and damson orchards were also developed at this time. Very little attention was paid to small fruit production apart

[19] 'Royal Commission on agriculture', *British Parliamentary Papers*, xvi (1894), report of Dr. Fream on the Maidstone district, para. 67.
[20] Original book of the 1851 Census, *Public Record Office* HO/107 ii (1616), 253.
[21] *Southeastern Gazette*, 26th May, 1863.
[22] C. Whitehead, *op. cit.* (1883-4), p. 163.

from a brief development of black currant production during the 1890s.

North-west Kent. North-west Kent had certainly possessed a fruit industry since the early seventeenth century. By 1800 there appear to have been two centres of production. The Thames-side parishes of Erith and Plumstead were famous for their cherries, while there was a more diversified form of production in the parishes of Wilmington, Sutton-at-Hone, St. Mary and St. Paul Cray.[23] The former area was gradually swallowed up by the expansion of London's suburbia during the nineteenth century, but the latter became the centre of the soft fruit producing industry in the British Isles by 1900. Cobbett noted in 1825 that the country around St. Mary Cray was 'a series of fruit gardens; cherries, or apples, or pears, or plums, above, and gooseberries, currants, raspberries or filberts beneath'.[24] This great variety of production was closely associated with proximity to the London market for all forms of produce were easily transported by road to Covent Garden. Other literary evidence suggests that there was a scatter of fruit production (mainly cherries) on the favourable soils between Darenth and Higham.[25]

It is very difficult to establish the history of development in this district from 1800 to 1840, for we possess no direct evidence. By 1840, however, there were many specialist fruit holdings in the area, while many of the large farms possessed a small acreage of fruit. The tithe award for Sutton-at-Hone thus records 46 acres of raspberry plantation, while gooseberries, currants and even loganberries are also recorded in other awards. After 1840 the pattern of development can be more easily established. Certainly the depression in the fruit trade after 1838 had little effect upon this district for although orchards were grubbed up, these were quickly replaced by soft fruits.[26]

The expansion of soft fruit production, however, mainly took place in those parishes that were within easy reach of the London market and which possessed areas of undeveloped wood or scrubland. In the district around Chelsfield, Halstead, Orpington, Chislehurst and Eynesford the fruit industry expanded rapidly over areas that had been poor scrubland or wood. As John Wood pointed out in 1906, 'wheat was then at 60s. a quarter and many of us had to take a bit of woodland to get a bit of land to begin with'.[27] In Eynesford it was reported that there had been extensive grubbing of woodland by 'the industrious little fruit

[23] See the comments in H. Hunter, *A history of London and its environs* (1811), ii, 187; A. Young, 'A journey to Dover', *Annals of Agriculture* vii (1786), p. 563; and J. Bannister, *A synopsis of husbandry* (1799).

[24] W. Cobbett, *Rural Rides* (1930 Edn. edited by G. D. H. and Margaret Cole), p. 252.

[25] See, e.g., R. Arnold, *A Yeoman of Kent* (1949).

[26] Fresh Fruit Commission (1839), *op. cit.*, questions 2183-4.

[27] Report on the Fruit Industry (1906), *op. cit.*, question 1535.

growers' between 1836 and 1881.[28] A return for 1886 indicates that in eight parishes around the Cray valley the area under fruit had risen from 629 acres *circa* 1836 to 1,455 acres in 1886. Webb reported that over a thousand acres of raspberries had been planted throughout north-west Kent in the period 1855 to 1875. Thus although the exact details are perhaps elusive, there is no doubt that north-west Kent had become a major soft fruit producer by 1870 or so.[29]

After 1870 the rate of expansion increased as the London jam industry rose to international importance. A report of 1882 stated that the largest additions to the soft fruit acreage in Kent 'have been in the neighbourhood of the Crays, and near Dartford, Orpington, Chelsfield and Farnboro . . . these consist in the main of raspberries, currants and gooseberries'. Another report stated that there were over 2,000 acres of strawberries in this district by 1882 and most of these had been planted up in the preceding decade.[30] By 1900 some of the fruit farms in this district were enormous—Messrs. Wood, for example, had nearly 2,000 acres given over to fruit production alone—and the industry was dominated by the 'highly specialized fruit grower, having possibly 500 to 1,000 acres of fruit in mixed plantations'.[31] This scale of production was a far cry from the small scale output of a few farmers which had been characteristic of the area in 1840. By 1900 north-west Kent dominated the soft fruit production in Kent, and only later in the twentieth century did the advent of motor transport and surburban sprawl of London lead to a decline of the industry. Undoubtedly this district with the advantages of proximity to London and a large area of undeveloped land, quickly adapted itself to meet the very rapid increase in demand for fruit and fruit products during the nineteenth century.

North Kent. The development of the fruit industry on the fertile tract of soils between Rainham and Boughton-under-Blean during the nineteenth century was slow. As late as 1880 fruit cultivation, particularly cherry production, was an addendum to the large scale arable and sheep farming, rather than a specialized industry.

This district is credited as being the centre of a revived fruit industry in the sixteenth century, but although there are many subsequent references to it, there is not much evidence as to its importance in 1800. Boys does not mention it and Marshall only comments that 'the Faversham part of it excepted . . . (it) is not a fruit country'. In 1874,

[28] *Southeastern Gazette*, 15th August, 1881.
[29] G. Webb, 'Fruit cultivation and management in Kent', *Trans. of the Royal Inst. of Surveyors*, viii (1875-6), p. 44.
[30] See the report from the Mark Lane Express quoted in *Southeastern Gazette*, 11th September, 1882; and C. Whitehead, *op. cit.* (1883-4), p. 155-6.
[31] W. E. Bear, 'Flower and fruit farming in England—part 3', *Journal of the Royal Ag. Soc. of Eng.*, 3rd series, x (1899), 46; and Report on the Fruit Industry (1905), *op. cit.*, para 13.

however, Hasted commented that there had been a decline in orchard cultivation within this area 'within living memory' as decaying orchards had been grubbed out and replaced by the more profitable hops.[32] The evidence suggests, therefore, that fruit production was not of any great commercial significance in this district in 1800. Cultivation was probably mainly confined to cherries and these were probably marketed in London by water. Cherry production is a very long term form of investment and contemporary leases suggest that it was a landlord rather that a tenant interest. Because of this, cherry production was not easily responsive to any short-term changes in demand, and the evidence suggests that the acreage remained remarkably stable throughout the century. Traditionally the cherry orchards were laid down to grass and used as sheep pasture—still not an uncommon feature in the district. It appears that although landlords controlled cherry production, most of them did not take a great deal of interest in it; few bothered to make their own marketing arrangements and the annual fruit auctions where the fruit was sold 'off the tree' were a regular feature. In 1874 two firms of auctioneers sold the crop from over 1,000 acres in this way.[33] Thus, although there was a marked increase in demand for cherries, particularly after 1870, there was only a small increase in the cherry acreage.

The history of other forms of production is more obscure. By 1840 the tithe returns indicate two small centres of diversified fruit production—one between Rainham and Sittingbourne, and the other in and around Boughton-under-Blean. After 1870 these two areas developed even more and the Sittingbourne area came to specialize on plum and greengage production as well as on several varieties of small fruit. Most of this specialized production was in the hands of smallholders, many of whom were owner-occupiers. Only after the agricultural depression of the 1880s had bitten deep into the economy of the area did any large-scale turnover from the traditional arable-sheep husbandry begin. Thus, although the area had a substantial acreage of fruit by 1900, it was by no means the dominant form of production in the district.

East Kent. The favourable soils for fruit cultivation in East Kent—mainly around Canterbury and Sandwich—had long been given over to intensive forms of cultivation such as hop growing or the cultivation of market garden products. But even as late as 1840 fruit growing was very little developed in the area compared with other parts of Kent. In the vicinity of Canterbury small scale specialist producers could be found but the overall acreage was not very large. After 1850 a more specialized

---

[32] W. Marshall, *A review of the reports to the Board of Agriculture* (*Southern and Peninsular England*) (1817), 445; and E. Hasted, *A history and topographical survey of the county of Kent*, ii (1788), 535, 560 and 568.

[33] See, e.g., the fruit sale advertisements in the summer editions of the *South-eastern Gazette* for 1874.

fruit industry began to emerge, particularly around the parish of Ash, where it was closely related to market gardening and oriented to the needs of the rapidly developing resorts of the Thanet coast. This trend continued until the latter part of the nineteenth century and even by 1900 the East Kent district was only slightly concerned with supplying the London market. This was partly a function of heavy transport costs and poor marketing facilities. One grower complained in 1889, for example, that it was costing him 8d. or 9d. to get his plums to market when the market price was under 2s.[34] At the same time there were acute difficulties over tenural arrangements in this district which led one writer to remark that 'fruit would be planted largely if there were a different system of security from that which now exists'.[35] The development of the fruit industry in East Kent was thus not very marked during the nineteenth century, and it was not until well into the twentieth century that fruit production became of any great significance within the economy of the area. But by 1900 a small localized industry had been developed, mainly oriented to the needs of the Thanet coastal resorts.

CONCLUSIONS

Broad economic, technical, and social changes led to a rapid rise in the demand for fruit during the nineteenth century. This increase was most significant between 1870 and 1900, and during this phase expansion of home production could not keep pace with the expansion of home demand—hence the rapid rise in imports of fruit. This failure on the part of the home industry to keep pace can be explained mainly in terms of technical difficulties, problems over land tenure, and difficulties of marketing. Within Kent development was also partly controlled by these factors. North-west Kent expanded most rapidly because it had a number of advantages in its favour—particularly low transport cost to the London market, new land for development, and a form of production that was least affected by problems of technique and land tenure. On the other hand development in Mid Kent was inhibited, partly by competition from the hop industry for the use of the land, and partly by technical, tenurial and marketing problems. The Weald suffered from similar difficulties as well as having to face all the problems inherent in opening up commercial production in an area which, before 1840, had had very little experience of this form of cultivation. North and East Kent suffered most of all from the high level of transport cost to the London market, and a landholding system that could not easily be adapted to the needs of fruit cultivation. In these terms the regional

[34] Royal Commission on Agriculture (1881), *op. cit.*, appendix to question 56, 491.
[35] Report on the Fruit Industry (1906), *op. cit.*, question 1062.

development of the fruit industry within Kent can be broadly understood.

Although the Kentish fruit industry had achieved much by 1900, it had failed to meet many of the opportunities offered by a rapid expansion in national demand. But by 1900 the basis for the subsequent expansion of the twentieth century had already been laid.

MAIDSTONE GENEVA

AN OLD MAIDSTONE INDUSTRY

By John W. Bridge, F.S.A.

The Hand-Writing upon the Wall, a caricature in colour, published by James Gillray in 1803, depicts Napoleon and his wife, Josephine, sitting at a table with members of their court, enjoying the spoils of England after the " invasion " by the French. A hand has written " *Mene, mene, tekel, upharsin* " on the wall, and the King's crown is outweighing Despotism to a cry of " *Vive le Roi* ".

Among the viands and wines shown on the table are the Bank of England, St. James's, The Tower of London, together with the Roast Beef of old England, Maraschino, and some red liquor in a bottle labelled " Maidstone ". The Maraschino, a liqueur made from the small black marasca cherries, was manufactured in England at this time, and might have been the forerunner of Maidstone's famous Cherry Brandy, as according to Walter Rowles' " Kentish Chronologer " of 1807, cherries were first planted at Teynham in Kent by Richard Haynes in 1520. Also, Evelyn records that " It was by the plain industry of one, Harris (a fruiterer to Henry VIII) that the fields and environs of about 30 towns in Kent only, were planted with fruit to the universal benefit and general improvement of that County to this day."

The bottle labelled " Maidstone ", however, was obviously intended to represent the well-known Maidstone Geneva, which was a very popular gin made in Maidstone at this time. If the liquor in the bottle had not been coloured, the bottle would appear to be empty, as the gin was colourless.

That this gin was exported to France is suggested by a second caricature in the writer's possession, by Woodward, engraved by Cruikshanks, and published by T. Tegg of Cheapside on 27th January, 1807.

The title is *The Giant Commerce overwhelming the Pigmy Blockade*. It shows John Bull throwing various goods of English manufacture across the English Channel to France, while he exclaims " Blockade my Country, indeed ! I'll shew you the Power of Commerce—take that, and that, and then to Breakfast with what appetite you may." Napoleon replies " Pray, Mr. Commerce, don't overwhelm me, and I will take off de Grande Blockade of Old England." The exports being thrown over to France include Fleecy Hosiery, Worcestershire Porcelain, Wedgewood Ware, Woodstock Gloves, Printed Calico, Leather, Derby Porcelain,

Birmingham Buttons, Wool, British Spirits, Sugar, Block Tin, Patent Coffins, London Porter, Staffordshire Ware, Norwich Shawls, Pig Iron, Cutlery, Combs, Shears, and a barrel marked " Maidstone Geneva ".

This blockade was a scheme of Napoleon to ruin Great Britain through her commercial trade, and was known as the Continental System, by which he attempted to exclude British goods from continental ports.

His Berlin Decree of 21st November, 1806, prohibited Spain, Italy, Holland and all French territory from direct or indirect commerce with Great Britain.

The British Order in Council of 7th January, 1807, countered this by forbidding all vessels, under pain of capture, from trading with any French port, or ports under the influence of France. Napoleon's scheme proved a failure, and even at the time when he was boasting of having struck a mortal blow, his own armies were being clothed from Leeds and Northampton.

Hasted writes in his *History of Kent*, " There has been within these few years a distillery erected and carried on here (Maidstone) to a very large extent, by Mr. George Bishop, from which is produced the well-known Maidstone Geneva, being of such a magnitude that no less than seven hundred hogs are kept from the surplus of the grains from it." These hogs were known as " squeakers " and were sometimes used to influence voters at elections. Geneva has no connection with a place of that name. It should be spelt with a small " g " as it comes from the Dutch *genever*, a corruption of the French *genièvre*, from the Latin *juniperus* = juniper, the berries of which were used for flavouring.

The word " Gin " is a contraction of " geneva ", and Geneverette is a continental wine made from wild fruits, flavoured with juniper.

Gin is an alcoholic liquor obtained from grain and molasses. The raw alcohol obtained from this source is re-distilled, then flavoured with the necessary material which varies with the brand, quality, etc., and re-distilled. It is flavoured with a large number of substances, such as angelica root, calamus root, sweet fennel, juniper, cinnamon, liquorice, etc. It is now usually sold at "70 proof", which is 30 "under proof", and it may not be sold below 35 " under proof ". When pure, it should be perfectly clear and colourless. Sweetened gin is produced by the addition of small quantities of pure sugar syrup added to the liquor. Hollands gin is a Dutch brand very largely imported into Great Britain. It is obtained from barley malt and is usually flavoured with juniper.

The origin of Proof Spirit goes back to the Middle Ages, when Proof Spirit was that mixture of pure alcohol and water, which when mixed with gunpowder, burned with a steady flame, and did not either explode, which was overproof, or extinguish, which was underproof.

rn, Excise Officers, first a Mr. Clarke in the middle of the eighteenth

PLATE I

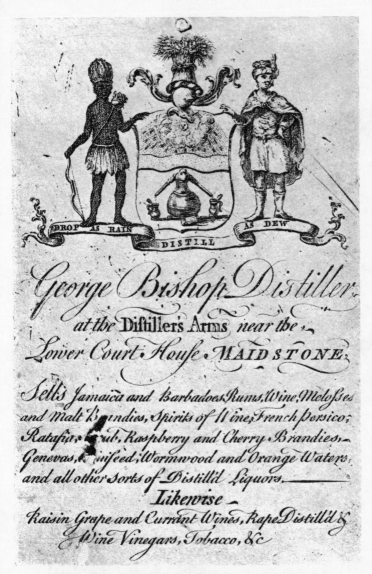

THE TRADE CARD OF GEORGE BISHOP

PLATE II

MENE, MENE,
TEKEL.
UPHARSIN

The Hand Writing upon the Wall

"The Hand-Writing upon the Wall"
By Gillray, 1803.

PLATE III

"The Giant Commerce overwhelming the Pigmy Blockade"
By Woodward, 1807.

century, and then a Mr. Sikes in 1816 invented an instrument, which by means of tables, could be more scientific than the "Gunpowder test". Both, however, used as Proof what was thought to be Proof at the time and as a result of this, the original test was used.

Proof spirit is defined as such spirit as at the temperature of 51° Fahrenheit shall weigh twelve thirteenths of an equal measure of distilled water. Application of this definition shows that Spirit of Proof strength contains very nearly equal weights of pure alcohol and water.

The proportions required to give Proof spirit are :

By weight. Pure alcohol $49 \cdot 28$
Water $50 \cdot 72$ $\Big\}$ at 60° Fahrenheit.

By volume the figures are pure alcohol $57 \cdot 1$ and water $46 \cdot 7$. Owing to the contraction in bulk, accompanied by a rise in temperature which takes place on mixing these figures for volume will give 100. Addition or reduction of the amounts of water as given above will give a mixture termed Under Proof or Over Proof, respectively. Thus 30 under proof means that 100 volumes contains 70 volumes of the proof spirit as defined by law. Thirty over proof means that 100 volumes of the 30 over proof liquid contain enough pure alcohol to make, by the addition of more water, a quantity of 130 volumes of proof spirit. In practice, the quantity of proof spirit in any mixture of pure alcohol and water is ascertained by the hydrometer invented by the Mr. Sikes referred to, using specific gravity tables in conjunction with the temperature of the mixture. It is on the proof spirit that all Customs and Excise duties are based. It is interesting to see that the normal gin and whisky sold to-day at 70 proof contains more water than pure alcohol.

The great popularity of Maidstone gin was because of its extra strength, it being made under a special Act of Parliament which allowed this. It was 83 proof, 13 per cent. stronger than the gin of to-day.

Excise duty was levied, based on the amount of spirit distilled from a given weight of " malt or other corn, including the bran thereof ", viz. 112 lb. avoirdupois which produced 120 gals. of " wash " or " wort " (the infusion of malt before fermentation) was charged " Two pounds, twelve shillings and fourpence ". If 30 gals. of the " wash ", when distilled by the Officer of the Excise, was found to produce " more than $2\frac{1}{8}$ gal. of spirits at the strength of one in six under Hydrometer Proof ", the duty charged was one shilling and fivepence. Additional duty was to be paid on the above, viz, 15s. and 6d. respectively until 12 months after " the Ratification of the Definitive Treaty of Peace ".

The writer has some of the original Maidstone gin made by George Bishop well over 100 years ago. It is crystal clear, colourless, and still very potent.

The effect of excessive gin-drinking is indicated by the following
" Epitaph on a Gin-Drinker ".

> " Half burnt alive ! beneath this Dung-hill lies
> A Wretch, whose memory the Sage despise.
> Her Brain all Tumult, ragged her Attire ;
> The Sport of Boys, when wallowing in the Mire,
> Life did, to her, as a wild Tempest seem ;
> And Death, as sinking to a horrid Dream.
> Hence learn, ye Brutes, who reel in human Shape,
> To you superior is the grinning Ape ;
> For Nature's wise Impulses they'll pursue,
> Whilst each dread Start of Frenzy governs you."

From Clement Taylor Smythe, writing in 1832, and from J. M.
Russell in his *History of Maidstone*, 1881, we learn that a distillery for
the making of Hollands gin was established in Maidstone by George
Bishop, a native of the town. He had for several years conducted a
distillery in Holland, and after acquiring the art of distilling the
celebrated Schiedam, he returned to England with the intention of
setting up a distillery in Maidstone. Finding that there were laws in
existence which would interfere materially with the needful operations,
he petitioned the Legislature for an Act of Parliament to enable him to
carry out his project, the realization of which, he pointed out, would
tend to prevent smuggling by rendering Hollands a home produce.
After much opposition, particularly by the Chancellor of the Exchequer
in the House of Commons, an Act of Parliament was obtained. Its
subsequent importance, however, was so great, that eight other Acts
were passed at different times, to continue and amend the powers which
had been granted (See 39 Geo. III. Cap. 105, etc.). The demand for
this spirit was very large, and it became in a short space of time a
principal article of sale in nearly every town and village in the country.
A large brick building with yards and other premises was erected on the
south side of Bank Street, near the Swan Inn and adjoining the old
Kentish Bank of Messrs. Brenchley & Co., and by the year 1789 the
distillery was in full operation. Maidstone Hollands gin was soon in
great demand. When the originator died, the concern was left in the
hands of his relatives, Sir William Bishop, George Bishop, and Argles
Bishop, whose affairs got into confusion through extravagance and
mismanagement, and in 1818, the distillery was sold. It was then
carried on by the purchasers under the management of George Bishop
for about a year, when in consequence of an application made by Argles
Bishop to carry on, under the same powers, an opposition distillery
which he had set up in premises in St. Peter Street, which have since
become part of the Medway Brewery, the Excise took the opportunity
of putting an end to both concerns, on the plea that the original distillery

233

having changed hands, the Act was inoperative. The premises behind Bank Street were afterwards converted into a steam corn-mill, shown as a " flour-mill " on an old map of Maidstone. The building, which was destroyed in 1926, can be seen in a view of Maidstone, published in *Kent's Capital* in 1898. Thomas Grant of Maidstone issued a handbill in 1857, a copy of which is in the Maidstone Museum, in which he gives the history of the manufacture of gin, based on the foregoing, to which he adds : " So highly was the gin esteemed, and the loss of it felt, that hundreds of Spirit Merchants, for many years after, professed to have a remnant ; and even to this date there are, as most persons can testify, numerous old public houses in London with " MAIDSTONE GIN " in large characters over their doors. In 1838 the father of the present proprietor began to distil this gin at Dover, and the celebrity it has again obtained since that period has induced the proprietor to erect a new distillery at Maidstone with all the improvements of modern times, including steam power. The chief recommendations in favour of this gin, in addition to its peculiarity of flavour are primarily, ITS WHOLE-SOMENESS—The peculiar care used in its first distillation from the grain, and the fact that it reaches the consumer in a state of genuine purity, are probably among the reasons why it agrees with the most delicate constitutions, and is generally admitted by medical men to be far more wholesome than ordinary gin. Secondly, ITS CHEAPNESS— for although nominally it is a trifle dearer than the BEST Common Gin, it is so much stronger in flavour, that for grog, little more than half the usual quantity is required. The price some time back lowered from 3s. to 2s. 8d. per bottle. It can be procured of most Spirit Merchants and Innkeepers throughout the Kingdom. The price is 14s. 6d. per gallon, or in bottles neatly labelled, at 2s. 8d. bottle included, 32s. per dozen, and to insure it being genuine, the corks are branded thus MAIDSTONE DISTILLERY. Where no agents are appointed, families can be supplied direct from the Distillery, in quantities not less than Two Gallons, or One Dozen Carriage paid to London or any Station on the South-eastern North Kent Railways. P.O. Orders, and correspondence to be addressed to " THOMAS GRANT, Distillery Maidstone."

In the Universal British Directory of 1791, George Bishop is mentioned as a Justice of the Peace, Sir William Bishop, Bart., as a Jurat, and George Bishop & Co., as malt-distillers.

George Bishop was Mayor of Maidstone in 1777 and 1786, and Sir William Bishop in 1778 and 1787. Sir William Bishop, Knight, distiller, who was knighted during his mayoralty by George III, lived in a house " standing back from the street, nearly opposite the Judges' Lodgings in Lower Stone Street ". He died in 1817 aged 83.

The following notices which are in the Maidstone Museum, giving the prices of spirits, are interesting :

MAIDSTONE HOLLANDS

Equal to any Imported.

Also best flavoured ENGLISH GIN, and fine, pure, clean SPIRITS that will mix with any Liquor in large Proportions without hurting the Flavours, and the best Wine Brandy Coniac flavour : Also CLEAN SPIRITS for the use of Apothecaries.

By GEORGE BISHOP ·
at his Distillery, Maidstone : and his warehouse :

No. 2.   RUSSIA COURT, Leadenhall Street, London.

Who only is authorised by Parliament.

No. 1.	Maidstone Hollands at per gallon		5s. 9d.
No. 2.	Ditto Cordial Gin.	,, ,,	5s. 6d.
No. 3.	Ditto best flavoured English Gin	,,	5s. 6d.
No. 4.	Ditto Clean Spirits	,,	5s. 6d.
No. 5.	Ditto best Wine Brandy	,,	6s. 6d.

N.B. Sold at the lawful strength, he being allowed by Law to sell Spirits stronger than any other Person.

A printed notice was sent to customers, probably because of the war conditions at that time, as follows :

Maidstone Distillery, June 20th. 1795.

Sir, We are sorry to say, there is a certainty of the Distilleries in England being stopped in six months—there is no stock of Spirits, and it is impossible for us to quote any prices at present.   We are,

Sir, Your obedient Servants,

Geo. Bishop and Co.

After this prices went up, and the following printed notices were sent to customers ordering gin.

Maidstone.

Sir, Your favour dated . . . came safe to hand, ordering . . . . Puncheon of Hollands ; we have thought it proper to advise you the present price before we forward the same, which is

7s. 0d. per Gallon   Money.

7s. 2d. Ditto.   2 months.

and we wait your further directions most respectfully.

Sir, Your obedient Servants,

Geo. Bishop and Co.

Later, this same notice was used, with the prices altered to 7s. 4d. and 7s. 6d. respectively.

The sale of Spirits by the Maidstone Distillery was discontinued about 1910, thus terminating the production of a commodity for which Maidstone was famous during the greater part of one hundred and fifty years.

235

MESSRS. BEST, BREWERS OF CHATHAM

By ROSEMARY A. KEEN, B.A.

IN these days when large firms of brewers with country-wide businesses are common it is interesting to contrast with them the beginnings of the small family firms now engulfed by them. The papers of one such family, the Best MSS.,[1] have been deposited in the Kent Archives Office. The Best brewery grew and flourished in the eighteenth century and was eventually taken over in 1851 by Winch and Winch, who later, as Style and Winch, were themselves merged with Courage and Barclay.

The Best family were established in Chatham from at least the mid-seventeenth century. Among the papers are the probate inventories of Thomas Best, who died in 1666, and his wife Dorothy Lott. Both owned brewing implements and probably they were the parents of the Thomas Best whose marriage to the daughter of John Mawdistley, a rich man, founded the family fortunes. It was this Thomas who "converted some small tenements, part of Dame Agrippina Bingley's house [in Chatham High Street] into a brewhouse and set up the business of a brewer in a small way". He married Elizabeth Thurston (*née* Mawdistley) whose father provided the money for rebuilding and expanding the premises, replacing the small tenements by a capital mansion house of brick ornamented with stone.

Thomas had one son, Mawdistley, who inherited the business, and five daughters, one of whom, Sarah, married Edward Vernon, the hero of Porto Bello and the Carthagena campaign. Mawdistley was head of the firm for only a few years for he died in 1744 leaving James, his younger son, to carry on.

It was during the eighteenth century, under the rule first of James Best and later his son James that the firm prospered most. James senior, second son of Mawdistley, was born in 1720. He had two sisters, Dorothy Sarah, and Frances, and two brothers, the elder of whom, Thomas, married Carolina Scott and lived at Chilston, the younger, Mawdistley, died as a boy. James must have been very fond of his young brother for there are some handwriting exercises and other papers, carefully kept, on which, in later life, James wrote " my dear brother Mawdistley wrote this ".

Very little survives to tell how James passed his childhood. One might guess that business affairs were in his blood, for a small account book methodically kept, gives details of how he spent his pocket-

[1] K.A.O. Ref. U480.

237

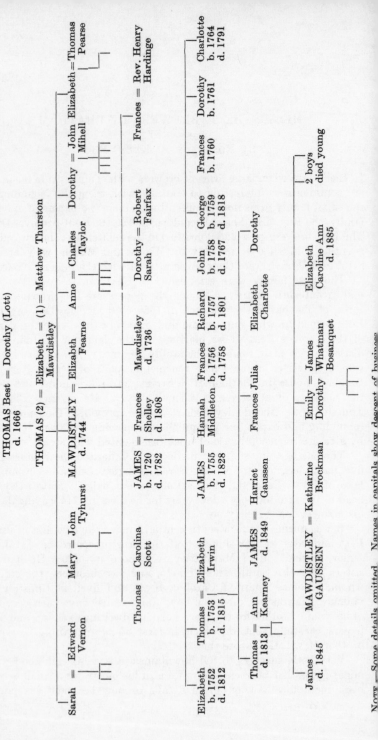

THE BEST FAMILY OF BOXLEY AND CHATHAM

NOTE.—Some details omitted. Names in capitals show descent of business.

money from Whitsuntide to Chatham fair in 1728. The entries are almost entirely for pennyworths of cherries, walnuts, or other eatables, according to the season, though once he bought an inkhorn and in September lavished twopence on some whipcord.

It is possible that he went to school in Chatham. Certainly letters from his school friends never come from far afield. One from George Peters in 1739, when presumably James had started work in the brewery, reminds him of how one of their friends, Lee, had " broke one of the beacons jumping over the furzes " while they were surveying at Bromley. He adds a sketch of himself and James laughing at Lee's misfortune.

James was blessed with a very happy marriage. As a young man he had fallen in love with a Miss Bartholomew, " my dearest Molly." Their engagement was apparently announced but the marriage was broken off. Judging by the copies of his letters which he kept it is probable that the lady's dowry was not sufficient. However, James' heart was not broken, for a few years later, in 1751, he married Frances, the daughter of John Shelley. This happy event came at the end of an exciting and costly year for him. He notes at the end of his accounts for 1751/2, " the occasion of my expenses being so high is this—part of the year I was sheriff, the other part I was married."

His accounts, indeed, reveal much not only about his personal taste and his family, but the effect which the growth of the business had on him. He was a man inclined to extravagance. Shortly before his marriage he had new-furnished his house at Chatham, in a style intended to be lavish. Thomas Gardner sent " an account what it will cost you furnishing your house in the most fashionable and Genteelest Tast as can be (Sparing no Cost which was your Orders to me) . . . [I] have included Plate China and all other things you may want ". The estimated cost for furnishing the fifteen rooms was £1,174 5s., the best parlour alone being over £200. Everything was of the latest fashion, even to the " two curious and carved flatt candle-sticks with snake handles " costing £8 10s. 9d. The wallpaper was very lovely. There was a fine yellow embossed damask with a gilt leather border, a printed sprig paper in a chain pattern, a fine crimson mohair embossed, and a fine blue on white Dutch tile paper. " I need not tell you," Gardner wrote, " Paper hangings are greatly in Taste and if you fix them a great Deal of money will be saved." James agreed with him. " The house may be furnished in a genteel Taste for half the sum," he continued, and James decided to economize, at least a little. He used some of his own furniture, had eight instead of ten " walnuttree large arms french chairs richly carved with Eagle claws stuffed up covered brass nailed backs," and ordered fine crimson worsted damask instead of Genoa for the sets of window curtains for

239

the dining room. This reduced the cost to £1,084 4s. and with this he was content.

A bundle of James' annual statements of accounts survive for the period 1748-1779. They reflect his gradual change of taste and standard of living as his business increasingly flourished. In 1751 his extraordinary expenses included not only money spent at the Assizes and on a present for his Chaplain during his term as sheriff, but also £80 on a new coach, £48 17s. for Mr. Whitby the cabinetmaker and £119 6s. 9d. spent in London, perhaps on his honeymoon. Then he notes " £1,000 for jewels not reckoned ". Gone are his bachelor days when he would spend £4 14s. 6d. on a pair of buckles or £3 4s. 6d. for the freight of his waistcoats. On 11th June comes the first entrance for Frances. " Paid my dear wife £5. 5s.", though ever afterwards she was always " my dear Fanny ". The following year expenses were again much larger as he furnished Boxley house. Fanny had a satin gown and other new clothes, amounting to over eighty pounds worth, and then there was the christening of his first child. It was in this year, too, that he started to pay for the schooling of six poor boys. With an increasing family there was no real chance for economy and from 1750 James' annual expenses increased fairly steadily and regularly, do what he could to prevent it. There was a trip to France in 1754 and new stabling in 1755. The number of servants increased and as the children grew older there were payments for their education. The boys graduated from Chatham to Eton and were also sent to France. His son James, who wanted a career in the army, needed £400 for his commission in 1776. James senior notes this as " an extraordinary charge " but despite equal expenses in later years he never mentions any further special expenses. Since his expenditure had risen from £1,500 to £2,600 per annum he had, perhaps, given up hope of economy.

James had almost certainly been bred up to the business, and when his father Mawdistley died in 1744 leaving the young man to carry on the firm alone he took up the task with relish and determination. During his headship profits from the firm almost doubled, his landed estates both private and business vastly increased and he was able to note with satisfaction that from 1765 to 1772 he paid more duty than all the other brewers put together.

James' gift lay partly in his willingness and eagerness to learn, and to use the most up-to-date methods. He was interested in every detail of the business and wrote for advice to people in many parts of the country. One of his most-valued correspondents was Mr. Combrune, a London porter brewer, who answered James' questions concerning his method of brewing " as I must suppose them to have been dictated by a spirit of curiosity, perhaps temptation, rather than want". James also had from him many notes and examples of how to keep his accounts, his method of striking a balance at Christmas and Midsummer, and notes on the brewing of his " guiles "[1] (giving the days of brewing, the quantity of malt used, the details of wort and hops, etc.). He even sent printed examples of his delivery notices, his vatts and butts' accounts and his method of reckonong his rough balance.

Mr. Combrune was not the only person whom James sought out. He prepared " six questions to ask a London porter brewer " and had them answered by J. Brest in 1772 and Isaac Jackson the following year. He wrote to men at Cambridge and Lowestoft, as well as near neighbours such as Mr. Baker, brewer at Rochester, who was a cooper at London. The last sent useful recipes on how to cure sour, ropy, or musty beer, to colour beer, cider or wine, to make mild beer stale, and to fine red port. James' method of approach is perhaps best illustrated by his dealings with Mrs. Ann Whitenhall of Faversham " who was a Yorkshire Woman and was used to brewing a great deal there, lived in many Gentlemen's familys and had always great Success. She brewed a great deal of good Beer in her small way, at her house at Faversham, where I first tasted it, and saw her; and after some Conversation upon brewing, and finding her quite expert in it: I got her to come over to Boxley and teach me her Method. My Lord Sonds and all the Gentlemen of the Neighbourhood used to stop, and drink some of her Beer; which She kept by her of all ages; It used to be extreamly fine and clear of the colour of a wheat straw, and well flavoured; it never used to be stale nor Stummy[2] but always drank mild and creamed ".

One of James' most important contacts was with a Mr. Henry Goodwin at Deptford. James brought away from Mr. Goodwin two small exercise books crammed with notes of " an account of several Brewings and the Methods made use of, by Henry Goodwin of Deptford Esq., given me by himself and with whom I went & stayed a week & saw his manner & Method of Brewing, and went to the Copper Side with Mr. Pyecraft his Brewer, and saw the whole Process and made several Brewings of Porter myself, which turned out very well and was much approved of ". This was in 1764 and it is noteworthy that Mr. Goodwin used a thermometer. The scientific brewing of beer was then in its infancy and the use of a thermometer was very up to date. Evidently it was some years before James made up his mind concerning its qualities as it was not until 1773 that two thermometers were sent from London, one for taking the liquors, the other for cleansing.

I have said that James was interested in all aspects of the business.

---

[1] gyle; the quantity brewed at one time: a brewing. *O.E.D.*
[2] *Cf.* " stum ", wine that has never fermented, *Blount* (*see* Halliwell, *Dictionary of Archaic and Provincial Words*).

His bundles of brewery notes include papers concerning casks. The choice of casks, both for the type of wood used and the size, was most important. " Mr. Jackson of Norwich " noted James " has got three more large casks made & finds them very useful—his observation upon them is to avoid filling them in very sharp weather & if compelled to it then start with more stomach—to have the Staves well seasoned or soiled before they are made, to take care the Piers are very stout to support them . . . never draw off in cold or frosty air." One opinion was not enough. Mr. Stewart considered " great casks are very useful for those who export beer and likewise for all returned Beers, always have the largest end of your cask uppermost like a churn ".

There is also amongst these papers a small bundle of recipes for killing rats, a perennial nuisance in a place where so much grain was kept. These had been collected by James from many places. There is a printed advertisement of 1774, by Mrs. Mary Smith of 77 Dean Street, Soho, for " Swain's paste for rats and mice to be had of Mr. Davis bookseller, Sackville Street, Piccadilly ". In 1764 Hudson the waterman provided a recipe which he had from the ratcatcher of Sheerness yard. Another recipe was that of S. Read, butler to the Duchess of St. Albans.

The business expanded considerably throughout these years. In 1751 Mrs. Waites brewhouse was purchased by James Best. Three years later he went into partnership with Samuel Waring, who was one of the senior clerks in the office. This was intended to last for twenty-one years but was dissolved in 1763 since Waring felt himself too old to be able to continue to share the responsibility. From that time to his death James continued alone. He bought Colonel Frederick's trade in 1767, apparently the last time that an actual merger occurred until Best himself sold to Winch in 1891.

In 1782 James died. He left a thriving business, a prosperous and extensive landed estate both at Chatham and Boxley, and a large and flourishing family. One of his sons, Richard, was to inherit the firm, as he thought. The future, however, did not turn out to be as bright as might have been expected.

James, Richard and George inherited the business jointly on their father's death, though George withdrew from it in 1795. Richard and James continued in partnership, though James probably had little hand in it as he was an Army officer and " wanted nothing to do with it ". The early partnership was not very successful. In 1784 the brothers commissioned the building of a brig *Concord*. She was to be used presumably to increase their overseas commerce. The surviving bills and correspondence give every detail of her building and fitting out as well as the costs of meals, wages and mooring expenses. With her gilded Medusa figurehead with its green snakes and blue draperies, the festoons of barley, leaves and flowers for the stern and badges, and the " blue ensign with the brewers arms painted on it both sides " she must have been a fine looking ship.   The captain, Mr. Dove, took the *Concord* to Madeira and Antigua, but the venture was not a success.   The beer went stale in the hot climate, Captain Dove was in debt to an Irishman for the ship's stores and landed up in prison, and in 1786 the ship was sold.   Despite this disaster the brothers apparently made no effort to recoup their losses.   For many years they drew far more than their allowances from the business with dire results.

In January, 1801, the blow fell.   William and Edward Twopenny, the family solicitors, wrote a respectful but stern letter to the heads of the firm.   They had had meetings with the brothers both together and individually and it had been suggested that Messrs. Twopenny should take over the business " from such investigation and a consideration of your affairs in general " they continued " we conceive the difficulties under which you now labour have in a great measure arisen from the various means that have been continually adopted by you all of withdrawing from the Estates and the trade divers sums of Money and a variety of articles purchased in the trade to apply to your respective uses instead of defraying the charge of them out of your own pockets.   Some of these that particularly strike us are as follows vizt—

Cash taken over and above the annuall allowances you were entitled to under your father's will.

Cash drawn from the Landed Estate Account as net produce of it when a great if not the major part of the Expences of buildings etc. in it were borne by the trade.

Cash drawn from the farm account under the idea of profit when in fact the major part of the Expence of it was born by the trade and charged in that account.

Articles consumed in your respective families & in the keep of carriages, pleasure Horses, Hounds & in various ways such as Beer, Coals, Hay, Corn, Rent, Taxes, etc. provided by & at the charge of the trade.

And sums expended in various articles of fancy about your respective Dwellinghouses.

What may be the amount of Cash & its value thus consumed in the period of now about 18 or 19 years we cannot precisely say but from the best judgment we can form it appears to us alarmingly large & sufficient to have not only prevented your present difficulties but to have enabled you advantageously to carry on your trade & your affairs and to have placed them and you at this time in a very commanding situation of trade ".

The suggested solution was for the family to confine itself to its

243

allowances. In addition " a present Sum of money is essentially necessary to be thrown into the trade . . . . We lament the necessity of using language so strong as this may appear to be but the importance of the subject & the friendship and attachment we have for you and various branches of your family & the sincere & earnest zeal which we feel for you for them & for your concerns require us to act the part of true friends in thus stating to you the result of our investigation and your real situation in their true light and without reserve ".

The immediate result of this sharp reproof was that Messrs. Twopenny took over the business and until 1807 ran it in trust for the brothers. It is possible that some gaps in the series of records are caused by this and that some books were retained in the solicitor's office after the business was returned to James.[1] Certainly many surviving series start in 1807, and the entire method of book-keeping becomes more careful and detailed after that date.

Very little information survives to give insight into James junior's career as a brewer although there is an amusing note by him in the front of the stock account book for 1818-23. For some years he had been unable to balance his stock and eventually one of his men was caught in the act of stealing beer, by tapping the casks with an elder-tube which he nicknamed a " pony ". He confessed that it was a regular practice with the men and that to avoid detection they would afterwards fill the barrels again by mixing stale beer with the good. James decided that since all the men had taken part in the fraud they should all be equally punished. He therefore reduced their beer allowance to one pot a day and cut their wages by two shillings a week.

James died in 1828 when the business passed to his only surviving nephew James (the son of his brother Thomas), who was later better known as Colonel Best. There is an interesting document in the collection dating from the 1840's concerning the desire of Colonel Best's tenants to sell London porter. In this Colonel Best is described as " one of the most Considerable Land Proprietors in the County . . . and the owner of a large Brewery Establishment at Chatham, which has no Competitor in the County ". It is ironical in view of recent developments that he was advised to open negotiations with Messrs. Barclay !

After the death of Colonel Best in 1849, despite the firm's prosperity, it was decided to lease the business to Messrs. Winch and, although the actual sale did not occur till 1891, the family relinquished personal interest in the firm from 1851. The series of business records come to an end, and even the family and estate papers dwindle in bulk and variety. Indeed, it might be said that as the Best brewery had come

[1] Richard died in 1801. James was not left alone in charge of the business till 25th March, 1809.

to the height of its fortunes with the first James as its head so it came to an end on the death of the third James.

NOTE ON BUSINESS RECORDS

The earliest surviving business papers date from the time when James was head of the firm. Probably the first series to be kept were the ledgers, grand cash accounts, and the corresponding brewhouse vouchers.

The ledgers include accounts for all aspects of business, besides the customers' accounts and tradesmen's bills. There are details of hops, with the names of the suppliers, and accounts for isinglass, malt and coals needed for the actual brewing. Freight expenses and excise dues are included, as well as oats and beans for the horses. There are also all kinds of taxes, due not only for the brewery site but also for the inns and other premises acquired as the business grew in size, church and poor cess, land tax, gaol rate (from 1818) and highways and lamps tax.

The earliest ledger also gives many more details for items, which are either no longer mentioned in the later ledgers, or, like yeast and yeast stores, become a separate series on their own. Some of these items may be included because of rebuilding or expansion of the premises, for there are details of bricks, lime, timber and lathes, sand, stone and tiles.

The earliest surviving cash account, like the ledger, is not the first of the series, and there are some gaps in the series during the eighteenth century. Some of these can be filled by recourse to James's private accounts, where business and personal items are intermingled with a note " brewing," beside the business entries.

The series of order books was begun in 1811 and runs complete to 1851. The entries are almost entirely for beer, etc., though some orders for hay are included. After 1843 the entries are arranged in columns, giving customers' names, quantity of beer or amber, date of delivery and the name of the carrier.

The petty cash accounts were made up weekly. The entries are mainly for wages, extra labour, letters and parcels, turnpike dues and payments for the starting of beer at $\frac{1}{2}$d. per barrel. There are occasional entries for the watchman, who was paid one shilling per night to watch the beer during the brewing of a guile. Some pierage dues are also included, and amongst the vouchers are rent receipts, and bills for stationery, iron work and the teaching of six poor boys. This last had been begun by James senior privately. Many entries are replaced in later years by separate accounts which were begun as the business grew. Extras accounts begin in 1823 and postage and letter accounts in 1827. Winch's allowances, 1d. per barrel, survive from 1829. No explanation is given for this allowance but probably he had a share in the firm. It is possible that he was a relation of the firm who eventually took over the business. There is also a book labelled " pots of beer," an account of the men's beer allowance, including bread and cheese for the men at Boxley, when extra workmen went over at harvest and other busy times.

Two of the most interesting volumes give details of the goods bought for the brewery. In one, 1801-45, the information is set out in columns, giving the name of the person or firm from whom the goods were purchased, the method of delivery (generally by wagon, sometimes by hoy or more rarely by barge) and the article purchased. Naturally this was usually hops and malt, but there were also butts and coals, isinglass seed, fodder, straw, cinquefoil and saintfoin. In the other volume, 1807-51, the entries are chronological and partly duplicate the entries in the first volume except that sometimes the names of the hoys and their owners are given. In this book purchase of equipment was entered, strakes for the wagons, tire nails, butt taps, barrel bungs, hose and old leather pipe. Some complaints are noted, though usually complaints were added in the order books. Much equipment was brought from London and a new back, needed in 1817, was ordered from a firm in Broseley, Shropshire. Agreements for employing men were also included, either to work in the brewery itself or as odd men at Boxley or Chatham.

Finally in the main series are the stock and general rest accounts. These, though interesting, contain nothing unusual. The general rest give customers' names with the number and value of barrels in their possession and a brief summary of the debts due to the firm and owing to the tradesmen and excise, with the amount of stock and utensils in trade. The stock accounts were made up weekly. The number of the storehouses is given till 1818, though only a few appear to be used. There is an interesting development in the type of drink brewed. From 1807 beer and amber were the only drinks until 1818 when ale was introduced. This was dropped again in 1838 and in 1849 porter and stout were introduced and the stock of beer and amber was gradually used up.

The minor series of accounts include items which would only be found in a brewery business. There are malt accounts, giving the names of the maltsters and the number of the lofts in which the malt was stored, a note of the date when the malt and hops were used in the brewing and the quantity taken. Accounts for the finings were entered in the petty cash. They were sold to inn-keepers and others at one shilling a pailful. The books list the names of the men with the number of pailfuls supplied daily. One volume of length accounts, giving details of the guiles, survives for 1807-14. Lastly there are the grains accounts which give the date of brewing, the quality (whether porter or amber, etc.), the quantity, amount paid and, until 1814, Messrs. Best's share. After 1829 only the names of the purchasers with the dates and the amount paid are given. A register of certificates for the delivery of beer, etc., was kept from at least 1827. These give details of the delivery rounds and divisions, the number of casks and quantity of beer and the officers or traders signatures. The system was discontinued early in 1830.

NOTE ON BEST ESTATES

The Best estates centred on Chatham and Boxley though for many years Chatham was more important because of the business interests and Boxley was used as a country residence and useful source for supplies of produce for the business.

Thomas Best had lived in his capital mansion house next door to his business. In 1735 he obtained a mortgage on Rome House which he settled on his son-in-law, John Mihell. His son, Mawdistley, had plans for building a new house. In fact he went so far as to write to his step-sister, Elizabeth Thurston, offering her the chests and pictures from his home that presumably would not fit the new house. His death in 1744 prevented his seeing the fruition of his scheme, but his plans were inherited by James senior who in 1750 commissioned Thomas Gardner to furnish the house, which, known as Chatham House, was finally completed in 1758, and which remained the family home until 1820 when it was burnt down. In 1774 James was able to pay off the mortgage on Rome House but did not make it his home until 1820. It was at this time, too, that the acquisition of business premises was at its height. There is an extensive series of rentals and rent books for the estates leased from or by James Best and the parishes covered include Frindsbury, Gillingham, High Halstow, and Rochester.

The Boxley estate developed earlier though not so swiftly as the estate at Chatham. Mawdistley bought Park House in 1720 and made it his home. There is some confusion over the exact site of the house. Old Park House which was occupied by Samuel Athawes and owned by John and later Pawlet St. John was probably somewhere near the present Park House farm. The house in which Mawdistley lived was south of the modern Park House and before the highway diversion of 1884 fronted the road. The last Park House, which has only recently been pulled down, was originally called Boxley Lodge and was purchased by Mawdistley Gaussen Best from George Rashleigh in 1838.

247

KENTISH TRADESMEN IN THE EARLY NINETEENTH CENTURY

By Elizabeth Melling, B.A.

AMONG the County Records in the Kent Archives Office, County Hall, Maidstone, is a very large series of account books and papers of insolvent debtors covering the first half of the nineteenth century in date.[1] The survival of such a group as this appears to be unique among County Records, and should provide an interesting source of information concerning the small tradesman and businessman of one particular area in the early nineteenth century. The records of large and important businesses with a continuous history have a good chance of survival, but the records of the small tradesman, particularly if unsuccessful, are not so easily found, a fact which adds to the importance of this collection.

From the end of the seventeenth century Acts of Parliament for the relief of insolvent debtors were passed regularly, the execution of these Acts being carried out by the Courts of Quarter Sessions. In 1820, by an Act of 1 George IV c. 119, a change was made in the system and a new court called " The Court for Relief of Insolvent Debtors " was set up, three commissioners being appointed to preside over it. The court could direct final examinations of debtors to be taken at Quarter Sessions and it is probable that much of its work was delegated to the justices in Quarter Sessions. In 1824, however, an amending Act was passed (5 George IV, c. 61), and the jurisdiction of the justices in Quarter Sessions over insolvent debtors was ended. The number of commissioners was increased from three to four and the commissioners were to make circuits separately to hold courts. The clerk of the peace or his deputy was to attend the courts held in his county and to act as clerk to the commissioner. Schedules and books belonging to debtors were to be lodged with the clerk of the peace so that they could be inspected by creditors.

This Act appears to be the origin of the formation of the collection under consideration and thus these documents and books of insolvent debtors are, strictly speaking, records of the clerk of the peace and not of Quarter Sessions. The bulk of the books and papers were filed with the clerk of the peace between 1830 and 1846, though the outside dates of deposit, as far as can be ascertained are 1825 and 1856. The outside

[1] Ref. Q/CI.

dates covered by the contents of the books themselves (as opposed to the dates when the books were deposited) are 1737 and 1855, but the bulk of the books concern the years 1820 to 1845. The books and papers of approximately 540 insolvent debtors have survived. For many of them only one or two books were deposited, but for some half a dozen or a dozen are found, and in one case forty-five. There are thus well over a thousand books. The papers are far fewer and consist of conveyances, leases, copies of wills, assignments of property for the benefit of creditors, bills, letters and odd memoranda.

Most of the books and some of the papers were endorsed, presumably by the lawyer acting for the debtor, with the name of the debtor, the prison where he was lodged, the number of books and papers deposited and the name of the lawyer. Some lawyers also added the date when the documents were filed with the clerk of the peace. The bulk of the books are also marked with a serial number, which, with some exceptions, corresponds to the chronological order in which they were deposited. There are, however, some books and papers to which no serial number has been given, and some which have no endorsement at all.

No detailed examination of all this material has yet been attempted, nor is it possible in a short article to do more than indicate a few points of interest which even a cursory examination has revealed and to mention a few of the more interesting items found in the collection. The five hundred and more debtors in question were engaged in many different trades, but as might be expected the number of traders engaged in the more common trades who became insolvent, is greater than the number of those engaged in the less usual ones. There are many bakers, grocers, butchers, tailors, cobblers, carpenters, builders, carriers, and horse-dealers to be found, though the largest number of tradesmen engaged in any one trade who became insolvent at this date were decorators cum glaziers cum plumbers cum carpenters. The number of publicans is also high. The relaxation of the licencing laws in 1828 and 1830 may have encouraged a sudden increase in the number of innkeepers and many evidently fell into debt. A number of traders were engaged in more than one trade at the same time. One man appears to have been both a coal merchant and a builder and joiner ; a certain baker and grocer also kept and trained gun dogs. Several publicans had an additional occupation, one for instance as a cobbler, another as a cobbler and brushmaker and hirer of horses and chaises. Letting lodgings was also an extra source of income to some of these debtors.

Some of the account books give the names and addresses of customers and thus afford information of over how wide an area a particular tradesman carried on his trade. In many cases this was over a radius of several miles and sometimes a tradesman's customers might be scattered over half the county. The radius of trade was naturally affected by the type of trade carried on. A supplier of food such as a butcher or baker usually served a smaller area than a carpenter, builder or tailor, while wine merchants and sellers of ale and porter seem to have had particularly large areas of trade. Gunsmiths and grain-merchants also seem to have drawn their customers from a fairly wide area, and professional men such as lawyers, auctioneers and valuers had clients from a large part of the county. A certain brandy merchant of Greenwich, called John Slee, had a very extensive trade. He supplied brandy to inns all over the country including many in the Midlands, Lancashire and Cheshire. A number of the debtors came from that part of Kent which is now in the London area, and some even from within London itself. Two account books and a letter book of a London merchant importing muslin from the Low Countries, France and Germany, are among the more interesting items in the collection. As might be expected, close trading connections between Kent and London are apparent. Kent tradesmen bought goods from London tradesmen, presumably wholesale, in order to resell them, and London tradesmen naturally had customers in Kent. The contents of some of the account books in which important local families figure as customers, supplement information provided by the account books of the same families among the private estate and family collections in the Archives Office.

In almost all cases where the name of the prison is given, the debtors were imprisoned at Maidstone, no matter where they lived. There are only three instances where another prison is noted, namely, Canterbury, Gravesend, and " The Debtors' Prison " at Hoo. Maidstone lawyers appear to have had almost a monopoly of dealing with the debtors' cases. Where the lawyer's name is given, five, four of them definitely styled " of Maidstone," dealt with the bulk of the cases, two others dealt with a few cases and six other names appear once only.

Many of the account books of these debtors are exceedingly rough and some are almost incomprehensible. In some cases it is by no means easy to find out in what trade the accountant was engaged. There are two main types of account book, rough Day Books giving details of the items sold, or the work done on a particular day and the amount of money charged, and ledgers with the accounts arranged under the names of the customers. The knowledge of book-keeping displayed is in most cases rudimentary, and judging by this it is not surprising that the owners of these books became insolvent. The accounts were seldom balanced and the tradesmen can have had little idea of an overall picture of his financial affairs at any one time. Often the books deposited for one particular tradesman only cover a few years so that it is not possible to follow the fluctuation and ultimate decline of his affairs over a long period. Some of the books also are completely undated or else give no year dates.

On the whole the debtors in question were merely small local tradesmen and their books and papers show mainly details of their day-to-day business, but some contain items of more general interest. There is, for instance, an account book of a Thames River Pilot, dated 1841-42, and at the back of the book are set out directions for the navigation of the River Thames. Or there is the Tunbridge Wells glazier and decorator who did work for the Duchess of Kent at Mount Pleasant House, Tunbridge Wells ; " 2 Sq^{rs} in Princeses Room 17½-12½ " were supplied on the 10th September, 1834, at a cost of ten shillings. A publican in East Kent had occasion to supply " the celebrated Lord Byron," as he described him, with several pots of beer and glasses of gin during March, 1822.

An interesting set of account books are those of William Slater, a schoolmaster. When the accounts begin in 1823, he evidently kept a boarding school for young ladies in Ilford, Essex. The accounts for the board, tuition, stationery, haircutting, shoemending and medical attention of the girls are set out, and whether they were parlour boarders. By 1827, William Slater had crossed the river to Greenhithe in Kent, and was teaching boys, most of them day pupils. From 1829 to 1832, he is found in charge of the National School at Greenhithe with both boys and girls for pupils. In addition, from 1827 to 1831, he ran an Evening School. At the same time he also took some private pupils both day and boarding. His educational activities were thus many and varied. Yet another interesting account book is that of Stephen Stevens of Hastings, who, between 1833 and 1838, hired thirty toll-gates on turnpike roads in Kent and Sussex. The accounts show that this was not a paying proposition. He seldom made more than a few pounds profit per annum on any one gate and in many cases he did not receive in tolls as much as he paid in rent for a particular gate.

The most interesting and exciting of all the books is one which is marked on the front " Re Skinner " and contains at the beginning and end very rough accounts, apparently of a carrier, dated between 1819 and 1827. The bulk of the book, however, consists of a detailed log of a ship, H.M.S. *Valontaire*, running from May, 1810, to January, 1811, while the ship was on active service in the Western Mediterranean patrolling the coast of Spain. Here is set out each day the state of the weather, the position of the ship, the details of setting the sails, what other ships were sighted, punishments given to members of the crew, and the general activities of the ship : how privateers were chased and boarded, French troops on the shore engaged, Spanish troops carried from one place to another, how the ship was supplied with food and how she was refitted in port. Such details as the firing of a twenty-one gun salute on the 30th May, 1810, in honour of the King of Spain's birthday, are noted, or how on the 18th October, 1810, marines were sent on shore to assist in levying contributions on the inhabitants of Cadequees. Here hidden among the petty accounts of small local tradesmen lies an enthralling story.

Apart, however, from items of special note, this whole collection should be of interest to the general economic historian and to the student of local history, and may well present the pattern of lesser business life in an unusual light.

THE ROAD BETWEEN DARTFORD, GRAVESEND AND STROOD

By R. H. HISCOCK, LL.B.

FROM the Roman era and possibly earlier the main road from London to Dover has followed approximately the line of what was later known as Watling Street. In the medieval period one major deviation from the Watling Street occurred between Dartford and Strood where the road was diverted through the town of Gravesend and Watling Street became a by-road and footpath until the arterial road, now the A2 or M2, was opened in 1924.

This article deals with the road between Dartford and Strood and the various Turnpike Acts under which it was maintained during the eighteenth and nineteenth centuries.

THE VARIATIONS IN THE COURSE OF THE ROAD

This was governed by two geographical features. First the Ebbsfleet which in Roman times seems to have been navigable as far as Springhead where the important settlement of Vagniacae grew up. This was the natural point for the road to make for between the Medway crossing at Rochester and the Darenth crossing at Dartford, as any line further north would have had to make a diversion to the south to cross the Ebbsfleet here. Secondly, the origin of the town of Gravesend as the eastern terminus of the Long Ferry on the Thames from London, which was in existence prior to 1293, from the evidence of a lawsuit in that year. This caused travellers from the Continent and East Kent to make for Gravesend. At about the same period the Ebbsfleet seems to have silted up and a bridge or causeway across it was built near its junction with the Thames at Stonebridge, Northfleet, enabling travellers to continue direct from Gravesend to rejoin Watling Street at Brent, Dartford.

By the end of the sixteenth century the Dover Road followed two courses between Chalk and Northfleet, one now known as Old Road, Gravesend, and Dover Road, Northfleet, about a mile to the south of the town of Gravesend and the other from Chalk to Gravesend water-side and then across the chalk cliffs near the river to Northfleet. The 'Old Road' is probably the earlier of the two and its course may have been dictated by the flooding of the valley below Milton Church at high tides prior to the building of the Sea Walls. The Domesday tide mill at Milton seems to have been near the Church, 'Millers Field' adjoined the

255

churchyard to the north and the tide must have flowed up to this point. It is interesting to note that the similar Mill at Northfleet was on the Creek near Stonebridge. Both these roads are shown in Symonson's map of 1596. This map marks the windmill on Windmill Hill, Gravesend, with a road running to the south of it and a loop road to the north. Philip Symonson was a Rochester man and would know the area. The course of the Watling Street between Strood and Dartford is not marked and certainly by the eighteenth century, and probably earlier, it had become a footpath between Park Corner, Swanscombe, and Sandy Lane, Betsham, but its site remained as the parish boundary between Southfleet and Swanscombe.

Chalk was dug at Gravesend at least as early as the fifteenth century and these diggings have from time to time interfered with the course of the road between Gravesend and Northfleet. A plan of 1693 in the Darnley Collection at the Kent Archives Office shows a new road 'set back from the waterside to the east of Gravesend town' the old road having been quarried away. On 23rd May, 1688, the Corporation Minutes refer to a letter to be written by the Mayor to Mr. Francis Brooke to empower him to enter a caveat in the Corporation's name for 'preventing the turning of the way near Northfleet, provided the said Corporation be at no charge'. A later Cobham Estate map shows the 'new road' of 1693 as 'old road' and a 'road to Northfleet cut *c.* 1716' further south, in addition to the proposed site for the 'New Road' which was cut in 1801 and is the present New Road—Overcliffe— London Road between Gravesend and Northfleet. Throughout the eighteenth century there were variations in the route between Gravesend and Northfleet due to the chalk diggings. Robert Pocock, the Gravesend historian, writing in 1797, states that the road across the cliffs was dangerous and almost disused.

In addition to the main road there is some evidence of a number of parallel or loop roads. There was a road through Stone and Greenhithe to Craylands (now in part only a footpath) and thence as the Lower Road to the Black Eagle, Northfleet. This Lower Road between Craylands and the Black Eagle, Northfleet, is reputed to have been the main road prior to the present road, having been cut by the Turnpike Commissioners, but there is no documentary evidence of this. From Chalk a Lower Road runs through Higham and Bill Street to Strood. There is a road between Watling Street near Springhead and Chalk connecting with this Lower Road which, judging from the original junction with the Old Turnpike Road near Echo Square, Gravesend, may well be older than the line of the Old Road, possibly connecting Roman settlements at Higham with those at Springhead. A deviation round Chalk Church and a road from Deadman's Bottom, Shorne, to Shorne Village and thence to Gadshill may also represent an earlier road.

The Turnpike Acts

The Turnpike Acts were passed to carry out improvements to the trunk roads of the country made necessary by the increase in travel and improvement of vehicles which took place in the seventeenth and eighteenth centuries and the need to have one authority responsible for a length of main road, instead of a number of parishes.

The road between Northfleet and Strood was turnpiked in 1711 and was the second Kent road to be so treated.

The Act recited that 'the greatest part of the highway between the towns of North-fleet Gravesend and Rochester . . . about seven miles in length and being an ancient Post and Coach Road as well for Carts and Carriages between London Rochester Maidstone Canterbury Dover Deal and Margrett is in many places too narrow and become very hollow and dangerous for Passengers and often occasions long stops to the Post and others travelling thereon and is prejudicial to trade . . .'. It then makes provision for the Justices of the Peace in Quarter Sessions to appoint Surveyors and gives them powers to pay and appoint labourers and require carts and persons who are liable to maintain the road by Statute to work on the road, and also gives powers to dig gravel and levy tolls.

The roads to which the Act applied are not set out in detail but the Trustees took over the road from Stonebridge through Northfleet and along the line of the Old Road between Northfleet and Strood. It also took over the course of the road across the chalk cliffs from the Queen's Head, Northfleet, to Gravesend and probably that between Gravesend and Chalk. Apparently the Commissioners made an alteration in the line of this road as in the Gravesend Corporation accounts for 1713-14 there is an entry on 12th April, 1714, for drawing and engrossing two orders, one for Northfleet survey and the other for Gravesend survey, to stop up the highway or road leading from Gravesend to Northfleet as agreed, 2s., and there are entries for 'biscake bear and tobacco 2s. 5d.' for 'wine' 13s., and for 'coffee and sugr' 1s., when 'viewing the highway'. This would seem to be the alteration of 1716 shown on the Darnley plan. The Act does not give any express powers to make deviations in the existing course of the road but only power to widen it, but not over ten yards nor to pull down any houses or take over any orchards or gardens, but the Trustees assumed power to deviate.

There is a short length of unmade road between Stuart Road and Bath Street, Gravesend, now known as Clifton Road, which, until the end of the nineteenth century, was known as the Old Main, which is the last remaining section of this road of 1716. The rest of its course except between Pier Road and Burch Road, Rosherville, has been quarried away.

The 1711 Act was for thirteen years but if the highway was sufficiently repaired before this and the monies for the work repaid the Tolls were to cease. In 1724 another Act was passed extending the term for fifteen years from 6th June, 1725. There was again a somewhat optimistic provision in this Act that if before fifteen years the roads were sufficiently 'amended' then the Justices in Quarter Sessions could direct that the Tolls were to cease. This Act also provided for a sum of £100 per annum to be appropriated for repair of the road from Chatham to Boughton after all expenses of the Northfleet and Strood road had been paid. This sum was allotted by Quarter Sessions between the various parishes concerned. (See *Kentish Sources, Some Roads and Bridges*, E. Melling, 1959, p. 20.)

In 1737 a further Act was passed extending the period for twenty-one years from 6th June, 1740, and the Trust was extended to take over the road from 'the east end of Dartford Bridge through the Parish of Dartford and the several Parishes of Stone Swanscombe and Northfleet and the great main road from the said Parish of Northfleet to the Pump near the Parish Church of Strood'. A question had arisen as to whether the previous Acts applied to the road across the chalk cliffs from Northfleet to Gravesend and the Act continued 'and for as much as certain doubts have arisen with relation to the road leading from Northfleet to Gravesend whether the same is comprised within the first above mentioned Acts or either of them . . . be it therefore hereby enacted and declared that the main road leading from The Queen's Head at Northfleet by the Chalk Clift (now occupied by the Society of Bricklayers) to the Town of Gravesend is and ought to be deemed and taken as part of the road directed to be repaired . . .'. There was also an express provision that tolls were not liable for County bridges. This was inserted to make it clear that the Trustees were not liable to contribute towards Stonebridge at Northfleet for which the County was liable under the Statute of Bridges of 1531. In 1835 the Trustees took over this bridge subject to the County paying them £16 per annum. In 1863 there was some trouble due to flooding and the Trustees found that the County had only paid £16 for two years. After some correspondence the County agreed to put the bridge in repair after which the Trustees were to be paid £16 per annum to keep it in repair.

In 1761 a further Act was passed in which the road was defined as from 'Dartford to Northfleet and Gravesend and from Gravesend to Chalk and from Northfleet to Chalk and thence to Stones end near the Parish Church of Strood'. The reference to 'Stones end' probably relates to the end of the paving in Strood High Street, although the Paving Act for Strood and Rochester was not passed until 1768. This is the first Act which refers specifically to the road from Gravesend to Chalk but it seems that this road was maintained under the earlier

Acts as there are references in them to Tide Coaches (see below, p. 245). The Act also recites that part of the roads were 'so extremely bad and dangerous that it is become necessary to divert and alter the present course of that part of the said Roads and to purchase further land for the purpose'. This was the section of road across the chalk cliffs which had been undermined and damaged due to quarrying. The Act contained provisions to prevent this and to stop diggings within fifteen feet of the road and to have the pits fenced. The road across the chalk cliffs was in such a bad condition that the Trustees at their meeting on 17th April, 1761, resolved to 'take over the road from Queen Mary's Green by John Goldsmith's farm houses to the Manor Pound at the upper end of Gravesend Town' as this was considered the most eligible road to Gravesend. This followed the course of the present Pelham Road, at one time known as Styles Lane from a Tenant Farmer of that name, from the Old Road to its junction with the present Darnley Road. It then turned eastwards and ran along what are now the back gardens of the houses on the North side of Cobham Street, the northern boundary of the road following the line of the back fences and thence curved round into Windmill Street. This curve is still clearly visible in the curved frontage of two shops (Numbers 2 and 3 Wrotham Road) and the northern boundary of the offices of the Gravesend Rubber Company (Number 4 Wrotham Road) which are on the site of the road. This section of the road was known as Blackberry Lane. On 1st May it was reported at the Trustees' meeting that the road from Queen Mary's Green passed John Goldsmith's house to the Manor Pound was provided and repaired. Queen Mary's Green was in Pelham Road opposite the present White Post public house. It was originally 'The green near the old Parish Church of St. Mary's' and is sometimes referred to as St. Mary's Green. The church became derelict in the sixteenth century and according to a manuscript note of Robert Pocock the last ruins and the churchyard walls were grubbed up in 1797 by James Bayley, the tenant of the Manor Farm. Further material from the old church was used to repair the road in 1822 after the Parish had resumed responsibility for it. John Goldsmith's house was the old Manor Farm in Pelham Road, pulled down about 1880, and stood on the site of Numbers 4, 6 and 8 Pelham Road. The Manor Pound was at the junction of Manor Road and Windmill Street on the north-west corner.

The Trustees carried out a number of improvements under this Act in addition to the above. In November, 1763, the lower part of Leather Bottle Lane (now Springhead Road), Northfleet, was widened and made 'a large commodious sweep'. At the same meeting the road between the bottom of Sir John Falstaff's Hill (now Gadshill) and Maze Sole Pond, Frindsbury, was ordered to be widened. In October,

1764, the road near the Coach and Horses, Chalk, was ordered to be widened and made straight and also near the Crown, Shorne, and Chalk church.

In 1777 a straight road was made through Chalk village. Previously the road at Chalk (east to west) had turned sharp right opposite the Parsonage (now the Old Manor House) into Vicarage Lane and then sharp left into Lower Higham Road, opposite Great Clayne Farm (recently demolished and formerly the Vicarage). At their meeting in October, 1777, the Trustees ordered that as soon as convenient to the Trust the road at Chalk Turnpike Gate should be diverted and turned to go (east to west) from the parsonage house at Chalk behind the barn there in the occupation of Mr. Benjamin Hubble upon a straight line to come out near the sign of the King of Prussia in Chalk Street, and at the same time the present Toll House and Gate there be taken down and removed to some convenient place near the Blacksmith's Forge in Chalk Street. This is the line of the present road, although the former is still also a road forming together a triangle of Lower Higham Road, Chalk Street and Vicarage Lane.

In May, 1775, the Trustees ordered a pond for washing sheep to be built at Northfleet Bridge for the benefit of farmers who had built the former pond there which had been taken away when the drain was made, 'the same to be repaired by the farmers as previously'. This pond figures in a number of nineteenth-century prints and photographs and occupied the triangle of road now used for a 'bus park at the junction with Grove Road adjoining Northfleet football ground.

In 1778 the Trustees agreed to widen the road between the front of Mr. Holmes's house at Denton in the road beginning at the foot of the hill leading to Paddock and thence to the cottage belonging to Mr. Joynes in the parish of Gravesend. Both these houses have been demolished. Mr. Holmes's house was probably the house known as Upper Denton to the south of the Old Road which had been demolished by the early nineteenth century and Mr. Joynes's cottage was the house he built and resided in known as Mount Pleasant Place, adjoining Singlewell Road, which was demolished in 1821 after his death, and it had been purchased by Colonel Dalton of Parrock Hall.

In October, 1781, the Trustees decided to apply for a new Act and in January, 1782, to insert a clause 'to turn the road from Northfleet Street by the top of Gravesend Town to Chalk Street'. This would have followed the line of the present road, but in February they rescinded the proposal as they were 'fully satisfied that such alteration was not for the benefit of the public and would increase the great debt'. The latter was presumably the more compelling reason. The Gravesend Corporation, at a meeting on 11th January, had already decided to oppose the Act unless the direct line through the town was agreed and asked

Lady Darnley to concur. Their opposition was not successful and the Act was passed without provision for the direct road.

In 1783 there was another diversion of the road across the chalk cliffs near Gravesend through lands belonging to the Earl of Darnley and Messrs. Wellington. From a plan in the Gravesend Library, apparently prepared for the Corporation to show the advantages of the direct line for a road between Gravesend and Northfleet, this road is shown along the edge of the cliffs at Rosherville where, at a later period, was the Upper Walk in Rosherville Gardens. Its course may also be followed by the present Cross Road at Rosherville between Burch Road and Pier Road and the entry now leading to some garages on the east side of Pier Road. It left the Old Main or Clifton Road at its junction with Bath Street running in a south-west direction. There was a further deviation at the Gravesend end in 1789.

In 1787 an alteration in the line of the road at Denton cut through the churchyard of the ruined church of St. Mary, and Robert Pocock records in a manuscript note that a fragment of the churchyard wall could be seen on the south side of the road. The ruins of the church (rebuilt in 1901) were on the north side.

In 1790 as a result of a Petition from the principal inhabitants of Dartford the Trustees agreed to improve East Hill, which was 'narrow, crooked and steep'. In July, 1795, part of the causeway of the road at the Chalk Hole near Gravel Hill (Swanscombe) fell in and the Trustees agreed to divert the course of the road to prevent further trouble. In April, 1796, the Trustees referred the proposed alteration to the Justices to settle. In the same year an alteration was made in the road near the present Echo Square, Gravesend, of which there is a plan in the Archives Office (reproduced in *Kentish Sources, Some Roads and Bridges*, by E. Melling, p. 44). The effect was to bring the road direct to the junction with the Cobham Road (Echo Square) instead of joining the road from Springhead (now Cross Lane, formerly Cut Throat Lane), some way to the west. A row of cottages were built on this slip of land or sand bank between the roads in 1868 which still exist.

In October, 1796, the Trustees agreed to apply for a further Act. The Gravesend Corporation once more brought forward proposals for a direct road from Northfleet, and Mr. Evans, the Town Clerk, attended a meeting of the Trustees to press for a road from the Leather Bottle, Northfleet, through King Street, Gravesend, to Chalk. The Trustees agreed to apply for optional powers but this did not satisfy the Corporation, who wanted the Trustees to undertake to carry the powers into effect as soon as possible. On 18th February, 1797, the Trustees resolved that if the Corporation were not satisfied with the optional clause they would suspend their application, which they did.

In September, 1800, the Trustees gave the Corporation notice of their intention to apply for a new Act. The Town Clerk was instructed to watch their proceedings in order to provide for the new road. On 25th May, 1801, the Corporation agreed to Petition the House of Commons that the Trustees should be directed to cause the road between Northfleet and Gravesend to be carried in a straight line from the Leather Bottle, Northfleet, to and through King Street in the town of Gravesend. A copy of the Petition appears in the Corporation Minutes. The Corporation Minutes of 1st September, 1801, report that their efforts had been attended with complete success and that the thanks of the Court be conveyed to Alderman Curtis and others who had assisted. In addition to entries in the Minutes there are a number of items in the Accounts for expenses in connection with this matter. The Corporation agreed to find funds to be advanced to the Trustees to a total of about £750.

The Trustees applied for the Act and in November, 1801, appointed Mr. Collins, of Leybourne, to survey the road. The road was to be thirty-four feet in width, footpaths on each side six feet at bottom and five feet at top. Mr. Collins' price for the work was £2,826 8s. 0d. and was accepted by the Trustees who, at this period, were meeting at the Queen's Head, Northfleet, presumably so as to be near the work. At one meeting they agreed to have a footpath on the north side of the road only, but both paths were constructed. The provisions against chalk pits were extended from fifteen feet to thirty feet, but these seem to have been disregarded.

Payments were made to Mr. Collins on account from time to time and the Trustees authorized the final payment to be made to him of £226 8s. 0d. on 22nd January, 1803.

Some difficulties arose over the junction of the new road with High Street, Gravesend. On 20th September, 1802, the Trustees agreed to buy two messuages belonging to Edward Martin and William Laurence at the top of the High Street for £697 15s. 0d. and in March, 1803, there was a suggestion for rounding the corner at the top of High Street and setting back the Carpenter's Arms. This was discussed further in July, when it was agreed to widen King Street, and plans were prepared by Mr. Coast. This bottleneck at the top of High Street was not finally eliminated until after the Trust finished when the Nelson was rebuilt in 1878 and set back in line with the south side of the road. Two of the oldest photographs of the town show the old Nelson jutting into the New Road shortly before its demolition.

In 1838 the Trustees of Pinnock's Charity pulled down the old almshouses in King Street and, in rebuilding them, set back in order to widen the road. There was some correspondence with their Clerk as the Almshouse Trustees claimed that the Turnpike Trustees had promised to pay them for this. The Gravesend Improvement Commissioners maintained the pavements in King Street and Milton Road, which were part of the turnpike, and in 1841 there was a threat of proceedings as the Trustees claimed that the Commissioners had encroached on the road.

In June, 1803, a Mr. Asser was appointed to prepare plans of the old road across the chalk cliffs showing the names of the adjoining owners and whether they had any other means of access, and in August a Committee was appointed to dispose of this road.

In 1804 the Trustees resolved to offer part of the road to Northfleet via the White Post (Blackberry Lane) to Mrs. Tadman, its site having been purchased from her late husband. She did not wish to buy and in August, 1808, the site of Blackberry Lane was sold to Laurence Ruck for £125. He was the owner of the adjoining lands and a house known as 'Rucklands', now the Masonic Hall in Wrotham Road. Prior to this sale in March, 1808, the Trustees' Surveyor had been instructed to take so much of the materials from Blackberry Lane as he could make use of to repair the New Road. The parish resumed responsibility for Styles Lane again and in 1811 they took steps to prevent Mr. Styles and a Mr. Assiter from encroaching on the road by ploughing, and in 1829 resolved to repair Styles Lane and fence the pond to prevent accidents.

The construction of the New Road in 1801 was the last major diversion in the course of the road made by the Trustees.

When the South Eastern Railway built the North Kent line (opened in 1849) a level-crossing was built at Milton Road, Gravesend, which caused trouble. From the start, the Trustees were opposed to this crossing and finally in 1864 the Company agreed to replace it with a bridge, resulting in a small diversion of the road.

In 1852 there was trouble with the European and American Electric Printing Telegraph Company who had left the footpath in 'a very insufficient state producing great public annoyance in so populous a locality'. The Mayor of Gravesend also joined in the complaints. In 1863 the British Electric Telegraph Company erected posts for over-head wires and once more the Trustees objected.

In 1859 there was some correspondence with Charles Dickens, apparently in connection with his tunnel under the road at Gads Hill, between his house and The Wilderness on the south side of the road, to which the Trustees agreed. The Rector of Milton (the Rev. Johnstone) was not so fortunate when he paved a crossing from the church to his new Rectory opposite in 1865, and the Trustees objected and requested him to remove it.

FINANCES AND TOLLS

The first Act of 1711 imposed the following tolls:
For every horse 1d.

For every coach chariot calash chaise and wagon 1s.

For every cart 6d.

For every score of Sheep or Lambs 4d.

For every score of Calves 4d.

For every score of Hogs 6d. and so for every greater or lesser number of Sheep Lambs Calves or Hogs proportionably [not being under five].

For [every] score of Oxen and Neat Cattle 8d. and so for every greater or lesser number [proportionably].

There is a note in the printed copy of the Act at the Record Office that the words in square brackets were 'interlined on the Roll'.

Soldiers, Postmen and Postboys were exempt and 'Horses loaden [sic] with Fish only for London and the said Horses returning back' were also exempt.

There were provisions for distraining on persons who refused to pay the Tolls and for Surveyors and collectors to account to Quarter Sessions half yearly and power to mortgage the Tolls at interest not exceeding 6 per cent. There are accounts for the years 1719-1744 among the Quarter Sessions Papers in the Kent Archives Office Q/SB. They are not very informative, the items consisting merely of 'Tolls collected' on one side and 'payments made to Treasurer' on the other. The average during this period is about £200 per half year, e.g. March to October 1719 Receipts £211 19s. 8d. Payments £203 3s. 4d. 1739 March to October £181 1s. 4½d. paid £172 19s. 10d. 1739 receipts £193 17s. 1d. expenses £167 18s. 10d. The highest receipts for a half year were in 1732 when £258 2s. 9d. was received.

The Justices were empowered to set up toll-gates, but the only gate set up under this Act was at Chalk at a point on the Lower Higham Road between its junction with Chalk Street and Vicarage Lane.

The Act of 1724 did not alter the rates of tolls but provided that they should be paid before passage. There were also some rather complicated provisions that Tolls were not to be paid twice in twenty-four hours for the same horse etcetera or with a coach chariot calash chaise waggon or other carriage drawn with the same horse or horses or 'the greater part of the same horses' or in the case of stage coaches, if the coach should not be the same yet if the horses are the same. There was also a penalty of 10s. for persons near gates allowing animals or vehicles to pass through their grounds thus avoiding payment of tolls.

This was also the first Act to allot £100 per annum to the repair of the road from Chatham to Boughton.

The Act of 1737 altered the tolls from 6th June, 1740, as follows:

For every coach Berlin landau Chariot Chaise Calash or other carriage drawn by six horses or more the sum of one shilling and sixpence.

For every coach Berlin landau Chariot Chaise Calash or other carriage drawn by four horses one shilling.

For every coach Berlin landau Chariot Chaise Calash or other carriage drawn by two horses sixpence.

For every Chaise Calash Chair or other carriage drawn by one horse only the sum of four pence.

The remaining Tolls were to be 'as in the former Acts'.

There was a provision for the Trustees to compound with owners of Tide Coaches from Gravesend to Chatham and Rochester (see below p. 245). There was also a provision for free passage on election days.

This Act which extended the Trust's road from Stonebridge to Dartford provided for one or more gate or gates on the additional road but no such gate to the westward of Stonebridge. (It would seem that this ought to have read 'eastward'.) No additional gate was set up under this Act.

The Act of 1761 altered the description of the vehicles and the Tolls of cattle (which were still governed by the 1711 Act) as follows:

For every Coach Berlin Landau Chariot Chaise Calash Caravan Hearse Waggon Wain Cart Dray or other carriage drawn by six horses One shilling and six pence.

For every Coach Berlin Landau Chariot Chaise Calash Caravan Hearse Waggon Wain Cart Dray or other carriage drawn by four horses One shilling.

For every Coach Berlin Landau Chariot Chaise Calash Caravan Hearse Waggon Wain Cart Dray or other carriage drawn by two horses Sixpence.

For every Coach Berlin Landau Chariot Chaise Calash Caravan Hearse Waggon Wain Cart Dray or other carriage drawn by one horse Fourpence.

For every horse mare gelding mule or ass laden or unladen and not drawing One penny.

For every drove of Oxen cows or neat cattle Eightpence by the score and so in proportion.

For every drove of calves sheep or lambs Fivepence by the score and so in proportion.

For every drove of hogs Sixpence by the score and so in proportion.

If Tolls were paid at one gate and a note or ticket produced then no toll should be paid at any other gate. The exemptions were also extended to cover animals and vehicles engaged in local husbandry, repairs to the roads, carrying mail or vagrants with passes.

The Act of 1761 gave the Trustees power to install a weighing engine. There is no reference to this in the Minutes, but on 19th March, 1764, Henry Green of Northfleet, a shopkeeper, petitioned John Calcraft (of Ingress Abbey, Greenhithe), Lord of the Manor, to set up an engine on

265

the waste at Northfleet Hill for weighing sainfoin hay and fodder which farmers sold and delivered at the Chalk Wharves (on the Thames) and other places. The Petition was signed by a number of landowners or farmers in Northfleet, at least one of whom was a Trustee and endorsed with the approval of John Calcraft and entered and recorded at the Kent Quarter Sessions at Maidstone on 1st May, 1764. Cooke in his *History of Northfleet* states that this weighbridge was on the London side of the gate set up at Northfleet in 1860 and in charge of the gatekeeper named Wilkinson.

The first meeting of the Trustees under this Act was on 17th April, 1761, at the George (later the Lord Nelson), Chalk. They agreed to keep the existing gate at Chalk and erect another at John in the Hole, near Dartford. This was at Stone, near the Welsh Tavern, and a road nearby is called Tollgate Road. At the Trustees' meeting on 1st May it was reported that this gate was open and that the Tolls from 8th April to 16th May amounted to £52 18s. 6d. In 1769 it was agreed to let the two gates to James Pearson for four years at £630 per annum. In the same year the Trustees agreed to borrow £488 10s. 0d. at 4½ per cent. and there is a minute that the existing debt at that date was £1,311 19s. 2d. By 1775 the Tolls were being let at £900 per annum. In 1761 the Clerk and Surveyor was paid £20 per annum, and in 1770 when the offices were separated, the Surveyor, Thomas Brandon, was paid £30 per annum.

In 1780 a Mr. Thomas Elliott objected to payment of Tolls on exchange of horses at Gravesend between the two gates. The Trustees took Counsel's opinion which was against them and when the next Act was obtained in 1782 it was expressly provided that persons were not to be exempt unless the same horses, etc., were used, but otherwise this Act did not alter the Tolls.

In 1781 the Tollhouse at John in the Hole was pulled down and a new one erected. This Tollhouse and gate were again rebuilt in 1811 and there is a drawing and plan in the Kent Archives Office which is reproduced in *Some Roads and Bridges*, page 44.

In 1791 the Mail Coach guard shot at the collector (William Rogers) at John in the Hole. He escaped serious injury, but another 'violent assault' took place in 1795 by Jeremy Lock of Canterbury which led to a prosecution by the Trustees. Rogers survived until 1800 and on his death, his widow was appointed collector.

The Act of 1801 altered the method of assessing the Tolls by charging so much per animal and not charging for the vehicle as follows:

For every Horse, Mare, Gelding or mule drawing any coach, Chariot, Phaeton, Calash, Curricle, Vis-a-Vis, Chaise, Diligence, Caravan, Hearse or litter the sum of Sixpence.

THE ROAD BETWEEN DARTFORD, GRAVESEND AND STROOD

For every Horse, Mare, Gelding, mule or beast of burden drawing any wagon wain cart or other such like carriage the sum of Fourpence.

For every Horse, Mare, Gelding mule or beast of burden not drawing Twopence.

For each Ass drawing any kind of carriage twopence.

For each Ass not drawing One penny.

For every Drove of Oxen, Cows, or Neat Cattle One shilling and fourpence per Score.

For every Drove of Calves sheep lambs or hogs Tenpence per score.

And in the case of Oxen drawing any carriage two Oxen shall be considered and paid for as one horse.

There were elaborate penalties for evading Tolls by going round gates or handing over tickets.

In 1803 Mr. Brandon the Surveyor's salary was increased to £50 and when he retired in 1807 his successor John Westbrook was paid £105.

An account for 1811 shows the total debts at £9,702 5s. 6d. and interest £620 1s. 11d. The rents from letting the Tolls were £2,560.

The last local Act was passed in 1822 and revoked all the previous Acts and was for a period of 21 years.

There was a general power to erect new gates as well as maintaining the existing gates or side bars and to enclose suitable gardens up to a quarter of an acre for the Toll Houses and that a lamp or lamps should be erected near the Toll Houses. The Tolls were almost identical with those in the 1801 Act, although there was a provision for receipts to be given *gratis* entitling the holder to pass through the other gates. There was also power for the Trustees to make the Tolls payable as to half at each gate.

The exemptions were wider than in the previous Acts and included the Royal Family and rectors, vicars and curates going to or returning from the church or chapel at which they officiated or visiting sick parishioners and any person attending divine service at his usual place of worship on Sunday if 'tolerated by law'.

On expiry this Act was renewed from year to year by the Annual Turnpike Acts until 1871.

An auction of the Tolls of the gates at Chalk and John's Hole with the side 'bars' or gates at Horns Cross for one year from 19th August, 1842, produced a successful bid by Lewis Levy of £3,410, the rent to be paid monthly in advance at 'the Western Door of Rochester Cathedral between the hours of ten and twelve in the forenoon'. The Clerk at the time was George Essell who was also Chapter Clerk and occupied the offices in the Precinct. There was trouble with the side bars, which were across the two side roads at Horns Cross. One of them blocked access to the yard at the rear of the public house and in 1838

267

there was a claim for Tolls when horses were taken round to the stables from the front of the inn, to which strong objection was taken.

A further series of Annual Accounts at the Kent Archives Office run from 1823 to the end of the Trust in 1871. The income for 1823 is as follows:

	£	s.	d.
Income brought forward	£1,884	4	8¾
Balance in Surveyor's hands	79	14	6½
Rents from Tolls	£3,550	0	0
Incidentals	8	0	0
	£5,521	19	3¼

The expenditure.

	£	s.	d.
Day Labour for maintenance and repairs	536	18	8
Team Labour	89	13	1
Gravel Hill balance of unliquidated account	432	16	0
Maintenance of buildings, houses, gates or bridges	£1,202	17	11¾
Land purchase and damage done	210	0	0
Salaries, Surveyors, Clerks, etc.	161	5	0
Printing and Stationery	1	7	0
Interest on Debt	169	10	0
Incidentals	73	19	8
Maidstone Road	100	0	0
Principal Debt paid off	£1,000	0	0
	£3,978	7	4¾
Total Balance carried forward	£1,543	11	10½
Amount of Debt secured on Tolls	£3,150	0	0
Purchase money lands at Northfleet	228	0	0
Purchase money land at Milton	210	0	0
Purchase money the site of houses at Milton	175	0	0
Balance of Contract for improvement of How Wood Hill (Stone)	700	0	0
Printers work	12	7	0

From this date the Tolls seem to have gradually declined. In 1824 they were £3,380; in 1827, £2,907; in 1832, £2,474. In 1843 there was an increase to £3,094 but the next year they dropped to £2,308. The opening of the North Kent line from London via Dartford to Gravesend and Strood (then called Rochester and Chatham) in 1849 lead to a drop from £1,808 in 1848 to £1,489 in 1850, £1,015 in 1852, £817 in 1854, £723 in 1858. There was a slight rise to £788 in 1859 but the Trustees decided it was necessary to take drastic action, and in 1860 they erected an additional gate on the Hill at Northfleet on the site of the old stocks opposite the present Roman Catholic Church. The cost of erecting this new Toll house and gate was £191 15s. 8d. The work was done by a Mr. Gould, a well-known builder and architect of Gravesend, and a Mr. J. K. White of 51 Orchard Road, Brentford, took the gate. The Northfleet local board objected to the siting of the gate, but without avail. In the Gravesend Free Press for 18th February, 1865, there was a letter complaining that owing to this gate it cost 8d. to pass from one part of Northfleet to the other.

The gate was financially successful, as in 1860 the Tolls went up to £1,010, and in 1865 to £1,156. These fell to £927 in 1870, the last full year of the Trust.

So far as expenditure is concerned there were improvements at Dartford Hill in 1825 and a purchase of cottages at Northfleet for £250 to improve the road in 1828. The last major expenditure was lowering West Hill and filling up the valley which cost £1,500 in 1828 and a further £2,109 in 1829. It is not clear where 'West Hill' was, but it may relate to what is now Gads Hill. This work resulted in the total debt going up to £8,650 in 1829. The debt was, however, gradually reduced and the Trust ended up with a surplus. The final account from 1st January, 1871, to the expiration of the Trust is as follows:

INCOME:

	£	s.	d.
Balance in Treasurer's Hands—brought forward	£147	3	1
Balance in Surveyor's Hands—brought forward	£5	13	0
Sale of Toll Houses surplus lands etc.	£218	18	6
Miscellaneous	£74	7	0
Revenue from Tolls	£878	15	0
	£1,325	6	7

There is a note that all surplus property of the Trust had been sold and all money due had been got in and all debts discharged.

EXPENDITURE:

	£	s.	d.
Manual Labour	£161	2	7
Team Labour and carriage of materials	£9	11	6
Materials for surface repairs	£491	0	5
Tradesmen's Bills	£28	17	11
Clerk, including allowance	£72	10	0
Surveyor, including allowance	£102	10	0
Law charges	£33	11	5
Incidental expenses	£28	11	11

269

Balance due from Treasurer*	£397	10	7
(There is a note.) * The above balance will be			
distributed.			
Dartford Highway Board	£130	8	5
Gravesend and Milton Improvement Commissioners	£43	2	8
Rochester Highway Board	£196	17	10
Highway Surveyors, Strood	£27	1	8
	£397	10	7

This Trust paid its way and ended with a surplus which was paid over to the bodies who took over the Trust's liabilities. The road was classed as a 'Main Road' under the Highway Act, 1878. This meant that the County was entitled to claim a moiety of the cost of repairs. A return of 2nd April, 1879, gives the cost of maintenance as £602 for the previous year and the length as 13 miles.

MILESTONES

The Act of 1737 contains penalties for defacing the milestones, but the Minutes for this period are lost and there is no record of the date when milestones were first placed on this road. The Act of 1822 provided for stones to be put up one mile apart and for direction posts to be erected, but stones had been set up long before this. In 1780 the Trustees directed the stones to be repainted and in 1803 after the New Road had been opened the Trustees directed the Surveyors to move the stones from the Old Road to the New Road.

From those still in existence it appears that at first they had the mileage from London in Roman figures engraved on one or sometimes two sides without any town name or the word 'miles'. At some date probably in the nineteenth century the stones were turned round so that the Roman figures are now at the back and plates were put on with the mileage from London Bridge and Gravesend or Rochester. These plates were removed during the 1939-1945 War, but in some cases, new plates of varying designs have been affixed to the stones since 1945.

The following stones still exist:

The sixteenth on Dartford Brent with figure 'VI' on the two rear sides. This may have been 'XVI' as the remaining figures are very faint, or possibly it refers to the distance from Gravesend which is six miles, but if so, it is the only stone to have a figure based not on London. There are modern plates on the front. The seventeenth has 'XVII' on the two rear sides and one modern plate. The eighteenth is likewise, but with two modern plates. The nineteenth has no engraved figures and may be a newer stone, neither has it any plates, only the marks where they were removed. The twentieth and twenty-first stones are both missing, but there are modern plates attached to a nearby house and a garden wall respectively. The twenty-second and twenty-third have both been removed, although their sites are known. The plates from the twenty-second, which was in Milton Road, Gravesend, at numbers 153/154 Milton Road are stored in the magazines at the Fort Gardens and are inscribed '22 miles to London', '7 miles to Rochester', although they are no longer accessible. The twenty-fourth has 'XXIV' on one rear side only; the twenty-fifth has no engraved figures but both have marks on the front where the old plates were removed. The twenty-sixth seems to have disappeared. The twenty-seventh has 'XXVII' on one rear side and the marks of plates on the front. The twenty-eighth has been removed.

COACH TRAFFIC

Colonel H. C. B. Rogers in *Turnpike to Iron Road* (1961) states that the first coaches were introduced about 1640. By 1647 Tide Coaches were running between Gravesend and Rochester in connection with the Long Ferry as in that year the Gravesend Corporation made an order forbidding such coaches and other public vehicles from plying elsewhere than in the 'inns or houses where their coaches or carts shall be'. The importance of this traffic was recognized in the Act of 1737 in which the Trustees were given powers to compound with the owners of Tide Coaches running from Gravesend to Rochester and Chatham and back, and which would pass through the Chalk gate.

Some evidence of the London traffic appears from the various Gravesend guide-books. The earliest published in 1817 states that coaches pass almost every hour to or from London.

The *Gravesend Gazetteer and Guide* of 1840, p. 14, lists some ten named coaches between London and Gravesend and continuing to Dover, Faversham, Canterbury and Brompton, and gives the up and down times in addition to Pearle's Omnibus. The Gravesend coach offices were at the Lord Nelson on the north-west corner of Windmill Street (on the site of the present Nelson) and the Prince of Orange on the south-west corner of High Street opposite (the site now being occupied by Burton's and the yard and stables by Chiesman's). This was usually known as the 'New' Prince of Orange to distinguish it from the 'Old' Prince of Orange at the junction of Windmill Street and the Old Road, and which at an earlier date was used as the coaching inn by vehicles on the Old Road.

Vehicles referred to in the Acts, from the *Shorter Oxford Dictionary*, are as follow:

271

FIG. 2.

Coaches at New Prince of Orange and Lord Nelson, New Road,
Gravesend, *c.* 1830.

Chariot—a light, four-wheeled vehicle with only back seats, 1661.

Calash—a light carriage with low wheels having a removable folding
hood, 1666.

Chaise—a light, open carriage for one or two persons, 1701.

Berlin—an old-fashioned four-wheeled covered carriage with a seat
behind covered with a hood, 1731.

Landau—a four-wheeled carriage with top in two parts so that it may
be closed or thrown half or entirely open, 1743.

Chair—a vehicle for one person; a sedan carried on poles, 1836; a light
chaise drawn by one horse, 1821; a chariot or car, 1814.

Caravan—a covered carriage or cart, a house on wheels as those used by
gipsies and showmen, 1674.

Hearse—a carriage or car constructed to carry a coffin, 1650.

Wain—a large open vehicle usually four-wheeled used for carrying
heavy loads.

Dray—a low cart without sides for carrying heavy loads, especially
that used by brewers, 1581.

Phaeton—a species of light four-wheeled open carriage usually drawn
by a pair of horses with one or two seats facing forward, 1742.

Curricle—a light two-wheeled carriage usually drawn by two horses abreast, 1756.

Vis-à-Vis—a light carriage for two persons sitting face to face, 1753.

Diligence—a public stage-coach, 1742.

Litter—a vehicle containing a couch shut in by curtains and carried on men's shoulders or by animals, 1774.

SOURCES AND ACKNOWLEDGMENTS

There are copies of all the local Turnpike Acts except the 1711 Act in the Gravesend Public Library. There is a copy of the 1711 Act in the Public Record Office. In the Archives Office are Accounts for most of the years from 1711 to 1744 among the Quarter Sessions Papers Q/SB. There is another series from 1823-1871 with the Chalk Turnpike Papers T.7. There are also the Minutes from 1761-1809 and a Letter Book, 1837-1866 T.7.A.11, in addition to other miscellaneous papers. Use has also been made of R. P. Cruden's *Manuscript Collection* in the Gravesend Public Library for Corporation references to the road, and the inter-leaved copy of R. Pocock's *History of Gravesend*, 1797, which contains his additional manuscript notes.

My thanks are due to the Staff at the Kent Archives Office at Maidstone and Public Library, Gravesend, and to Messrs. J. Benson and E. Tilley for various references, Mr. F. J. G. Foot and the Gravesend Historical Society and the Dartford Antiquarian Society, and my brother, Mr. D. H. Hiscock, A.R.I.B.A., for the plans.

THE OLD TELEGRAPH FROM LONDON TO THE COAST OF KENT.

BY MISS A. G. HARDY.

THE device of conveying messages by a chain of visible signals is probably nearly as old as time, and the origins of it, like the origins of most things, can certainly be traced back to the Greeks. So far as Kent is concerned, however, the earliest system of which we have definite information is the network of beacons extending over the whole of the shire, described, with a plan of the stations, by Lambarde in his *Perambulation of Kent* (1576) ; but it was no novelty then, for he himself remarks that it had been reorganised as far back as 1338 :[1]

> I find that before the time of King Edward the third they [the signals] were made of great stacks of wood (of which sort I my self have seen some in Wiltshire) but about the eleventh yeer of his reign it was ordeined that in our Shire they should be high Standards with their Pitch-pots.

Lambarde also tells us how,

> for the more speedie spreading of the knowledge of the enemies comming, they were assisted with some Horsemen (anciently called of their Hobies or Nags Hobeliers) that besides the fire (which in a bright shining day is not so well descried) might also run from Beacon to Beacon, and supply that notice of the danger at hand.[2]

[1] Mr. S. E. Winbolt conjectures that these very beacons may well have been established on the same hills that had served the Romans fifteen centuries earlier.

[2] Lists of " Hobilliers " are included in the memorandum of the Wards of Kent in the *Textus Roffensis* (Hearn's edition, 1720, pp. 236 *et seq.*) under the date 1338.

It is well known that beacon signals of this sort were used to spread the news of the defeat of the Armada. But this primitive system served only to attract attention, and was incapable of conveying actual messages. During the seventeenth century several projects were set afoot, one by the Marquis of Worcester in 1663, and one by a Dr. Hooke in 1684, for establishing a regular code of flag signals, the one ultimately adopted, however, being that originated by James II when Duke of York, and systematised by Kempenfeldt in 1780.

The credit for the invention of the telegraph proper is generally attributed to a Frenchman, Claude Chappe, who devised a machine which he wished to call the " Tachygraphe ", and on it the first real " telegram " was spelt out from Montmartre, Paris, on August 15th, 1794, informing the French Government of an important recapture from the Austrians. It took the form of a beam pivoted at the top of a mast and having extensions on swivels at its ends.

In the following year—1795—a telegraph system on a different principle was devised in England almost simultaneously by two independent investigators—Gamble and Lord George Murray. Both their machines were submitted to the Lords of the Admiralty, who decided to adopt Murray's, regarding it as the better machine, as it had six shutters giving sixty-three changes, as against Gamble's five shutters giving thirty-one. Figure I gives some idea of the method of working the machine ; the six shutters were revolved on pulleys worked from inside the cabin.

That same year Mr. George Roebuck, a surveyor, was given a contract to erect twelve stations from London to Deal, with a branch to Sheerness. The stations were as follows : *Admiralty ; St. George's Fields ; New Cross ; Shooter's Hill ; Swanscombe ; Gad's Hill ; Beacon Hill ; Shottenden Hill ; Barham Downs ; Betteshanger ; Deal.* The branch line ran from *Beacon Hill* to the Battery at *Sheerness* via *Tong* and *Furze Hill.* He was to receive £215 for each of the stations, which were to consist of two small rooms, and to contain, in addition to the telegraph apparatus, a stove, an eight-guinea clock and two twelve-guinea telescopes. By June, 1796, this line was finished, the yearly cost of operating it being estimated at £2,950.

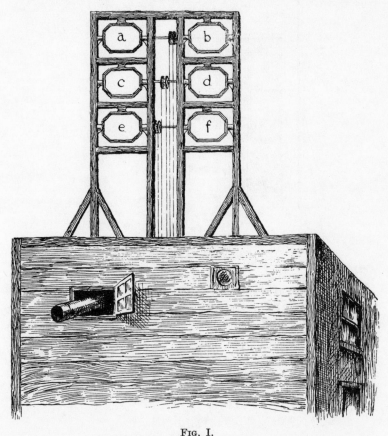

FIG. I.

TELEGRAPH ERECTED ON THE ADMIRALTY OFFICE, CHARING CROSS, in February, 1796.

In the year 1804, Colonel Pasley, when enquiring into the subject of telegraphs, found that the shutter system was inferior to the naval system of flags and pennants, the latter being capable of exhibiting three letters or numbers at the same time, whereas the land telegraph could exhibit only

277

one. Whereupon Lord George Murray invented the two-armed telegraph, and was granted the management of the telegraph system at the various seaports. This system was

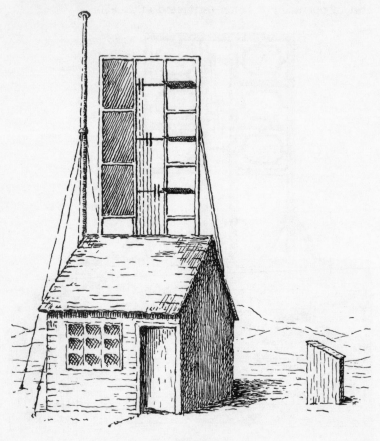

Fig. II.
TELEGRAPH AT NEW CROSS, 1796.
(Shooter's Hill in the background.)

improved upon by Colonel Pasley in the following year—1805.

In 1809, Colonel Pasley observed that the French Coast Telegraph, known by the name of the Semaphore, resembled very closely his method. It had three arms exhibiting positions similar to his, but placed on separate pivots vertically over each other upon the same post.

A temporary check was put to the progress by the Peace of 1814, and Napoleon's banishment to Elba, which led to a reduction of the War Establishment and the optimistic order from the Admiralty that the line from London to Sheerness and Deal was to be discontinued. Five months later Napoleon escaped, and orders were promptly given for its re-establishment.

Meanwhile, Admiral Sir Home Popham had been working for more than thirty years at an alphabetical system of flag signals ; his code was already in use in the fleet, and it was on it that Nelson's famous signal at Trafalgar had been made. In 1816, however, he appeared as the champion of the Semaphore, and proposed that this method of working should replace the balls and flag system between the North Foreland and Land's End. The Admiralty adopted his suggestion, and empowered him to choose the sites for a line of semaphores to be set up between the Admiralty and the dockyard at Chatham.

He did not follow Lord George Murray's route beyond his first station, the house (still in existence) numbered 34 *West Square, Southwark.* His next station was *Telegraph Hill, Nunhead,* near New Cross, where there is now an open space still remembered as its site. Thence the line ran slightly southwards to *Red Hill,* an elevation of some 260 feet just over a mile north-west of Chislehurst Church, and from there to *Row Hill,* or more correctly Rue Hill, near Wilmington, in the grounds of Leslie G. Wates, Esq., J.P. This hill, incidentally, and the adjacent Green Hill, were the two fortresses of Duromagus, the city of Cadwallon, and it was here that the British chieftain made his last stand against the Romans. The next station was at *Betsham,* and the last before Chatham itself was *Gad's Hill,* where there is an eminence still known as " Telegraph Hill ".

This line began working on July 3rd, 1816. The new system was soon found to surpass the shutter telegraph in quickness and clearness of reading, and Sir Home Popham was thanked for his invention and awarded £2,000 by the Admiralty.

Sir Home Popham's semaphores consisted of two metal arms, seven or eight feet long, playing in a groove at the top of the same upright post and worked by handles near its foot. Fig. III shows the arms in positions 1 and 2 of the

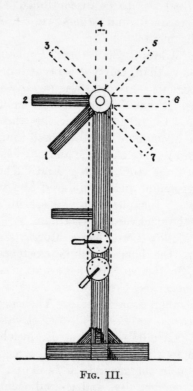

Fig. III.

seven possible, with the two indicators below standing in the corresponding positions.

It will be noticed that the stations are not more than six or eight miles apart, that being found to be the longest distance at which the arms could be seen, even through a telescope, under normal climatic conditions in this country.

In 1816 the Admiralty expressed their intention of building a permanent line of semaphores from London to

Sheerness, Deal and Dover. One Goddard surveyed the land in 1820, and the plans went so far as the purchase of sites from various owners. The sites were marked with boundary stones bearing the broad arrow, which, it may be, are there still, but nothing further was done.

The increasing density of the atmosphere in London made it only a question of time before the visual system of telegraph must come to a natural end, but it lingered on until the invention of the electric telegraph, the stations being finally closed at the end of the year 1847. In 1849 London was in electric communication with the Admiralty Office at Portsmouth.

I am indebted to the Librarians of the Admiralty and the War Office for affording me facilities for obtaining information and copying drawings; and to Instructor Captain Oswald T. Tuck, R.N., for information as to Chappe's machine; also to the Public Record Office for the study of manuscripts.

[The illustrations have very kindly been made by Eng.-Capt. J. B. Hewitt, R.N., from sketches by Miss Hardy.—ED.]

A KENTISH HOLIDAY, 1823

Edited by F. HULL, B.A., Ph.D.

IN 1955 I published in *Arch. Cant.*, vol. lxix, 'A Tour into Kent, 1759', being the journal kept during a holiday spent touring this county by members of the Mount family of London. This brief diary had been found among the Mount MSS. deposited by Sir William Mount, Bt., in the Berkshire Record Office. Recently a somewhat similar document has been brought to my notice among the papers of the Powell family of Speldhurst, deposited in the Kent Archives Office by S. K. M. Powell, Esq., J.P., of Shadwell in that parish. In offering this journal for publication I am well aware of its imperfections, but as a comparison with the Mount diary, although later in date, and on account of the occasional glimpses of Kent in the reign of George IV, it may prove of some interest.

The author was Charles Powell, second son of Baden Powell of Speldhurst and Hester, daughter of James Powell of Clapton. He was born in 1807 and so was sixteen years of age when this holiday was taken. In later life he was a J.P. for Kent and was uncle to Robert Stephenson Smyth Powell who became 1st Baron Baden-Powell and was founder of the Scout movement.

The text itself requires little comment. There are a few difficult readings and on three occasions very rough plans of churches visited are inserted in the original. The punctuation is chaotic and it has been necessary to modify this in order to provide a more readable account. Charles Powell's unusual method of recording half and quarter hours has been retained as have his occasional mis-spellings. Its merit lies mainly in the unexpected: the gaol as a showpiece; the first impressions of the sea; the number of steam vessels already afloat in 1823; the glimpse of the future Queen at the age of four riding on a donkey, but suitably attended; and the visit to a naval vessel at Chatham. Occasional inaccuracies, Charles Powell was not over critical of guides and their tales, can be forgiven in this record of a youth's first visit to much of his home county.

DIARY OF CHARLES POWELL OF SPELDHURST, 1823[1]

Friday 19 [September]. Sisters set off to Newick about 12—at the same time Uncle and Aunt Sikes and I to Maidstone—stopt at Tunbridge at Miss St. Croix—then we turned up by the Church

[1] Kent Archives Office: U934 F8.

thro' a flat country to Hadlow, by Goose Green to Mereworth.
Saw the House (belonging to Lord Le de Spencer)[2] thro' the
trees it is divided into three parts Stables, Kitchen and
Dwelling [*inserted:* a handsome London church at Mereworth].
Stopt at the Inn where Papa, Mama and H. in our carriage
came up to water the horses—we set off before them from
there through Teston and Wateringbury, Barming Cross and
the Bower to Maidstone. At Teston a pretty bridge on the
road to Goudhurst. Large hopgrounds with very few hops
almost all the way from Tonbridge. Arrived at Maidstone at
4 o'clock to Bell Inn, Papa came in soon after us, then we all
walked to the New Jail[3] a fine stone building—went into the
wards and chapel—saw the prisoners spining, weaving, making
mats, string, ropes, etc., then we came in to dinner. After
dinner H.[4] and I walked with Papa by moon light down
[2] Gabriel Hill up Stone Street then turned down Knightrider
Street to the Church which is very large [*rough plan inserted
in text*] and some old buildings called the College. Came in and
had our tea. In the Prison we saw the solitary cells and [in]
one of them quite dark was a boy confined there 6 days for
disobedience.

Maidstone seems a large town and the Jail a large, strong,
melancholy and clean place of punishment.

Saturday 20th. Had breakfast at $7\frac{1}{4}$ and then set off for Hithe
thro Harrietsham and Lenham to Charing where we changed
horses—then thro' Ashford to Marsham where we turned
up to Mr. Longdale's, stayed there a while and returned to
the high road again. Sir E. Knatchbull lives at Marsham
Court where there is a fine park. Watered the horses at
Stone Hill, Smeeth and then thro' Sellinge to Hithe, Swan
Inn. On the hill above Hithe a fine view of the Sea—almost
calm with a great many small brigs on it.

A little beyond Maidstone the Moat, Lord Romney's on the
right—then Leeds Castle, Mr. Martin's on the right before we
[3] came to Harrietsham, an old castle standing in a lake, lately
repaired and modernized.[5] It formerly belonged to General
Fairfax in Cromwell's time.[6]

[2] Thos. Stapleton, Lord Le Despencer, 1766-1831, by this time resident
abroad. See *Arch. Cant.*, vol. lxxvi (1961), 169-179.

[3] The new gaol was begun in 1812 and the prisoners were transferred on
8th March 1819.

[4] Henry Powell, M.D., 1809-67, brother of Charles.

[5] The castle was altered and modernized in 1822.

[6] This is an error. The Fairfax connection resulted from the marriage of
Catherine Culpeper and Thomas 5th Lord Fairfax who succeeded to the estate
in 1688 on the death of the second Lord Culpeper.

On the left near Newin Green some old Barrows.[7] As soon
as we got to Hithe we went and walked on the shingles—the
tide had just begun to ebb—saw a small fishing boat launched
—we went into a Martello Tower of which there are a great
many all round the coast, wherever there is a weak place
that an enemy might attack. These are generally inhabited
by the preventive service which is called the coast blockade,
but the one we went into was held by a pensioner. There are
no guns up all round the coast, the wall is 7 feet thick, there
are 3 different floors in it, the lowest a coal hole, the next
above it a magazine and the third a dwelling. The gun is
fixed on a pivot on the top landing and is turned round to any
point. Dinner at 3—then we all walked up hill by the church
to go to Saltwood castle. Uncle and Aunt stopt and we went
[4]   in to the Castle which is a fine ruin belonging to Mr. Croft
and inhabited by a farmer. Came back and had our tea—a
moonlight night. Hithe is 67 miles from London.

This was the first time I had seen the Sea and I thought it
looked beautiful and much *higher* than I expected. From the
Hill going up to Saltwood I saw the French cliffs and coast
very clearly with the telescope—Dungeness—lighthouse—
Romney and Lidd—and Sandgate—Rode a bit to [?].[8]

Sunday 21—Went down to the Sea with Mama before breakfast,
Papa joined us, the sea was ebbing—saw a machine let into
the sea, picked a few common shells and seaweed, came back
to breakfast, read the Gospel to Mama and went to church,
which is an old building, the chancel was part of an old
abbey[9] with small Bethersden marble pillars round the large
stone ones, very handsome, the roof has been groined but is
now plain, no pews in the chancel. Under it is a small crypt
with a handsome groined ceiling, full of sculls and bones
[5]   piled up supposed to be[10] [*rough plan of church inserted*].
Mr. Croft the rector, Mr. Crawford, curate, who did the duty.
After service the clerk shewed us the crypt. Went to dinner:
began to rain. After dinner to church and then down to the
sea in the rain and a brisk gale and had a fine blow. (Just

[7] This reference is mysterious. The nearest known sites are near Belle Vue
Farm, Lympne and at Stowting; neither would appear to be applicable.
[8] The word written looks like 'Sistors', 'Tiston', or 'Iston'. It would appear
that this phrase was added later and remains obscure.
[9] This was Leland's interpretation copied by Hasted, but see Canon Livett,
'The Church of St. Leonard, Hythe', *Arch. Cant.*, xxx, 273.
[10] This sentence is unfinished. Legend has it that they are the remains of
the 'combatants slain in a sanguinary battle between the ancient Britons under
King Vortimer, and the Saxons, about the year 456'. [Ireland, *History of Kent*,
Vol. II, p. 229.]

before church went down to the sea to find Uncle and H. but could not see them, the sea was then up to the bank, after I came in Uncle came. Lost the top of my umbrella.) Came home to tea, read part of Walton's life of G. Gilbert, wrote, etc. There is a small organ in the church and the children sing. In the side aisle there is a curious old circular table inlaided like a mariner's compass. [*Rough sketch inserted*].

Monday 22. Breakfasted at $7\frac{1}{2}$, set off $8\frac{1}{2}$ to Dover thro' Sandgate and Folkestone—arrived at Payn's York Hotel about 11. At Sandgate there is a fort or castle built in Henry 8th.

[6]   times. It looks modern. Sandgate consists of a long row of houses built on each side of the road close on the beach and seems a pleasant place. From the top of Folkestone hills is a very fine view of the town and sea and coast. All the way till within 2 miles of Dover a magnificent view of the sea. As soon as we got to Dover we went on the beach and the two piers and round the basons saw steam packets[11] lying there. H. and I walked with Papa, up the Shakespeare Cliff to the top by Hearts hill fort and the citadel where we sat and took views—then came down to dinner about $2\frac{1}{2}$. A little rain, walked with William on the pier.

Tuesday 23. Walked with Papa and Mama on the old pier before breakfast, then went to the Harbour and saw two steam vessels set off, the first the Brittania, 2nd the government packet. Walked with Mama and Aunt (Papa and Uncle went to call on Mr. Stride) through the streets home, then had a donkey chaise and went up to the castle, which consists of a grand keep which is a square tower with a square tower at each corner. It is surrounded with a yard, barracks among which is the governor's house, and a walk, then a deep foss

[7]   over which is a draw bridge and an outer wall. An old warder shewed us over the castle—there were no guns mounted—all the magazines were full—only 7 soldiers there now. We saw the old keys of the castle and an old Roman sword of state and 2 Elizabeth pocket Pistol 8 ins. long, and part of the old towers and walls of Hubert de Berg. From the cliff a fine view of the town and the coast of France—there are there piles of canon balls and shells.

When we came down I walked with Papa to look at the shaft which is a winding staircase, round a *well* with windows looking into it, reaching from the top to the bottom of the cliff. Then to the Eagle Steam packet, went all over it—in it

---

[11] Steam vessels were first used on the Channel crossing in 1821.

we found Uncle, Aunt, Mama and H. Looked at the Steam Engine, which is two connected, each equal to 20 horse power —waited to see it set off for Ramsgate. Dinner about 4. After dinner went down to the beach the Sovereign, 'no faith', the Monarch packet come in. It anchored some distance from the beach and the Dover boats went off to fetch the passengers. Then there was a fine bit of fun, all the Inn Keepers crowding round the passengers as they landed to ask them to their hotels and the custom house officers inspecting etc. Afterwards Uncle, Papa, H. and I walked round the bason thro' the town home. Tea at 7. The keep of the Castle was built in William 1st's time and the barracks round to George 2nd—the older part by the Saxons. The magazines are excavated in the Chalk, the shaft up the cliff was built by government and leads up to the Barracks on the top.

[8]

Wednesday 24. Got up in the morning H. and I went up and down the Shaft then with Uncle Sikes to the old pier—then breakfast—set off about 10 to Ramsgate through Walmer, Deal and Sandwich. Stopt at Walmer and walked to see the Castle which belongs to the Lord Warden of the Cinque Ports, at this time Lord Liverpool.[12] The Castle is near the sea and is built in the form of a circle with some smaller ones bulging from it. The Top is planted as a garden. We then had lunch at Mr. Brich's. Mr. Pitt[13] used to live at Warmer [sic] castle, he had the modern part of the dwelling built and the shrubberies planted. At Deal a castle like Walmer. The town is large and the streets narrow—changed horses there.

[9]

Sandwich seems a clean town, it used to be fortified, there is an old gateway on the Canterbury road.[14]

Got to King's Head Hotel, Ramsgate $3\frac{1}{2}$, walked on the Piers, saw 2 packets come in, one from France the other from London. Walked on the sands, saw Prince Leopold, the Duchess of Kent and her son and daughter—Prince Feodore.[15] Dinner $5\frac{1}{2}$. The Piers are fine structures begun by Smeaton and continued by Rennie and not quite finished yet. At the end of the western pier is the light house. Capt. Cotton is one of the principal trustees.

[10]

A little beyond Sandwich, Richborough castle an old Roman ruin.

[12] Robert Banks Jenkinson, 2nd Earl of Liverpool, 1770-1828, Prime Minister.
[13] William Pitt, 1759-1806, Prime Minister.
[14] See *Arch. Journal*, vol. 86 (1929), 289-90 and also plate XV.
[15] The Duchess had two children by her first husband, Charles Frederick, b. 1804, Prince of Leiningen and Anne Feodorowna, b. 1807. Her brother Leopold became King of the Belgians.

Thursday 25. Went down to the Sands then Papa took H. and I to see the Lighthouse which has oil lights [argond lamps, *inserted*] each having a polished reflector behind it—lighted when there is 10 ft. of water at the entrance. Then we went up the Western cliff, then home. Then H. and I went down to the Sands to Mama, Uncle and Aunt. Saw the Prince and little princess Alexandrina Victoria[16] riding on a donkey, attended by 2 grooms and ladies. Set off at 12 for Margate through Broadstairs where we saw Mr. Mrs. and Miss Twining who were staying there. Got to York Hotel, Margate, looking into the Harbour 1½. Walked on the pier which is smaller than that of Ramsgate, but handsome, with a small lighthouse at the end. Walked up the cliff, bought shells, dinner at 3. Saw the Eclipse by steam come in. I walked with Papa up the town and down the town, the toll for walking on the pier is 1d. a day for each person.

[11] Friday 26. Set off about 8¼ to Kings Head, Canterbury where we arrived 11½. Walked to the Cathedral which is a fine building but some of its towers are much spoiled by having their tops [. . .].[17] The inside is being handsomely repaired by the Dean and Chapter. On the right hand side of the high tower is St. Michael's chapel w[h]ere several warriors are buried; on the left the dean's chapel from which is a door to the cloisters on the left of the nave. Behind the altar is the chapel of the Holy Trinity or Becket's, in it was Becket's tomb which Henry 8th burned, and the Steps worn by the feet of pilgrims and the stones hollowed out by their knees, the tombs of Edward the Black Prince and Henry 4th and a very rich East Window. The Quire is made of Oak, the screen behind the altar was given by Q. Mary, but the face of it is now reversed being thought too popish. The oak-carving is by Gibbon, the small pillars about the nitches etc. of the Cathedral are of Petworth marble. Under the quire is St. Mary's chapel [*written above* the crypt *struck through*] and the French protes-

[12] tant church given by Q. Elizabeth.

The service on week days is performed in the chapter houses without music. The roof of this place is of Irish oak, the Dean's set is of stone with a curiously worked cushion. In Becket's chapel is an old stone throne on which the Saxon Kings were crowned and where the archbishops are enthroned. On the side of the chapel is H[enry] 4's private chapel. In the high tower is the great Bell Harry. The architecture is very

---

[16] The future Queen Victoria, b. 1819.
[17] There is a gap at this point but the letters 'dec:' have been added in pencil.

mixed, but much of it Saxon, the cathedral was founded by Ethelbert.

On each side of the entrance to the quire are 3 statues of Kings, on the right 3 Edwards, on the left Ethelbert with a model of the cathedral, King John and another. In the nave is a staple to which [?] Odo tied his horses. The roof all over the cathedral is very beautiful. Canterbury is a county and town of itself.

[13] Walked on the Dane John's walk on the old wall and up the mount. On the wall are several old towers, then by the castle home. Dined at 3.

There are 16 parishes at Cänterbury.[18] Set off at 4 for Sittingbourn through the Westgate of Canterbury by Broughton hill where is a fine view of Isle of Sheppy, by Faversham, thro' Greenstreet and Bapchild. Got to the George, Sittingbourne at 6½, had tea.

In the Cathedral are monuments of Dean Wooton who was minister to E[dward] 6, H[enry] 8, Q[ueen] M[ary] and Q[ueen] E[lizabeth].[19] It was executed by an Italian and is reckoned a very fine piece of sculpture. Dean Fetherby whose tomb is covered with all the human bones carved out in marble.[20]

Saturday 27. Breakfasted at 7½, set off about 8½ for Rochester through Newington and Key Street. Arrived at the Bull about 11. Papa and Uncle went to call on Capt. Parry of the Prince Regent, who came and took us, Papa, Uncle, H. and I in the Admiralty barge down to the Prince Regent one of the five largest men of war in the navy, of three tiers of guns of

[14] which there were 120, the length of the ship was 230 and that of the mizzen mast from the deck 192. There were 3 tiers of store rooms and four of cabins in the stern: 1st. the captain, 2nd. Admiral, 3 officers, 4, the lowest, the midshipmen. The stores were all placed in exact order. The guns were 32 and 24 pounders, one of the links of the great chain cables weighed about 34 lbs., the full complement of men 900. The captain's and admiral's cabins are very handsomely fitted up with mahogany. On our way we passed by the dockyards and the sheds under which they build ships, and the ships of war that were not wanted laid up in ordinary with covers. Got home just before 5, Captain Parry dined with us.

[18] It is difficult to see how this figure was arrived at. Hasted records twelve parish churches and formerly five others plus the suburbs. The 1881 census indicates the whole or part of 34 parishes as within Canterbury.
[19] Nicholas Wotton, 1497?-1567, secretary of state.
[20] Charles Fotherby, d. 1619.

In the chain cable is a clever joint to free the Ship from its moorings in case of fire etc. invented by Sir Robert Seppings[21] commissioner of Portsmouth harbour.

[15] Sunday 28. Went to the Cathedral both morning and afternoon. A minor Canon did the duty alone. Service in the morning at 10½, afternoon at 3. There is a good organ and chanting. The Cathedral is a very old building and was very much spoiled by Cromwell, but has been patched up since. All the brass off the tombs has been taken away. There are tombs of Walter de Merton, Bp. of Rochester founder of Merton Col. Oxford and of Bp. Warner who founded Bishop's College, Bromley.[22] The roof of the nave is of wood and lead, quite modern. Some of the walls are out of the upright and supported by buttresses. Went into the chapter house which is modern, the old one having been burnt down—the cloisters are all destroyed—the altar piece is the angels appearing to the shepherds, by B. West.[23]

After morning service Capt. Parry shewed us his house and the Dean's.

Walked with Papa etc. by the river and thro' the town by the old walls after Evening Service.

Rochester Cathedral looks very poor and dirty after Canterbury and seems as if no one cared about it, there are several old tombs of Bishops and Abbots about the Cathedral, all of which have been opened by O[liver] C[romwell] for rings etc.

[16] Monday 29. After breakfast at 8½, Capt. Parry came and took us all in the barge to the docks about 2 miles by the river. He first took us to see the saw mills which are moved by steam, some are circular the rest like common ones but cutting 5 or 6 planks from a log at a time. Next we saw logs lifted from the mast pool by an iron machine and carried to the yard by a carriage down an inclined plane—all by steam. The smithery, a large building containing a great many forges where they were making anchors, knees,[24] bolts etc. The slips or sheds under which they were building ships, saw one whose ribs were being put on and another with all its timbers on. The we met with Capt. McCleod, then we walked up to Mr. Parkins, the Head Ship Wright who shewed us the model of a ship being launched, and several other models of masts. Left

---

[21] Sir Robert Seppings, 1767-1840, naval architect, knighted, 1819.
[22] Walter de Merton, d. 1277 and John Warner, 1581-1666.
[23] (?) Benjamin West, 1738-1820, artist.
[24] A piece of metal having an angular bend, used in shipbuilding.—O.E.D.

Mama, Aunt and H. at the Surgeons to be recruited, and we
went on to the block machines which are not in use, then to
the lead mill where we saw lead pressed out and pipes extended
[17]   and the bore pulled out. Saw the steam engine which moves
the saws and timber carriage, it is an 80 horse power. The saw
machinery, the timber carriage, the block machines were
invented by Mr. Bruell, Capt. Raine's son in law. Among the
docks was a new one just made, of granite about 35 ft. deep
and 4 below the bed of the river. The Royal George and
the Tremendous [84 guns *inserted*] were being built chiefly of
English oak, soaked in salt water as an experiment against
the dry rot. In digging a new dock they had found two old
vessels sunk in the mud. The keel a vessel is built on is always
taken off and a new one put on before it is used. The keelson
is a piece of timber which is placed on top of the keel through
its whole length into which the ribs are fastened. Capt.
Parry and McCleod dined with us.

Tuesday 30. Set off at 8½. Uncle and Aunt to Clapton and we home
through Maidstone and Tunbridge at each of which we changed
horses. A few miles from Rochester went down Blue Bell
hills by the side of which in a field on the right stands Kit's
[18]   coity house consisting of a hut built of four large stones [*rough
sketch inserted*] supposed to be a druidical tomb. From these hills
is a fine view. The country between Rochester and Maidstone is
much finer than any we had seen before after we left Tunbridge
first, except Folkestone hills. Went up to Bidborough, got
home by a little after 1. Dined at 3, rain.

Wednesday October 1. Rain.

[*Added in pencil*]:		
	Maidstone	22
	Charing	12
	Hythe	18
	Dover	12
	Deal	8
	Ramsgate	12
	Margate	8
	Canterbury	15
	Sittingbourne	18
	Rochester	14
	Maidstone	9
	Home	22
		170

INDEX

Acts of Parliament, bridges, 258; distilling, 233, 234; enclosure, 193–206; harbours, 120, 121; improvement, 258; insolvent debtors, 249; poor law, 200; turnpikes, 255–73

Adisham, 193; manor of, 44–5, 49–50

Agney Cum Orgarswick, manor of, 42, 44–5, 49–50

Agricultural Depression, 15th century, 56

Aldington, manor of, 25

Andrews, J. H., 119–26, 127–133

Animal Husbandry, 31, 57, 63, 78, 196; folding of, 29–30

Appledore, manor of, 41, 42, 44–5, 49–50

Apples, 214, 215–6, 220, 221

Apprenticeship, 73, 74, 106, 107, 110, 117

Archaelogia Cantiana, 1, 2, 10, 171, 204

Archaeology, 1, 6, 9

Ash, 61, 225

Ashford, 61, 63, 65, 66, 67, 68, 69, 70, 284; population, 89; poverty, 97

Baker, 95–6, 107, 114, 116, 117, 250

Baker, A. R. H., 11–35

Banking, 161, 162–3

Barfriston, 5, 193

Barham Downs, 181, 190, 276

Barking (Essex), 69

Barksore, manor of, 41, 44–5, 49–50

Barley, cultivation, 39–50, 54–6, 63, 80, 109; trade in, 104, 123, 130

Bartoner's Accounts, 43

Beadle's Rolls, 37–9

Beans, cultivation, 41, 43–4, 46, 49–50, 55, 79–80, 109; trade in, 130, 245

Bedfordshire, 77, 82

Bekesbourne, 5, 30

Berkshire, 82; -Record Office, 185

Best (family of brewers), 108, 237–47; Estates at Boxley, 240–2, 246–7

Betteshanger, 30, 276

Bexley, 4, 25, 58, 203

Bibliotheca Cantiana, 6

Bishop, G. (Maidstone distiller), 228, 229, 233, 234, 235, 236

Bishop, T. M., 37, 42

Black Death, 75

Blackheath, 79, 199–200, 201

Blacksmith, 65, 91, 96, 116

Blean, manor of, 39, 44–5, 49–50

Blome, R., 132, 198

Boulogne, 138, 139, 162, 163, 164, 181, 197

Boys, William, 1; -John, 30, 199, 200, 217, 220, 223

Brenchley, 210, 219, 221; – Iron work, 86–7

Brewer, 65, 95–6; Best of Chatham, 237–47; Medway brewery, 234; Messrs. Winch, 237, 244, 246

Brewing, 42, 43, 87, 108, 113, 115, 237–47

Bricklayer, 65, 116

Brickyards, 106

Bridge, J. W., 207–11, 227–36

Brighton (Sussex), 71–2, 73

Bristol (Somerset), 147, 172

British Museum, manuscripts, 171, 174

Broadstairs, 119, 121, 123, 124, 125; harbour, 119, 121; shipping, 121, 124; visitors at, 288

Bromley, 175–6, 192, 203

Brook, manor of, 41, 42, 44–5, 47, 49–50

Browne, J. (ironmaster), 87

Buckatzsch, E. J., 88

Building Trade, 96, 107, 116, 250

Business Records, Best of Chatham, 237–47; tradesmen, 249–53

Butcher, 65, 91–3, 95–6, 114–6, 117, 250

Cade's Rebellion, 62, 66, 67, 68

Calais, 70, 105, 129, 138, 139, 140, 142, 143, 145, 152, 158, 162, 163, 164, 181, 183, 189

Cambridge, 171, 172, 173, 174, 241; -shire, 82, 131, 175

Camden Society, 171

Camden, William, 4, 123

Canterbury, 37, 43, 48, 66, 68, 76, 77, 78, 81, 85, 86, 110, 139, 141, 172,

293